REFUGEE COMMUNITY ORGANISATIONS AND DISPERSAL

Networks, resources and social capital

David Griffiths, Nando Sigona and Roger Zetter

First published in Great Britain in October 2005 by

The Policy Press
University of Bristol
Fourth Floor
Beacon House
Queen's Road
Bristol BS8 1QU, UK

Tel +44 (0)117 331 4054
Fax +44 (0)117 331 4093
e-mail tpp-info@bristol.ac.uk
www.policypress.org.uk

© David Griffiths, Nando Sigona and Roger Zetter 2005

British Library Cataloguing in Publication Data
A catalogue record for this book is available from the British Library.

Library of Congress Cataloging-in-Publication Data
A catalog record for this book has been requested.

ISBN 1 86134 633 6 paperback

A hardcover version of this book is also available

Cover design by Qube Design Associates, Bristol.
Front cover: photograph supplied by kind permission of
www.thirdavenue.co.uk
Printed and bound in Great Britain by Hobbs the Printers, Southampton.

Contents

List of tables and boxes   v

Acknowledgements   vi

Glossary   vii

one **Introduction**   1

    The institutional and policy context   1

    Theoretical questions   6

two **Refugee community organisations: paradigms and**   11
      perspectives

    The role of migrant organisations: the sociological tradition   12

    RCOs: dominant paradigms and empirical studies   14

    Challenging the paradigm: ethnic community, RCOs   21
      and the state

    New perspectives   25

    Conclusions   35

three **Dispersal: policy and practice**   37

    The dispersal of quota and programme refugees   37

    The changing legislative framework in the 1990s   38

    Dispersal under the 1999 Immigration and Asylum Act   44

    The 2002 Nationality, Immigration and Asylum Act   48

    Refugee settlement   50

    Dispersal and RCOs   58

    Conclusions   63

four **Refugee community organisations in London:**   65
      consolidation and competition

    Methodology   66

    Refugee settlement in London   72

    RCOs in London   74

    Resource base and organisational issues   75

    The impacts of dispersal   95

    Conclusions   102

five   **The institutional and policy framework in the regions**   105

Socioeconomic characteristics of the regions   105
Structure of the consortia   107
NASS and the impacts of dispersal   111
Asylum seekers and refugees in the regions   119
Conclusions   126

six   **The development of RCOs in the regions**   129

RCOs in the West Midlands: emerging organisational forms   129
Birmingham Refugee Network   144
RCOs in the North West: fragmentation and unity in refugee communities   151
The impacts of dispersal and legislative change   170
Conclusions   174

seven **Dispersal, RCOs and refugee communities**   179

The institutional framework   179
The development of RCOs   184
The impacts of dispersal   193
Conclusions   197

eight **Conclusions**   199

The integrative role of RCOs   199
Opportunity structures and modes of migrant incorporation   204
Networks, resources and social capital   206
Social cohesion, immigration and refugee integration   211

References   221
Appendix: RCOs interviewed by location   239
Index   241

List of tables and boxes

Tables

4.1   Summary of RCOs interviewed in London   76
5.1   Top five nationalities dispersed by NASS in the West   113
      Midlands as at the end of 2002
5.2   Top five nationalities dispersed by NASS in the North West   115
      as at the end of 2002
5.3   Numbers of asylum seekers in the West Midlands as at   119
      March 2003
5.4   Numbers of asylum seekers in the North West as at the   124
      end of September 2003
6.1   Summary of RCOs interviewed in the West Midlands   131
6.2   Summary of RCOs interviewed in the North West   154

Boxes

3.1   The 1999 Immigration and Asylum Act   41
3.2   The main principles of dispersal   45
3.3   Deficiencies of the dispersal process   46
3.4   The principal NGOs assisting refugees and asylum seekers   52
3.5   Refugee integration: a partnership model   54
6.1   The Midlands Refugee Council   145

Acknowledgements

Special thanks to Azim El-Hassan for his expert guidance on the fieldwork and to all the refugee organisations and individuals in London and the regions who generously gave up their time and energy to assist in the research. The authors would also like to thank the ESRC for the funding of the initial research project upon which the book is based.

Glossary

ASD	Asylum Support Directorate
BHUK	Bosnia Herzegovina UK
BME	black and minority ethnic
BRF	Birmingham Refugee Forum
COTASS	Coordinators Training and Support Scheme
ECB	Ethiopian Community in Britain
ECHR	European Convention on Human Rights
ESOL	English for Speakers of Other Languages
EUMS	European Union member states
IAA99	Immigration and Asylum Act 1999
IAP	Interagency Partnership
ICAR	Information Centre about Asylum and Refugees in the UK
IND	Immigration and Nationality Directorate (of the Home Office)
IRSS	Immigration Research and Statistics Service (of the Home Office)
LASAR	Liverpool Asylum Seekers and Refugees Development Project
LGA	Local Government Association
LNC	Liverpool Network for Change
LRV	London Refugee Voice
MARIM	Multi-Agency for Refugee Integration in Manchester
MARSN	Manchester Refugee Support Network
MRC	Midlands Refugee Council
MRSN	Merseyside Refugee Support Network
NASS	National Asylum Support Service
NGO	non-governmental organisation
NMSO	North Manchester Somali Organisation
NRIF	National Refugee Integration Forum
OSS	One-Stop Service
RA	Refugee Action
RC	Refugee Council
RCO	Refugee Community Organisation
RCODP	RCOs Development Project
RSI	Refugee-Specific Initiative
RWP	Refugee Working Party

SUG	Somali Umbrella Group
VCO	Voluntary and Community Organisation
VSU	Voluntary Services Unit (of the Home Office)
WDRS	Westminster Diocese Refugee Service
WMCARS	West Midlands Consortium for Asylum Seeker and Refugee Support
WUS	World University Service

ONE

Introduction

This book examines refugee community organisations (RCOs) in London and the regions in a period of rapid change in asylum policy in the UK. Drawing upon fieldwork in London, the West Midlands and the North West, and based upon a critical review of the literature, this book focuses upon the growth in refugee communities and the number of RCOs, particularly outside of London. Furthermore, it examines the resource and organisational constraints affecting RCOs and the contested process of defining and representing refugee communities within the local political and policy environment. While providing a detailed account of a highly topical policy issue, this book is also situated within and framed by a range of theoretical questions. In the first case, these concern the contribution of RCOs to the integration of refugees, conceived as a two-way process between the refugee community and receiving society. The role of informal networks in refugee communities and the distribution of resources are also central themes addressed throughout the book. The concept of social capital in particular is critically examined as a means of analysing the role of networks and resources in refugee communities, in addition to the relationship of RCOs to the key agencies involved in the settlement and integration of refugees.

This introductory chapter addresses the broader institutional and policy context affecting the development of RCOs before providing a brief overview of the theoretical questions, which are discussed in greater detail in Chapter Two.

The institutional and policy context

The period since the late 1980s has witnessed the transformation of the UK from a marginal recipient of asylum seekers to one of the most significant in the European Union (EU) (UNHCR, 2004; Zetter et al, 2003a). The policy response has been reactive on the whole, introducing restrictive legislation as the number of applications increased dramatically from 1988 onwards. Between 1993 and 2003, four major asylum and immigration Acts were passed, with a fifth introduced in July 2004. The general trends have been to reinforce pre-entry controls and to accelerate the erosion of the welfare rights of asylum seekers and their withdrawal from the mainstream benefits system. The rationale for the latter has been both to reduce welfare spending and to act as a deterrent to future asylum applications. This is despite the fact that there is little evidence to suggest that welfare benefits act as an independent pull factor for asylum seekers to the UK (Schuster, 2000; Robinson and Segrott, 2002). Declining asylum applications in the UK since the summer of 2003 have only marginally reduced the political saliency of asylum and immigration, with the emphasis now more firmly upon the increased use of detention and the removal of failed asylum applicants.

One corollary of the increasingly restrictive policy environment from the late 1980s onwards has been growing evidence of the social marginalisation of asylum seekers and refugees, both in terms of their socioeconomic position and in relation to their diminishing rights and entitlements (Carey Wood et al, 1995; Zetter and Pearl, 1998, 2000). A sustained 'moral panic' around the issue of asylum in general and the effects of the current dispersal policy upon local services and populations in particular has also taken place. Robinson's reference to the terminology of 'moral panics', developed in the context of accounts of media amplification and deviancy in the 1970s, retains its significance in relation to current asylum policy (Robinson et al, 2003). In these terms, dispersal may be less a rational response to easing what is perceived as a 'burden' on local authorities in London and the South East than an attempt to remove asylum seekers from the public gaze and to purify "social space" (Robinson et al, 2003, p 171). Given that the spending on immigration and asylum amounts to a tiny fraction of public expenditure, it would appear that the scale of the anxiety elicited by the asylum issue cannot be explained in purely economic terms.

A variety of contributory factors may be involved in the extreme nature of the political and policy response to the increase in asylum applications, which has occurred in the UK since 1988. At the most abstract level, for example, many commentators point to the generalised fear of 'the Other' (see Rustin, 1991). This is a conventional mainstay of the literature on race and racism and draws upon a variety of psychological, psychoanalytic and sociological determinants and explanatory frameworks (Goldberg, 1993). Fear of 'the Other' may be particularly aggravated in relation to the crisis-driven and sporadic character of refugee flows. In a similar vein, the danger associated with proximity to strangers, which was described by Simmel at the turn of the 20th century (1971) and later elaborated by Z. Baumann

(1997) as one of defining features of postmodern uncertainty, may be a significant underlying factor in explaining the highly emotive character of the political and public response to the asylum issue. More concretely, several commentators have noted the specific political configuration of the post-Cold War era, and the extension of conventional security concerns to areas such as international migration and refugee flows in particular (Loescher, 1992; Weiner, 1995; Overbeek, 1996). In Europe, a parallel securitisation of migration has arisen as a result of political changes at the supranational level and the perceived erosion of national boundaries and identities (Balibar, 1991; Miles and Thranhardt, 1996). The Europeanisation of restrictive asylum policy has been one notable result of this process (Geddes, 2000; Zetter et al, 2003a). Geopolitical changes since 11 September 2001 and the continuing process of EU enlargement have heightened security concerns relating to unregulated migration and porous national borders.

In the UK, the evolution of a 'race relations' framework (analysed in detail in Chapter Two of this book) has provided one of the central axes for developments within the asylum field (Schuster and Solomos, 1999; Schuster, 2003). Anti-immigration rhetoric, short-term electoralism and concerns over mounting welfare budgets are the immediate context for the increased saliency of asylum in the domestic policy agenda. The 1993 and 1996 asylum legislation corresponded closely to election years in both cases. Legislation under New Labour has not been so tightly synchronised with electoral politics. Rather, it has been predicated on the need to preserve 'harmonious race relations' and to forestall the rise of the Far Right. Indirectly, electoralism can be viewed as an intrinsic component of this containment strategy, since 'getting tough on asylum' is generally perceived in terms of long-term electoral advantage. Spanning both Conservative and Labour governments, the asylum issue has typically been presented as a problem of numbers, growing burdens on local resources, the threat of cultural dilution and the weakening of national and societal security (Waever et al, 1994). The legislative response to the increase in asylum applications that occurred over the course of the 1990s and into the beginning of the new millennium is outlined more fully in Chapter Three of this book.

As we have argued elsewhere (Zetter et al, 2003a), in comparative EU terms, the UK had lagged behind in the pace of its legislative response during much of the 1990s, opting for an ad hoc mixture of pre-entry controls and in-country deterrence rather than the comprehensive overhaul of asylum policies that had taken place in Germany and the Netherlands in 1993 and 1994, for example. Only under the impact of steeply rising asylum applications towards the end of the decade and a generalised perception of administrative crisis was a radical overhaul of the asylum system set in train. Following legislation in 1993 and 1996, the 1999 Immigration and Asylum Act marked a radical point of departure in asylum policy by introducing a centrally coordinated system of support for asylum seekers dispersed to the regions under the National Asylum Support Service (NASS). This was based upon partnership arrangements between the NASS, local authority consortia, non-governmental organisations (NGOs), the voluntary sector, private sector and RCOs. Partnership arrangements between the agencies involved in reception are not new, but follow on from long-standing traditions of cooperation between the Home Office, NGOs and the voluntary sector in the reception and settlement of quota refugees. What is new, however, is the institutionalisation of partnership arrangements as the basis for the reception of new asylum seekers and the regionalisation of the settlement process under the newly formed local authority consortia. The formal incorporation of RCOs in the reception and integration arrangements (as 'stakeholders' in the local authority consortia) is also part of the more coordinated policy response to asylum introduced under the 1999 legislation. The dispersal framework, as this evolved out of policy changes in the 1990s, is discussed in greater detail in Chapter Three of this book.

The policy discourse on RCOs is generally informed by what we term in this book an integrative or dominant functional paradigm. Within this paradigm, RCOs are viewed as essential to the integration of refugees, as a neglected social and material resource and a vital mediating institution between the refugee community and host society. In classic sociological terms, they are instruments of functional adaptation for refugees newly arrived in the receiving society. Our perspective departs from this paradigm by raising a series of additional questions about the role and status of RCOs. A comparative framework is instructive here. The incidence and saliency of RCOs in the UK, compared to many of its neighbouring EU states, requires clarification. Distinctive to the UK is its mode of migrant incorporation and the race relations framework which allows for the representation of minority interests through designated community organisations (Soysal, 1994; Favell, 1999). These factors provide the structural and historical context for the analysis of RCOs which we undertake in this book. In addition, the pursuit of funding and representation within the local political and policy environment – the core questions of the control and allocation of resources – are potent driving forces behind the formation of RCOs which are also central to our analysis.

The policy and academic literature on RCOs, long dominated by an integrative framework which emphasises their functionality for refugee communities and the wider society of reception, is in need of revision. In this respect, it is necessary to emphasise that there is no automatic correspondence of interests between the different agencies involved in dispersal or the more general reception and settlement process. Analysis of power imbalances between the different actors involved – the Home Office, NGOs, the voluntary sector and the RCOs – is notable by its absence in the literature. By contrast, the conclusions reached in this book point to the significance of agenda setting and differences in the decision-making capacity of the agencies involved in the dispersal process. In particular, the control and allocation of resources is a fundamental consideration in the relationships between the different actors. Our starting point is a critical one: critical of the assumptions underlying the policy literature and of the institutional context within which refugee community organisations are formed. While our emphasis is not policy-led there are significant policy issues that stem from the research. These include the limited role that RCOs currently have in providing a platform for integration as a two-way process between the refugee community and the receiving society. Our conclusions suggest that informal networks may be more important than formally constituted organisations in the integration process. Above all, we argue that the broader framework of migrant incorporation centred on multicultural race relations is a principal determinant of the ways in which refugees organise in Britain. At a more fundamental level, it can be further questioned whether the designation of refugee community organisation itself militates against acceptance within the so-called 'mainstream'. On the other hand, as our fieldwork evidence suggests, while several of the newly developing organisations in the regions chose to organise outside recognised channels, the possibilities for doing so were limited and heavily dependent on the viability of own-community resources. These and other issues are more fully addressed in this book's conclusions.

The research upon which this book is based was funded by the Economic and Social Research Council, award reference number R000239583. Fieldwork for the research was conducted between June 2002 and June 2003 in the cities of London, Birmingham, Manchester and Liverpool. Our general aim was to investigate the changing position of RCOs in a period of radical legislative change. Within this framework, four specific objectives informed the fieldwork component of the research. These were, first, to examine how policy changes at the national level are impacting on the development of RCOs in established locations and new dispersal areas. Here the evidence suggested that the position of RCOs in dispersal areas was tenuous at best and strongly dependent upon networking with their more powerful partners in the statutory, NGO and voluntary sectors.

A second objective was to investigate how well equipped RCOs are in exercising their role to support asylum seekers and refugees within the new framework. In this respect, a significant degree of variation was evident between the locations and also according to the size and capacity of the organisation in question.

A third objective was to outline the institutional, organisational and resource constraints to effective networking and collaboration. Again, power imbalances and inequalities in access to basic resources were the main factors influencing RCOs across the three locations. A final objective was to examine the degree to which there is a conflict between the traditional settlement role of RCOs and the need to respond to the new pressures raised by legislative change. Stemming in part from a broader critique of the policy and academic literature, our position argues both for a critical reassessment of the role of RCOs in the integration process and for a close scrutiny of the institutional and political relations within which RCOs are embedded.

Informing these aims and objectives are a number of theoretical considerations that also bear directly upon the analysis and conclusions reached in this book.

Theoretical questions

To insist on the importance of theoretical reflection can often seem to be something of a luxury. The pragmatism of 'what works' now appears to drive asylum policy as much as the general policy arena (Maile and Hoggett, 2001). As Castles (2003) and Black (2001) have argued in relation to the incorporation of migration specialists into official policy frameworks, detachment from immediate policy imperatives is necessary both for the development of good policy and sound academic research. Currently, as various commentators have noted (IPPR, 2003; Robinson et al, 2003), government policy on asylum is not so much rooted in evidence-based research as in the generation of moral panics and the needs of short-term electoral politics.

Therefore, theoretical detachment is necessary but also subject to its own limitations. The current fragmentation of social theory suggests that recourse to a single master narrative is misplaced. The dangers of eclecticism beckon on the other side. Our own position is to draw selectively upon a range of perspectives that challenge the old and rather worn paradigm concerning the role of associations in migrant and refugee integration. This is not to suggest a grand paradigm shift but that a new set of questions needs to be raised concerning the status of RCOs. Our set of questions concerns the following three areas.

RCOs as integrative mechanisms

The role of RCOs in integrating refugees into the host society is a dominant feature in the literature. While we do not discount the essential work performed by RCOs, the degree to which they are instrumental in integrating refugees is an empirical question that requires further examination. Often taken as one of the credos of analysis, it is important to query the degree to which RCOs have the capacity to integrate refugees. How do we define integration in this sense and in what particular arenas does it occur? Are informal networks, not constituted as bureaucratic organisations, more or less significant for the integration of refugees? Does integration occur because of or in addition to the vital welfare work performed by RCOs?

Opportunity structures and the mode of migrant incorporation

The broader institutional framework affecting RCOs also needs to be brought into the centre of the analysis. Often implicit in the literature on RCOs, the modes of migrant incorporation (Soysal, 1994) are key determinants affecting the character of refugee organisations and the opportunity structures (Koopmans and Stratham, 2000), which are available for the mobilisation of refugee communities. The peculiarities of the British 'race relations' framework are a fundamental consideration here. Asylum as a whole has been absorbed into the framework of racialised immigration control, which has dominated the post-war scene in Britain. How does this broader framework constrain and enhance the possibilities for refugee organisation? In particular, how has dispersal impacted upon RCOs in London and the regions?

Networks, resources and social capital

The extensive literature on the significance of networks and resources in the migration field also needs to be made available to the analysis of RCOs. Again, this is more often implicit in the analysis of RCOs than expressly foregrounded. Our attention to networks is also informed by social capital analysis. As the research progressed, our initially positive orientation to the concept also shifted. Although the concept has come to dominate a range of policy-related fields, it is characterised by definitional confusion. The concept tends to raise more questions than it satisfactorily answers. Moreover, its various uses reflect a gamut of competing theoretical perspectives in social theory, including Marxism, rational choice theory and (in Putnam, 1993) a strand of pluralist functionalism. Our use of the term is therefore critical and primarily conceived as a convenient shorthand metaphor for the material and symbolic benefits deriving from participation in social networks. The degree to which networks cement relations of trust and norms of solidarity or, rather, are the fields upon which various conflicts are played out is one of the central empirical questions addressed in the analysis.

The order of this book is as follows. Chapter Two sets out to review the range of theoretical questions that inform the analysis. The areas covered include the literature on migrant organisations, the integrative role of RCOs, and the relevant research on social networks and social capital. The chapter also provides a critique of the literature and proposes alternative perspectives and questions relating to the role of RCOs that are developed throughout the book.

The third chapter consists of a brief overview of the dispersal framework for asylum seekers, which was introduced under the 1999 Immigration and Asylum Act. The partnership model which informs the reception and settlement of asylum seekers and refugees is central to the discussion, specifically as this involves RCOs as formal (if junior) partners in the new dispersal arrangements. Although there has been a long tradition of settlement programmes for quota and programme refugees in the UK, the current national refugee integration strategy is distinctive in being based upon the new dispersal arrangements for the reception of asylum seekers in the regions.

The organisation of the fieldwork chapters, which follow, is by case-study location and is also developed in terms of particular themes: consolidation and competition in relation to London; emerging organisational forms and fragmentation and unity in refugee communities, in the analysis of the regions. Chapter Four, which outlines the methodological underpinnings of the fieldwork, is focused on the position of RCOs in London. This comes before the examination of the effects of dispersal on RCOs in the regions, for two principal reasons. First, a range of more general theoretical issues is raised in this chapter; second, the London settlement experience in many ways predates and provides a background to the dispersal process. Chapter Five provides an overview of the institutional and policy framework in the regions, while Chapter Six is based upon fieldwork conducted with RCOs in the West Midlands and the North West respectively. Birmingham, Manchester and Liverpool are the main cities examined. In order to facilitate comparison, the sections on the different regions follow a broadly similar order, from an analysis of the number and structure of RCOs to a discussion of the principal themes covered in the interviews.

Chapter Seven compares and contrasts the experiences of RCOs in London and the regions, while the Conclusion (Chapter Eight) approaches the themes raised in the fieldwork chapters from a more theoretical perspective. In particular, the institutional constraints and opportunities for mobilisation affecting refugee communities; the role of networks, resources and social capital in the creation of refugee organisations; and the broader issue of refugee settlement and social cohesion in the UK are addressed in greater detail.

TWO

Refugee community organisations: paradigms and perspectives

There is an absence of generally accepted definitions relating to organisations in refugee communities. Many commentators refer to refugee associations (Joly, 1996) or refugee organisations (Gold, 1992). In other cases, refugee-based organisations is the preferred term (Salinas et al, 1987; Majka, 1991). More widespread now is the use of refugee community organisation (RCO) or refugee community-based organisation to designate organisational forms among refugee groups. Do definitions matter? Implicit in the term RCO is the rooting of organisational forms in broader social relationships. Zetter and Pearl (2000, p 676), for example, confine their definition of RCOs to

> organisations rooted within, and supported by, the ethnic or national refugee/asylum seeker communities they serve. Essentially, these RCOs are established by the refugees and asylum seekers themselves – or by their pre-established communities.

One of the problems in the literature hinges on the relationship between refugee organisations and the communities they are assumed to represent. In this respect, a clearer conception of the conflicting pressures faced by refugee organisations and the ambiguities surrounding their role is necessary. How in particular are the organisations formed by refugees affected by the broader framework of asylum and immigration policy? This question is particularly important in the context of dispersal and the growth in the refugee population outside London that has taken place since the introduction of the 1999 Immigration and Asylum Act. In general, the term RCO is used in this research as recognised shorthand for the complex, diverse and fragmentary social forms that characterise refugee organisations. Rather than assume at the outset that refugee organisations directly express the interests of their communities, it is necessary to put this assumption 'on hold'. The general ethnic relations literature is revealing on this point. Beginning with the classic sociological accounts of migrant communities, this chapter first reviews a range of literature bearing on the issue of migrant and refugee organisations. Second, the problem of 'community' is addressed, and finally, the theoretical perspectives which underpin our own analysis of RCOs are presented in more detail.

The role of migrant organisations: the sociological tradition

Reviewing the North American literature on migrant associations, Gold (1992) notes the move from the dominant assimilationist model in the 1920s and 1930s, which viewed associations in terms of a failure to assimilate, to a more nuanced integrationist conception in the 1960s, which regarded associations as a vital means of support and integration for migrants. Assimilation conventionally refers to the absorption of minorities into the host society on cultural, economic and social levels. Integration, also conventionally, refers to the full participation of minorities in the host society while at the same allowing for the retention of their distinctive cultural identities (Castles et al, 2003). Similarly, in the UK, Rex (1987), reviving earlier sociological debates about the role of associations which stem from the work of Tonnies (1955), believed that the study of migrant associations was principally concerned with the issue of identity in migrant communities. According to Rex, while Tonnies underplayed the role of associations (*Gesellschaft*) as secondary to primary community relationships (*Gemeinschaft*), Durkheim developed a more positive conception of associations as providing a source of identity in advanced societies. It should be recalled that, for Durkheim (1933), modern organic solidarity had resulted in a freeing of the individual from social bonds. Occupational groups were to supply a much-needed sense of belonging and identity for individuals, let loose from traditional forms of solidarity. For Parsons (1971), writing from the standpoint of 20th-century functionalist sociology, normative integration was firmly based upon the internalisation of appropriate norms and values. Migrant organisations would clearly supply one of the vehicles of normative integration in this framework. As Rex remarks (1987, pp 16-17):

> The immigrant associations which we are concerned with studying may perhaps be thought of as playing for immigrant populations something like the role which Durkheim assigned to occupational groups. Clearly they do play some role in the socialization of the individual and

offer him some kind of answer to the question 'Who am
I?'.

Again, within a primarily Durkheimian conception of social
integration, Rex (1987, p 17) argued that migrant organisations could
have an important role to play in integrating individuals both within
the migrant community and also within the wider social setting:

> It does make some sense then to see the immigrant
> associations and community structure as forming the
> intimate small-scale group which has moral influence over
> the individual and which yet integrates him with a larger
> society.

Within this framework, migrant associations are essentially modes of
adaptation to new social relationships and norms. Second-generation
migrants may move away from associations, yet they retain their
significance for newly arrived migrants who struggle to rebuild social
networks and identities. To the four main functions of community
associations which Rex lists (overcoming isolation, providing material
help, defending interests and promoting culture), he later added
maintaining links with the homeland as one of the primary aims of
migrant associations. While associations are central features of migrant
adaptation, they are not the exclusive focus of research. Ethnic networks
based upon family and other factors and the broader symbols of cultural
life are the other components of migrant adaptation that need to be
analysed alongside formal associations. The term 'association' was
understood to include workers' associations, churches, football clubs
– even the personnel of pubs, cafes, youth clubs, leisure activities and
so on. For Rex, there was a broad overlap between a general
anthropological analysis of migrant communities and the study of
associations. Associations, that is, have to be studied alongside informal
networks, kinship systems and symbols in migrant communities. The
key issues were the degree to which migrants were assimilated,
withdrew into ethnic enclaves or mobilised on the basis of ethnic
solidarity. In drawing attention to the relation between homeland
orientations and associations, Rex also anticipated the study of
transnational communities and global diasporas which gained
momentum throughout the 1990s (Cohen, 1997; Vertovec, 1999).

Specific empirical studies of migrant associations have been
developed within this general paradigm (Rex, Joly and Wilpert,
1987). The term 'paradigm' as applied here is borrowed from Kuhn

(1962) and refers to the set of assumptions collectively held by a specific scientific community, which informs the practice of 'normal science'. Although its application in the present context is not exact, the term captures the uniform and shared character of the assumptions informing the study of migrant and refugee associations. Cheetham (1985, p 47) for example, in her review of ethnic associations in Britain pinpointed the diversity of organisational types and the variety of functions they fulfilled, noting the firm link between the development of associations, the promotion of ethnic identity and migrants' integration into British society. According to Cheetham (1985, p 19), the functions of the associations included: direct provision of services, information-giving, advice, support groups for the young and elderly, referral and advocacy, lobbying and pressure group activity and promotion of the home culture. Explaining the origins of migrant associations, she argued that "desperate needs, disillusion with statutory agencies and an increasing wish not to lose ethnic roots and identity" (Cheetham, 1985, p 25), drove members of minority groups to develop their own organisations. In general she noted three types of organisation: cultural, cultural and welfare, and welfare-based. The largest group was that which combined cultural and welfare functions, providing 'culturally sensitive' services in a way that the statutory services were unable to match. The aims of the associations typically combined service provision with improving public understanding of the position of the particular migrant group. Cheetham (1985, p 20) concluded that "there is an inescapable link between cultural, political and welfare functions" in associations. The limitations of associations were also noted, including the effects of short-term funding, a lack of perceived legitimacy, resource constraints and the ongoing need for training and improved networking skills (Cheetham, 1985, pp 50-1). Rex and Josephides (1987), in their cross-national comparison of migrant associations, and Jenkins (1988), in her cross-national study of ethnic associations and the welfare state, similarly concluded that associations were vital instruments for the retention of culture and language *and* for integrating migrants into their new social settings.

RCOs: dominant paradigms and empirical studies

The classic sociological interpretation of the role of migrant associations has been highly influential in the study of refugee organisations. Marx (1990) in his analysis of the 'social world of refugees' explicitly draws upon Thomas and Znaniecki's (1918) classic study on Polish migrants in the US. The same phases as occurred in the study of Polish migrants were believed to apply in the case of refugees, where initial family-based socialisation gives way to the more formal organisational processes of the receiving state. As Marx argues (1990, p 210):

> Associations, then, attend a second phase in the adaptation of the immigrant, when his or her contacts with the new social environment have become more numerous and varied.

As in Rex, associations act to integrate refugees into their new social settings while allowing for the retention of cultural identities.

A significant strand within the North American literature on refugee associations (typically based upon large data sets, survey methods and multivariate analysis) conforms to this general paradigm. Dorais (1991), for example, bases his survey of Vietnamese, Laotians and Cambodians in Quebec City, on Rex's analysis of community associations as indicators of migrant organisation and adaptation. As Dorais (1991, p 567) argues:

> By setting up in the host country, social networks based on kinship and friendship, and by establishing ethnic associations and religious institutions, immigrants are able to respond quite adequately to their most important socio-cultural needs within a community that mediates between them and the larger society.

According to Dorais, the formation of effective community organisations depends on the existence of well-integrated individuals (the experience of upward social mobility in the receiving society), core values (traditions of organisation and leadership) and the support of the host or home society for their success. The most significant variable here is the level of economic integration although the cultural homogeneity of the group is also cited as important.

More qualitative studies in the fieldwork tradition have been undertaken by Sorenson (1990), who examined the question of ethnic identity in relation to the settlement of Eritrean refugees in Canada. Voluntary associations, he argues, are the main articulators of identity for Eritreans in exile. This involves a selective process of interpreting traditions and forging collective identities in exile, particularly for politically motivated refugees. Gold (1992, pp 18-23), again within the fieldwork tradition, in his comparative study of Vietnamese and Soviet Jews in California, notes that, although similar political orientations may unite refugees and foster the formation of refugee associations, they may equally lead to division and factionalism. The most significant factor is the "broader context of refugees' settlement" (Gold, 1992, p 23), including, as in Dorais (1991), the economic context and the role of state institutions in fostering refugee settlement. The importance of solidarity among refugee communities for their economic integration has been consistently noted within the literature (Rogg, 1974).

The theme of refugee organisations and their relation to cultural identities and homeland politics has been developed in a variety of national and comparative contexts. Vasquez (1989) writing on Chileans in France, and Eastmond (1993, 1998) on Chileans in the US and Bosnians in Sweden, have noted the extreme importance of the 'institutions of the diaspora' in reconstructing a sense of belonging and identity for refugees, particularly in the early phases of displacement. A process of adaptation to the receiving society typically accompanies the selective reconstruction of national and ethnic identities, including the reinterpretation of gender identities, according to these accounts. Refugee organisations change and adapt to the particular circumstances and histories of the group in question, and also in relation to changes in the receiving society and the group's country of origin. The underlying assumption of the functionality of refugee organisations in preserving national and ethnic identities while acting as a bridge to the new social setting is retained in most of these accounts. It is also a dominant assumption within the academic and policy-based literature on refugee community groups and RCOs in Britain reviewed below.

British-based studies of RCOs

In this context, it is useful to note that accounts of pre-war and post-war refugee settlement in Britain consistently point to the role of community organisations in cementing social bonds among refugees (Sword, 1989; Talai, 1989). Although the history of refugee dispersal in Britain is addressed more fully in Chapter Three, commentators have similarly noted the importance of community organisation for the Vietnamese settlement programme of the 1970s and 1980s (Jones, 1982).

Cheetham (1985, p 44), in a perceptive account, discussed the formation of RCOs in relation to minority ethnic associations, noting the special position of refugees and asylum seekers, the specific character of their needs and legal position and the failure of statutory authorities to understand their position. She recommended more use of refugees as settlement workers as they had inside knowledge of the problems faced by refugees.

In a later contribution on programme refugees, Joly (1996) compared Vietnamese and Chilean settlement in the UK and France. She interviewed a sample of associations in the UK and France based upon the main categories of association (cultural, political and advice-based). Following Rex, her interview schedule comprised several broad areas:

- basic data on the association (history, funding and structure);
- the character of the association including aims, activities, resources and membership;
- the relationship to country of origin;
- the relation to the reception country;
- and issues of identity and settlement.

The politicisation and home orientation of the Chilean organisations in France contrasted markedly with the weak organisation and orientation of the Vietnamese towards integration in the society of reception. Joly concluded that the relation to the country of origin is the decisive variable accounting for the effectiveness of community organisations. She also noted the role of the society of reception, which is different in either case (with more settlement problems encountered in the UK), and the importance of a settled community of co-ethnics (with the historic link between Vietnam and France proving beneficial in this respect).

In practice, Joly differentiates between refugee communities which possess a collective political project in the society of origin and those which do not, referring back to Kunz's (1981) earlier distinction between majority-identified and events-alienated refugees. Those refugee groups with a collective project might include national liberation movements, territorially based national and ethnic groups or those fleeing dictatorship. Those without a collective project could be victims of genocide or generalised violence, for example (Joly, 1996, p 155). This reproduces Zolberg et al's (1989) distinction between political activists, target minorities and victim groups. Joly's first refugee type has high degrees of community organisation, strong transnational linkages and an orientation to home that overrides integration in the host society. The second type is the polar opposite: having severed ties with the country of origin, the goal of integration becomes more significant for the group and with it the possibility of experiencing discrimination and marginalisation in the host society. The viability and coherence of this type depends on its existence as a group prior to flight and whether it has developed a cohesive consciousness. With weak networks and community organisation, marginalisation from both the society of origin and reception potentially awaits this type of refugee group.

In a study combining quota and 'spontaneous' refugee arrivals, Salinas et al (1987) interviewed 27 RCOs in London. These included early associations formed in the 1920s by Russian exiles and post-war refugees, as well as newer arrivals. Half of the sample was from refugee groups who had arrived on a quota basis, while 15 had arrived and organised during the 1980s. As Salinas et al (1987, p 1) argue:

> In this study, we assume that refugee-based organisations were formed to provide alternative sources of assistance for refugees and to meet the needs not provided for by existing organisations such as voluntary agencies or the statutory services.

The authors note a proliferation of RCOs in the early 1980s, specifically in London where their research was based. The underlying assumption of the research is that there is poor statutory understanding of refugees' needs and that RCOs may be better positioned to help their communities, particularly in the early phase of settlement. In addition, RCOs provide a support mechanism for forced migrants uncertain about the future, alleviate boredom, provide a sense of 'self-determination' and identify unmet needs in the community. They also act to counter the experience of discrimination and cultural insensitivity in service provision, which is common to both refugees and other migrants. As with Cheetham (1985), they found three main types of organisation: cultural, welfare-based and those which combined the two functions. The research also reviewed the main areas of work and support including language training, housing and income support and gaps in provision.

On a more critical note, Salinas et al (1987) also noted that factionalism in refugee communities is a central feature, pointing to this as the basis for a number of organisations forming from the same nationality. Politics, class and differences in the date of arrival of refugees of the same nationality are all factors that encourage fragmentation in refugee organisation. The authors also noted that the existence of RCOs formed by co-ethnics or co-nationals who arrived at an earlier date may also have a marked effect on the ability of newcomers to settle and adapt in a shorter time period (Rogg, 1974). The absence of pre-existing contacts may be a problem for new arrivals hoping to organise in the UK. In general, by providing a bridge to the receiving society, RCOs are seen as central to the integration process of refugees, although this is not defined in terms of assimilation but of cultural adaptation.

The literature on RCOs in Britain from the 1990s onwards indicates both continuities with the dominant paradigm and the emergence of new themes. The continuities with the earlier paradigm are reviewed in the remainder of this section, while the emergence of critical perspectives is addressed in the following part of this chapter. Duke (1996) reviewed quota and non-quota arrivals and based her analysis upon two surveys, one on Vietnamese refugees arriving between 1983 and 1992 and the other on non-quota refugees arriving between 1982 and 1989. She outlines the situation as it then was in relation to non-quota refugees and the arrangements in place from the Voluntary Services Unit (VSU) of the Home Office to support refugee community groups. The VSU funded the Refugee Council and Refugee Action in the regions and the regional refugee councils. The principle of community self-help in addition to statutory provision was central to government policy on refugee settlement. Duke (1996, p 9) reiterates the mediating role of RCOs:

> Their mediating role cannot be overstated, especially given the language problems that most new arrivals have. It is much easier for them to make contact with their community groups whose members speak their own language than it is for them to contact British agencies directly.

All of the communities in both the samples had community groups. The benefits of RCOs to refugees were consistently highlighted in the research. According to the refugees interviewed, RCOs act to build up networks and provide a means of obtaining employment through the development of contacts. The role of informal networks for the mental health of refugees was also very important. Duke finally notes the valuable contribution that RCOs can make in terms of assets, resources and skills and that these are currently under-utilised.

The 1995 Home Office study on refugee settlement (Carey-Wood et al, 1995) also alluded to the role of RCOs. This was further developed in Carey-Wood (1997), who found that the difficulties refugees face in accessing mainstream services leads them to develop refugee-specific initiatives (RSIs). These have the advantage of acting as a voice for refugees and providing flexible responses to their target populations' needs. Her research is based upon an analysis of RSIs, interviews with individuals from statutory, voluntary and community organisations and case studies of specific RSIs. She again outlines the prevailing community development approach of the Home Office as this operated through the VSU, Refugee Action, Refugee Council and regional refugee councils. The concept of partnership between the public, private and voluntary sectors was central to the community development approach advocated by the Home Office.

Summarising this literature, a list of positive and negative factors can be outlined. On the one hand, RCOs retain a vital, functional role including:

- empowerment for individual refugees;
- providing a communal voice and form of representation;
- a flexible and immediate response to local needs;
- a mediating role between refugees and service providers;
- building and sustaining community networks;
- provision of employment opportunities;
- filling gaps in existing service provision.

On the other hand, the downside of RCOs includes:

- problems around representation and the exclusion of certain groups (women, the elderly, political sub-groups);
- insecure funding and short-term aims;
- dependence on volunteers resulting in high staff turnover;
- an emphasis on individual case work (legal advice, housing advice, and so on) to the detriment of long-term community development and settlement work;
- dependence upon organisations rather than individual initiatives by refugees;
- raised expectations and ambiguities about roles;
- localised subgroup mobilisation rather than community-wide organisation.

Before turning to examine the new themes that have emerged in the analysis of RCOs, it is important to note that the research reviewed in this chapter refers to the situation in Britain prior to dispersal. The emerging literature on RCOs under dispersal is reviewed in Chapter Three.

Challenging the paradigm: ethnic community, RCOs and the state

The positive functionality of RCOs for the settlement and integration of refugees is the dominant paradigm informing the literature in this field. Concerning the British case, the limitations of RCOs, although noted in the literature, are seldom developed into a more nuanced understanding of the structural constraints affecting refugee organisations. Issues of representation and accountability relating to RCOs are significant themes in the literature but do not result in a sustained critique of the underlying assumptions informing the overall paradigm. RCOs, as the fieldwork in this research illustrates, are not naively representative of their communities and neither are they as automatically integrative as they are assumed in the literature. The broader state context of immigration and asylum policy is again noted in the literature, as in the case of Duke's (1996) and Carey-Wood's (1997) observations on the Home Office's relation to the voluntary sector, but not developed into a more coherent explanatory framework. Idealised, functional models of RCOs and unproblematic notions of community and representation predominate in much of the literature reviewed here. Conflictual relations within refugee communities or between refugee communities and the state are also notable by their absence. A certain parochialism of vision is also apparent in the lack of a comparative framework in most of these accounts. For example, why are RCOs a significant feature in Britain, but far less so in comparable EU states? The key issues raised by the literature therefore concern how the 'refugee community' is defined and the relation of RCOs to the broader context of migrant incorporation operating in the British context.

The term 'community' is one of the most contested concepts in the social sciences (Bell and Newby, 1971; Albrow et al, 1997). Within the classic sociological tradition the solidaristic bonds of community have typically been contrasted to the more formal and impersonal linkages which permeate contemporary societies. The dichotomies of *Gemeinschaft* versus *Gesellschaft*, mechanical solidarity versus organic solidarity, and particularism and ascription compared to universalism and achievement run throughout the literature. Copious North American and British empirical studies of communities based in particular localities have been undertaken which adhere in varying degrees to this overarching framework (Park, 1925; Albrow et al, 1997, p 22). Within the British ethnic relations literature, local studies of particular groups proliferated from the 1970s onwards (Watson, 1977;

Khan, 1979; Robinson, 1985; Werbner, 1991). Many of these studies were similarly rooted in the conception of communities as localised and territorially bounded. Theoretically innovative approaches from the 1980s onwards have increasingly challenged the notion of the localised, bounded community upon which much of this earlier research was based. Hall (1991, 1992), Gilroy (1987) and Bhabha (1990), among others, developed an approach that emphasised the importance of diasporic communities, 'new ethnicities' and transnational linkages in the formation of a sense of locality and ethnic community rooted in the realities of globalisation and the emergence of 'virtual communities' which span the globe (Albrow et al, 1997, p 23).

An important change, related to this broader context, is in the understanding of the relation of ethnic communities to the state and the implications this has for the forms of migrant mobilisation. Werbner and Anwar (1991, p 21), in their analysis of black and minority ethnic leaderships in Britain, argued that minority ethnic communities are 'imagined', in Anderson's (1983) sense, both by the state, "in order to control or allocate resources in an 'equitable' manner", and by minority ethnic leaderships "who claim to represent them". As Anderson had argued, all communities beyond situations of immediate face-to-face contact are imagined, the product of forms of representation. This conception of the 'ethnic-imagined community' has been extensively developed in the literature (Eade, 1991; Werbner, 1991) and is closely related to the assumptions embodied in the race relations framework and the tenets of multiculturalism that have dominated British immigration policy in the post-war period.

The race relations framework has been one of the most significant factors behind the increased saliency of asylum in the British domestic policy agenda. The notion of the race relations framework as used here is adopted from Miles (1993) and Solomos (1998), and as applied to the asylum field, from Miles and Cleary (1993), Schuster and Solomos (1999) and Schuster (2003). As Schuster (2003, p 132) notes, until the 1993 Asylum and Immigration Act asylum had been a subsidiary feature of the Immigration Rules and "had been treated as a type of immigration" throughout the 20th century. Asylum, as she notes further, has been incorporated within the dominant race relations approach to immigration in the post-war period. The British response to immigration (whether by labour migration or the specific case of refugees) is characterised above all by policy ambivalence, or a pronounced duality of approach. From the 1960s onwards, restriction on admissions, particularly of non-white entrants, has been combined with a race relations and multicultural approach to those allowed to settle in Britain. Favell (1999, p 4), in his analysis of British immigration policy, notes that race relations are founded on the representation of 'racial' group interests but without the guarantee of specific minority rights as such. In the British case, as Soysal (1994) has also argued in her comparative study of incorporation regimes, multicultural race relations involve the incorporation of minorities through devolving responsibility to designated community organisations and other forms of local representation. As Koopmans and Stratham (2000) have argued, the parameters of post-war race relations in Britain had been decisively shaped by the earlier experience of Empire and colonial rule.

The race relations framework and multiculturalism underpin asylum and refugee policy in several related ways. In the first instance, a restrictive approach to asylum applications has been framed within the language of increasing numbers, welfare strain and urban decay which is typical of the racialisation of immigration in the post-war period (Miles, 1993). In the second case, as we suggest at greater length in this book, RCOs have been absorbed within the multicultural framework of minority ethnic community representation and the discipline of funding regimes which structure the black and minority ethnic (BME) sector as a whole (McLeod et al, 2001).

Drawing upon the literature on ethnic representation and the state represented by Werbner (1991) and Goulbourne (1991) and applying this to the case of RCOs, Wahlbeck (1997) investigated the role of Kurdish community associations in Finland and Britain. The basic contrast was between the state-centred approach to refugee reception and settlement in Finland, which had a broadly assimilationist inflexion compared to the multicultural, race relations approach in Britain. Wahlbeck noted the greater diversity and variety of functions for the Kurdish associations in Britain, compared to the smaller number and limited functions of associations in Finland. This reflected the smaller number of Kurds in Finland and the distinctive reception and integration policies of the receiving states. Welfare institutions in Finland had effectively taken over the role played by RCOs in the British case. In both cases, however, the associations functioned as part of the broader diaspora organisation of Kurds. Wahlbeck (1998), writing specifically on the role of Kurdish associations in London, argued that although political divisions in refugee communities may provide obstacles to the development of "viable and unitary" associations (1998, p 216), they may at the same time provide the basis for effective ethnic mobilisation. While associations and broader ethnic networks are vital for refugee settlement, how far do political divisions block effective organisation? Wahlbeck concludes that political orientation to the homeland can be a useful resource for refugee organisations. He also outlines the multicultural assumptions of UK asylum policy and its incorporation within the broader race relations framework. The British 'communal option' (Goulbourne, 1991) creates artificial 'ethnic communities' out of segments, presupposing the existence of exclusive ethnic groups with defined boundaries and identities. The British policy of defining groups in ethnic terms imposes "artificial ethnic boundaries on a diverse and complex reality" (Walhbeck, 1998, p 220). Refugees, in particular, appear to lack clearly defined and homogenous ethnic communities but are similarly constrained to represent themselves as such.

The politicisation of the Kurdish organisations is based upon a common national identity that necessarily excludes minorities who fail to fully identify with the nationalist project. Consequently, associations may fail to provide for all members of their communities equally. This, Wahlbeck argues, is a direct result of the assumption of homogenous ethnic communities which is implicit in the multicultural framework. Albeit that the politicised Kurdish associations are only partial representations of communal interests, nevertheless they function well for "smaller groups within the wider community" (Wahlbeck, 1998, p 225). On the whole, the associations provided a platform for the development of informal networks, which were vital for new arrivals and for obtaining employment in the local garment trade. Politicisation in refugee communities does not result in a complete failure of organisation but may lead to the marginalisation of certain groups and individuals. For this reason, refugee associations and the services they provide have to be balanced by universal provision through the state.

In a similar vein, Kelly (2003), reviewing the government programme for the settlement of Bosnian refugees in the early 1990s, criticised the state-driven assumption of a unified Bosnian community and the 'disempowering' effects of this upon refugees. Drawing upon several related strands, Griffiths (2002) compared Somali and Kurdish community organisations in London and the role of RCOs in providing a platform for the public enunciation of identities. The issue of ethnic representation within the multicultural discourse of the state, the internal politics in refugee communities and the relation to the political conflict in the country of origin were highlighted as counters to the more simplistic notions of community solidarity and coherence which tend to dominate in the literature on RCOs.

Surveying this emerging literature, we can make several points. On the one hand, this research directly points to the significance of state-driven forms of migrant incorporation and their effects upon refugee organisations. Also highlighted here is the role of refugee networks, including internal divisions within refugee communities. This suggests the need for a multilayered approach to RCOs through the deployment of interlocked and crosscutting concepts. Structural resources and constraints clearly impinge upon the forms of refugee organisation. Yet organisational forms in turn derive from networking processes that occur within and across specific refugee communities. The concepts of opportunity structures, networks, resources and social capital that are reviewed later in this chapter, suggest alternative ways of conceptualising the role of refugee organisations, which are developed more extensively throughout this book.

New perspectives

The new institutionalism and opportunity structures

According to Hay (2002, p 105), "the new institutionalism emphasises the ordering (or structuring) of social and political relations in and through the operation of institutions and institutional constraints". The general emphasis is upon the normalising role of institutional habits, based upon the density of institutional networks and the definition of what is permissible, possible and feasible within them. Institutions are therefore conceived as normalising and regulatory in nature. Coming under the broad umbrella of the new institutionalism, the opportunity structure approach has been championed by Koopmans and Stratham (2000) in their comparative analysis of national integration paradigms. The focus here is on the political and institutional arrangements governing the sphere of immigration and ethnic relations (Koopmans and Stratham, 2000, p 30). What the authors term 'political opportunity structure' analysis is defined by "consistent – but not necessarily formal or permanent – dimensions of political environment that provide incentives for people to undertake collective action by affecting their expectations for success of failure" (Tarrow, 1994, p 85). It is the overarching context for mobilisation and action based upon available resources in the political environment.

Soysal's (1994) highly influential study of 'incorporation regimes' has suggested the ways in which dominant paradigms of incorporation, which are both discursively and institutionally organised, affect the forms of migrant mobilisation. As she argues (1994, pp 85-6), "my analyses suggest that the organising principles and incorporation styles of the host polity are crucial variables in accounting for the emerging organisational patterns of migrants". The dominant race relations paradigm in the UK is posited on an individualistic, liberal or market-based model of migrant incorporation. This results in a dispersed or localised pattern of migrant organisation and a resultant proliferation of minority ethnic voluntary organisations that provide a range of social services to their communities. In the absence of direct, state-based incorporation of migrants, localised migrant organisations tend to focus on welfare and social provision for their own communities. A striking contrast is with the corporatist approach in Germany, for example, where state and para-state institutions take the dominant role in migrant incorporation. In this case, migrant organisation, according to Soysal, tends to be less dispersed and localised and more closely anchored to representation at the level of the state.

Although it may not be possible to directly translate from Soysal's generalisations concerning migrant organisation to the specific case of refugees (there are distinctive legal criteria involved in the case of refugees, the experience of forced migration and distinctive nationalities, ethnic groups and patterns of settlement entailed), nevertheless there are certain inferences that can be drawn. One clear implication for the organisation of refugee groups in the UK is that they encounter a distinctive national tradition of migrant incorporation and ethnic representation, which provides their immediate 'opportunity structure', the terms under which they enter the public sphere of accountability and legitimate representation. The general framework of migrant incorporation affecting minority ethnic populations applies equally to the case of refugees. Moreover, the establishment of the Home Office (2004) *National refugee integration strategy*, developed in the context of the dispersal of asylum seekers to the regions, explicitly acknowledges the role played by RCOs in the integration of refugees. On a formal level at least, RCOs now find themselves increasingly embedded within a broader framework of institutional arrangements that aim to 'integrate' refugees. These points are developed further in later chapters of this book.

Networks, resources and social capital

As Koopmans and Stratham argue (2000, p 32), opportunity structure analysis is closely tied to resource mobilisation theory and in particular the ways in which the presence or absence of resources affects the capacity of migrant groups to mobilise. Al–Ali et al (2001), for example, have noted the importance of the resources available to particular groups in their capacity to organise on a transnational basis. Mobilisation of this type depends upon the capabilities and skills of a group, their length of time in a particular country and, as indicated earlier, the opportunity structures available. The internal organisation of migrant communities is also a significant variable. Drury (1994, p 19) has argued that resource mobilisation theory, closely associated with accounts of ethnic mobilisation (Rex, 1994), predicts that internally cohesive groups with high levels of organisational solidarity are more likely to mobilise than those lacking such resources. The definition used here follows Lin (2001, p 29) in defining resources "as material or symbolic goods". In particular, the significance of the interpretative level in relation to resources should not be underestimated. The acquisition of social status, for example, has a symbolic importance, which is not adequately captured in the notion of resources as material goods.

The clear implication in this context is that analysis of the institutional structures affecting refugee organisations has to be complemented by attention to the networks and resources available within refugee communities themselves. Within migration theory, network analysis has a long history and is central to many accounts of contemporary migration. Gurak and Caces (1992) provide a useful overview of the different approaches. Ritchey (1976) discusses the role of migrant networks in terms of decision making, suggesting three hypotheses:

- *Affinity:* the higher the density of networks at home the less likely migration will occur;
- *Facilitating:* networks facilitate migration through money lending and lowering transaction costs;
- *Information:* information provided through networks about potential destination countries can facilitate migration.

In these ways, networks can influence the selectivity of migrants and the timing and channelling of migrants to particular destinations (Koser and Pinkerton, 2002, p 10). Arango (2000, p 291) has similarly argued that:

> Migrant networks can be defined as sets of interpersonal relations that link migrants or returned migrants with relatives, friends or fellow countrymen at home. They convey information, provide financial assistance, facilitate employment and accommodation, and give support in various forms. In doing so they reduce the costs and uncertainty of migration and therefore facilitate it.

The study of refugee organisations, therefore, should be central to the analysis of networks in refugee communities.

More generally, as Vertovec (2001, p 6) notes, "as a method of abstraction and analysis, the social network approach sees each person as a 'node' linked with others to form a network". It may be regarded as a loose federation of approaches rather than a unified perspective. In general, networks provide both opportunities and constraints for social interaction. Networks can be analysed along a range of potential axes, including size, density, complexity, strength, duration and frequency. Social networks in this sense not only link people, but they also affect the circulation of resources. There is an important distinction to be made, moreover, between the use of network analysis in 'descriptive and metaphoric usage', as opposed to a rigorous mode of collecting and analysing data. Network analysis, in the sense used by Vertovec (2001, p 10) and as deployed here, implies the use of "network terms and concepts to order the research process and to significantly elucidate data", and not an abstract deductive schema.

Parallel to the notion of networks, 'social capital' has long been a mainstay of migration theory. According to Massey et al (1998, p 43):

> Network connections constitute a form of social capital that people can draw upon to gain access to various kinds of financial capital: foreign employment, high wages, and the possibility of accumulating savings and sending remittances.

Social capital refers here to the ways in which migration creates new relations and resources for later migrants. The initial placement of contacts abroad eases the process of migration and reduces transaction costs for future migrants. As Massey et al (1998, p 43) argue further:

> Thus the growth of networks that occurs through the progressive reduction of costs may also be explained theoretically by the progressive reduction of risks. Every new migrant expands the network and reduces the risks of movement for all those to whom he or she is related.

Arango (2000, p 8) similarly notes that:

> Migration networks can be seen as a form of social capital, in so far as they are social relations that permit access to

other goods of economic significance, such as employment and higher wages.

One of the more sophisticated and sustained uses of the concept is in Faist (2000), who combines the literature on social networks and social capital. According to Faist, network analysis on its own does not consider the dimensions of symbolic ties, obligations and forms of solidarity, in contrast to social capital. Consequently, for Faist (2000, p 102):

> Social capital are those resources that help people or groups to achieve their goals in ties and the assets inherent in patterned social and symbolic ties that allow actors to cooperate in networks and organisations, serving as a mechanism to integrate groups and symbolic communities.

It is important to note that these accounts often draw upon different strands and theorisations of the concept of social capital. There are three main points of origin to the concept, although the common-sense notion that 'it's not what you know but *who* you know that counts', has long historical roots (Harriss, 2002). The principal elaborators of the notion are, first, Bourdieu (1967), writing from a neo-Marxist position, Coleman (1988), who argues from a rational-choice individualist model of social action, and Putnam (1993), with a focus on norms and networks of trust that is strongly redolent of functionalist social theory. Each of these starting points is distinctive, although often blurred in subsequent accounts. A brief presentation and critique of the positions is followed by a discussion of the implications for the analysis of RCOs, which forms the basis of this book. It is important to note here that debates over the concept of social capital reflect much broader and long-standing differences within social theory as a whole, which can only be referenced here.

The earliest contribution is that of Bourdieu. In *Reproduction* (1967), Bourdieu introduces the idea of different forms of capital (economic, social, cultural and symbolic) as resources which individuals and groups compete over in different social fields. The notion of *habitus* is central to Bourdieu's account and refers to the historically acquired set of dispositions, reflexes and forms of behaviour people acquire through acting in society. This is part of how society reproduces itself but also provides the platform for social change as individuals seek to match their expectations to changed material and social circumstances. Conflict and change are 'built into' social relationships in this framework, leading to a strong emphasis on agency and forms of political intervention in Bourdieu's output (May, 1996, p 127). Fields in this context provide the arena for struggles over the different forms of capital, such as the 'artistic' and 'scientific' fields and the 'field of power' (May, 1996, p 129). Presented within a Marxist framework that seeks to revise Marx's own conception of 'capital' (Fine, 1999), *social capital* is defined as "the aggregate of the actual or potential resources which are linked to possession of a durable network of more or less institutionalised relationships of mutual acquaintance and recognition – which provides each of its members with the backing of collectively owned capital" (Bourdieu, 1986, p 51). In this account, social capital is a resource connected with group membership and social networks. As Siisiänen (2000, p 12) observes:

> Membership in groups, and involvement in the social networks developing within these and in the social relations arising from the membership can be utilised in efforts to improve the social position of the actors in a variety of different fields.

Two points can be made here. First, social capital in this perspective is closely linked to more general forms of struggle over resources in society. Second, social capital is based upon processes of recognition between agents that lend it a symbolic or interpretive character. As Fine (1999) has insisted, social capital in Bourdieu has to be understood primarily on the level of meaning rather than as a discrete material resource.

The difficulties in Bourdieu's account are legion. The reinterpretation of Marx has been challenged from within Marxism itself, while there is a continuing debate over the status of concepts such as *habitus* and 'field'. Does the *habitus* represent a resolution of the "problem of the relationship between structural conditioning and actors' freedom of choice" (Siisiänen, 2000, p 16) or another form of reductionism? Despite these problems, it can be argued that Bourdieu's contribution has been unfairly neglected in subsequent accounts of social capital. If Bourdieu represents a Marxism that is widely perceived to have 'failed' on both political and theoretical grounds, Coleman and Putnam, as illustrated now in this chapter, have chimed more comfortably with the prevailing assumptions informing mainstream social science.

Coleman (1988) aimed to combine sociological insights into social structure with the utility maximisation model of economics. Coleman argued that both disciplines have serious gaps: an account of purposive action in sociology and of the social bases of individual economic activity in economics. His goal was to import the rational basis of action into sociology proper, without discarding social organisation in the process. In this context, social capital constitutes a particular kind of resource available to an actor. It is not an entity but a variety of entities, facilitating social structures and action within social structures. In particular, it refers to "the value of these aspects of social structure to actors as resources that they can use to achieve their interests" (Coleman, 1998, p 101). His main focus was on social capital in the family and the community and its effects upon human capital in the next generation.

There are significant problems with Coleman's perspective. Portes (1995, p 5), for example, argues that Coleman fails to distinguish between membership of social structure, which might be termed 'social capital', and the resources acquired through such membership. In this context, Portes (1995, p 12) has argued that social capital is "the capacity of individuals to command scarce resources by virtue of their membership in networks or broader social structure....The resources themselves are not social capital; the concept refers instead to the individual's ability to mobilise them on demand". It has also been argued that Coleman focuses on dense ties – family and kinship – rather than 'weak ones'; that is, formal ties with institutions outside the immediate family which may be better placed to elaborate social capital (Granovetter, 1973). This failing in Coleman is to some degree rectified in Putnam's distinction between bonding, bridging and linking social capital, which is discussed more fully later in this chapter. In Coleman's account, social relations are resources used by actors, in particular those of trust, expectations and reciprocity, in order to realise their goals. In general, the 'social' is brought into the analysis only to be relegated to the role of functional adjunct to the primary role of individual, rational economic behaviour.

Putnam's work in part can be seen to address some of these deficiencies. In *Making democracy work* (1993), Putnam provides a comparative analysis of regional administrations in Italy. The basic distinction he draws is between the florescence of 'civic community' in the north of the country and the absence of strong networks and relations of trust in the south. This is also the basic reason he gives for the economic vitality of the North: put plainly, mutuality and civic responsibility result in a strong economy. The 'vibrancy of associational life' is used as one of the main indicators of civic participation (alongside voting activity and reading newspapers) and what he later in the book refers to as social capital. For Putnam (1996, p 34), "by 'social capital' I mean features of social life – *networks, norms and trust* – that enable participants to act together more effectively to pursue shared objectives". Trust relations – that is, a shared value basis that is founded on voluntary regulation of social relations between persons who are not personally related – are essential to the functioning of modern societies. Trust is the bedrock of reciprocity, networks and voluntary associations, which in turn generate further trust. There is therefore a virtuous circle of trust relations that is self-reinforcing, as much as there can be a vicious circle of distrust and 'non-civic community'.

A certain circularity of argument is already evident in this account. In practice, Putnam tends to identify trust or norms of reciprocity with intermediate voluntary associations (operating between state and civil society). In *Making democracy work*, the voluntary associations examined consist largely of sports clubs and cultural associations, which tend to directly promote social integration. The issue of non-integrative associations is not adequately addressed in this account. As Siisiänen (2002, p 5) argues, Putnam follows in a long line of commentators who regard voluntary associations as the "base for examining the relationship between civil society and the state. A plurality of crosscutting voluntary associations was understood as the main precondition for a stable democracy". Again, as she argues, the main problem concerns the question of distrust and conflict (that is, conflicts between different parts of civil society), which result in different types of association with conflicting aims and interests. In a similar vein, Putnam is silent on both the more general role of state institutions and the internal politics of voluntary associations. Discussion of the tendencies towards oligarchy and bureaucratisation in organisations is notable by its absence. In fact, Weber (1911, cited in Siisiänen, 2002) had documented discussion of power relations inside associations, between leadership and rank and file, and also towards outsider groups at a considerably earlier date.

Although massively influential, there are clearly serious deficiencies in Putnam's account. These include:

- *circularity:* social capital is the cause of social solidarity and economic benefits and "its existence is inferred from the same outcomes" (Portes, 1998, p 16);
- *a tendency to downplay the 'dark side' of social capital:* the exclusion of outsiders which may result from communal solidarity (Portes, 1998);
- *conservatism:* the emphasis on the role of values and norms is heavily redolent of Parsonian functionalist sociology;

- *weak empirical evidence:* Harriss (2002) in particular has challenged the historical accuracy of Putnam's account.

Responding to the charge of conservatism, it has already been noted that Putnam has made a distinction between *bonding, bridging* and *linking* forms of social capital that attempts to take power relationships into consideration.

- *Bonding social capital* refers to the level of intra-community relationships between family and friends.
- *Bridging social capital* describes the level of inter-community relationships that cohere contacts of a similar social background.
- *Linking social capital* aims to address the question of power, and what Granovetter (1973) has referred to as the importance of 'weak ties', by referring to relationships with those in power and official bodies.

In this research, we are primarily concerned with bridging and linking forms of social capital, relationships and networks between refugee groups and between refugee groups and official channels at both the NGO and statutory levels. A word of caution is required, however, as Putnam's conception of linking social capital tends towards the consensualism that informs his general position. Is the development of linking social capital an advantage for less powerful groups, or does it merely perpetuate forms of tokenism and dependency? These issues are critically addressed in the fieldwork.

In relation to the exhaustive critiques of the concept that are now available, two additional points are worth recounting. First, there is a need to discount an exact economic definition or significance given to the concept 'capital' in relation to the term 'social capital'. Social capital is not alienable as in the case of physical capital; neither does it involve present sacrifice for future gain, again as in the case of physical capital. Second, it is necessary to challenge the underpinning of social capital in the individualistic and utility maximisation model of social action that is prevalent in mainstream economics. Although they may have both intended and unintended economic benefits, social networks may not (on the whole) be built up for their prospective economic benefits for individuals.

Despite the logical and substantive difficulties with the concept of social capital, it has proven highly influential in recent international and national policy arenas, notably in the World Bank and in related policy fields (Harriss, 2002). This is despite the fact that the concept has proven difficult to operationalise in practice. In many cases, the very vagueness and elasticity of the term has been made into a virtue. In general, as Harriss argues, the popularity of the concept reflects the concerns of a neoliberal economic agenda which prioritises tight fiscal control and the erosion of welfare rights. In effect, if social capital can be used to mobilise popular resources then the rationale for state-administered welfare is further undermined. As we argue in Chapter Eight of this book, that this should be argued in the name of participation and democracy is one of the more ironic aspects of the case.

The approach taken here is more critical. Social capital, like the concept of the network, "is itself a metaphoric, shorthand notion" (Vertovec, 2001, p 11) for a complex variety of positions and embodies a range of theoretical assumptions and perspectives. Social capital may be defined as a convenient shorthand term for social networks and their role in enabling individuals and groups to access other forms of symbolic and material resources. It does not provide an overarching conceptualisation that is self-sufficient and free-standing. In this respect, as the discussion of Putnam indicates, it is important to acknowledge conflict and unequal power relations as much as the integrative effects of shared norms and reciprocity. In relation to the application of social capital analysis to the case of RCOs, a key question raised by this research is whether a consensual perspective which emphasises shared norms and trust (as in Putnam) is more or less appropriate than a conflictual model (as in Bourdieu) which emphasises competition over different types of resources. This forms a recurring theme in the research and will be more fully addressed in the concluding discussion.

If there is a tendency in social capital analysis to idealise community solidarity, the fieldwork conducted as part of this research indicates that real communities are "far more complex than the concept of social capital can capture" (Campbell, 2001, p 4). Yet as Campbell (2001, p 5) goes on to suggest, "the concept does have the potential to serve as a modest starting point for research seeking to conceptualise the community level of analysis in particular situations". Some work has already been undertaken which applies the concept of social capital to the refugee field. Loizos (2000) has given some useful hints concerning the utility of the concept. He is quick, however, to point to the deficiencies of social capital as a solution to overarching structural problems and to the need to place the concept within a broader range of approaches. As Loizos (2000, p 125) argues:

> In my view, the social capital emphasis cannot be plausible
> as comprehensive social theory: it can only add some
> harmonies to the melodic themes of political economy.

In his view, social capital is a 'complementary concept' and not one
that occupies centre stage in social theory. In reviewing the process of
adjustment to new situations in exile, refugees as 'social capitalists'
rebuild their networks in exile and use these as new means of support.
Social capital refers to the tendency of former villagers to 'stick
together':

> In short, [social capital] is the package of customs, beliefs
> and practices from before their dislocation which continued
> to serve them in diasporic adjustment. (Loizos, 2000, p 132)

In a situation of dislocation, refugees are compelled to turn to one
another to reconstruct a meaningful sense of social life and identity. In
sum, although social capital may be a useful complementary concept,
there is also the need to look at the broader context of resettlement
policies and asylum policy, including the specific model of minority
inclusion and representation. In the UK, for example, Loizos notes
the potentially damaging effects of dispersal upon the formation of
social capital in refugee communities: dispersal may act to prevent the
formation of effective refugee networks by placing asylum seekers
outside areas in which there are already established refugee
communities. This broader context is addressed in Chapter Three.

Conclusions

This chapter has outlined a number of different approaches to the
study of refugee organisations. Beginning with the sociological
literature on migrant associations, it was noted that the dominant
paradigm informing the field was predicated on the integrative and
adaptive functions of associations for migrants in new social settings.
Empirical studies of migrant and refugee associations have tended on
the whole to conform to this dominant paradigm. The downside of
refugee organisations in terms of factionalism, lack of
accountability, insecurity of funding and general 'structural
precariousness' has also been noted in the literature. More critical
approaches, which to varying degrees run counter to this dominant
paradigm, have highlighted the role of the state in setting the parameters
within which migrants and refugees organise. Assumptions of

'community' solidarity and unity and the race relations framework have been noted as the key determinants affecting refugee organisations in Britain. Building upon this critical approach, we propose alternative perspectives that provide distinctive insights into the factors determining refugee organisation. Following a broadly neo-institutionalist approach, these factors include the opportunity structures available to refugees (including here the incorporation regimes in play) and the possibilities which these provide for organisational activity. This again points us to the broader state context and framework affecting refugee organisation. Complementing the emphasis given to structural aspects is the importance of refugee networks and forms of social capital in refugee communities. Subject to a sustained critique, it has been suggested that the concept of social capital provides one possible point of entry to the discussion of networks and their benefits to refugees, albeit that this is set within a broader analysis of structural determinants and power relations. Increasingly, the integrative framework which has dominated the study of refugee organisations and which is implicit in many accounts of social capital, particularly those stemming from the work of Putnam, appears in need of revision.

Our own research is based upon attention to institutional constraints and a critical reading of the literature on social capital. This perspective highlights the extensive power relations and conflict which operate at a variety of micro and macro levels and which directly impinge upon the forms of refugee organisation and mobilisation. 'Power' is conceptualised in this research as a multi-faceted phenomenon that operates at a variety of levels (Goverde et al, 2000). Going beyond the conventional debate between pluralism and Marxism that dominated the 1970s, 'power' is increasingly conceptualised in terms of discourse and meaning (Foucault, 1980). Incorporation regimes for example, as Soysal (1994) has argued, are both discursive and institutional in character. An important distinction that informs the discussion is the difference between power as enabling and power as coercive – *'power to'*, versus *'power over'*. Institutional arrangements in this sense may provide 'opportunity structures' for action while acting to constrain mobilisation within specified limits. Lukes' (1974) distinction between power as decision making, agenda setting and the setting of preferences through forms of institutional bias (normative power) also retains its relevance and informs the analysis of institutions in this research.

THREE

Dispersal: policy and practice

This chapter reviews the background to current dispersal policy and practice in the UK. The principles, implementation and effects of dispersal under the 1999 Immigration and Asylum Act are examined. In particular, the development of new institutional arrangements for the reception and settlement of refugees is addressed. The chapter further reviews the main contents of the 2002 White Paper, *Secure borders, safe haven: Integration with diversity in modern Britain* (Home Office, 2002a), and the key provisions of the 2002 Nationality, Immigration and Asylum Act. The specific role of refugee community organisations (RCOs) within the new policy framework is then discussed in more detail. Under the broad heading of partnership arrangements between the central state, local authorities, non-governmental organisations (NGOs) and the private and voluntary sectors, RCOs have been formally incorporated into the emerging institutional framework. The chapter concludes with a review of the developing literature on the impacts of dispersal upon RCOs in London and the regions. This provides the context for the fieldwork results that are presented in the following chapters of this book.

The dispersal of quota and programme refugees

In contrast with comparable European Union (EU) states, the UK has only recently introduced organised reception and dispersal procedures for asylum seekers. This stands in marked contrast to the extensive experience in the dispersal of quota or programme refugees in the UK, in the Ugandan, Asian, Vietnamese and Chilean programmes in the 1970s and 1980s (Robinson, 1985; Joly, 1996) and more latterly in the case of the Bosnian and Kosovan programmes in the 1990s (Robinson and Coleman, 2000). The UK's general approach to reception and settlement policy up until the 1999 Immigration and Asylum Act, had in fact been largely decentralised and incremental in character. The decentralised approach to asylum in Britain was based upon distinctive national traditions of cooperation between the Community Relations Unit (now the Race Equality Unit) of the Home Office and voluntary bodies and NGOs (Kaye, 1992; Carey-

Wood et al, 1995).The pressure of rising numbers during the 1990s and increasing demands upon housing and welfare facilities in the major areas of settlement in London and the South East, provided the backdrop for the introduction of a coordinated approach to asylum (Home Office, 1998) and the development of new institutional arrangements for the reception and support of asylum seekers. As Boswell (2001) and Robinson et al (2003) have argued, the current dispersal system is based upon an ambiguous logic of 'burden sharing', which is closely linked to perceptions of public tolerance of asylum seekers and their visibility in the major areas of settlement. The limitations of the dispersal system in terms of its stated aims are discussed more fully later in this chapter.

The evidence on dispersal and the reception and settlement of quota and programme refugees had suggested systemic policy failure related to accommodation-led integration, without due attention to the broader social and economic infrastructure of the regions to which refugees were dispersed (Robinson et al, 2003).The programmes were 'front-loaded' in the sense of prioritising the availability of cheap surplus housing in the dispersal areas and neglecting the later settlement requirements of refugees (Robinson and Hale, 1989; Robinson, 1993a; Joly, 1996). High levels of secondary migration to London and other major conurbations indicated the failure of enforced dispersal to areas without adequate infrastructure or pre-existing forms of community support. By contrast, the Bosnian Programme of 1993 has been hailed as an example of effective settlement based upon cluster areas and the principle of ethnic community formation (Refugee Council, 1997; Robinson et al, 2003).Although persisting in the principle of dispersing refugees outside London, a more long-term perspective was also taken on the settlement needs of Bosnians in terms of housing and employment requirements in the cluster areas. Given the subsequent low levels of secondary migration of Bosnians, this suggests, as Robinson et al (2003, p 119) argue, "that carefully selected clustering was a superior policy to indiscriminate dispersal".

The changing legislative framework in the 1990s

The essential backdrop to the legislative changes that occurred throughout the 1990s is the dramatic increase in asylum applications in this period: from 26,205 applications in 1990 to 80,315 in 2000 (Home Office, 2000a). It is important to emphasise that these figures relate to principal applicants only. This is from a baseline of around 4,000 applications per year during the period 1980-88. Reviewing the key legislative changes, the 1993 Asylum and Immigration Appeals Act was the first primary legislation to deal with asylum in the UK. It was designed to deal with the backlog of asylum cases and aimed to introduce a streamlined approach to hasten decision making. The principal features of the Act included the reinforcement of carriers' sanctions which were first introduced in 1987, the introduction of the finger-printing of asylum seekers and their children and the withdrawal of mandatory provision of local authority housing for asylum seekers. For those who could make political capital from the asylum issue, the Act did not go far enough in stemming the 'rising tide' of asylum seekers. The 1996 Asylum and Immigration Act, formally announced in the Queen's Speech on 15 November 1995, coincided with the campaign for the 1997 General Election. The editorial in *The Guardian* (25 October 1995) was unequivocal in its verdict:

> Let us be clear that the only reason why we are about to have another Immigration and Asylum Bill is because it is deemed to be politically advantageous to the Conservative Party's electoral prospects for this to be so.

For the irate editor, it was seen to be another in a line of "last ditch desperate measures to save the Conservatives in the face of the Blair ascendancy". As in the case of the 1993 Act, the Conservative Party was set to play the race card in the run-up to the General Election in 1997.

In the event, the main provisions of the Act included the extension of 'fast-track' procedures for asylum seekers from designated 'safe countries', the so-called 'white list' and the withdrawal of benefits for those individuals who applied for asylum in-country or who were on-appeal against a negative decision. In addition, asylum seekers were excluded from local authority housing lists, a clause which was reinforced by the 1996 Housing Act. The Act therefore combined pre-entry restrictions with in-country deterrence. In practice, the benefits and housing clauses had the most immediate impact on the livelihood of asylum seekers and the system of welfare support available to them. In response to the withdrawal of centralised support, local authorities used the 1948 National Assistance Act to cater for destitute asylum seekers. London was characterised by a range of ad-hoc responses and the absence of coordinated support measures across boroughs (Medical Foundation, 1997). The increased costs over the benefit system and the acute housing shortage led to a situation during 1997 when the asylum support system was widely believed to be heading towards breakdown. This was the context for the New Labour review of the asylum system that was begun shortly after their taking office and continued until October 1997.

The government White Paper (Home Office, 1998), *Fairer, faster, firmer: A modern approach to immigration and asylum*, was published in July 1998. In many respects, it conforms to the broader process of centralisation in UK government, which has been noted by a variety of commentators (Stewart, 1993; Clarke et al, 2000). In particular, the proposed modernisation of the asylum system is of a piece with contemporary government initiatives that are documented in the White Paper, *Modernising government* (Cabinet Office, 1999), and its associated Best Value regime. As Maile and Hoggett (2001, pp 509-19) have argued:

> Local government (in the UK) is increasingly becoming a 'policy-free zone' and the role of local authorities (like many of their non-elected local counterparts) is to deliver centrally determined policies in a strategic way.

Asylum can be analysed in terms of a telescoping of these broader tendencies within government policy. Beginning with the 1998 White Paper and the subsequent 1999 legislation, the various statutory requirements to house asylum seekers have been taken away from local authorities while the powers of administration and budgetary control have moved to the Home Office. Centralisation of control is further illustrated in the increasing regulation of carriers and attempts to minimise financial motives for moving to the UK, as well as frequent references in the 1998 White Paper to the cost savings associated with such rationalisations. The presumption that all asylum seekers are potential 'economic migrants' is represented in terms of 'fairness' to those who are in 'genuine need' (Home Office, 1998).

The introduction of organised dispersal in the UK is a response to specific domestic policy issues as well as being part of a more general process of EU harmonisation in reception policies (Zetter et al, 2003a). In the first case, as Robinson (Robinson et al, 2003, p 105) has noted, debates around the efficacy and desirability of dispersing minority ethnic groups in the UK are longstanding.

Box 3.1: The 1999 Immigration and Asylum Act

The 1999 Immigration and Asylum Act, based upon the 1998 White Paper, marks a radical point of departure in UK asylum policy. In contrast to the incremental approach to the reinforcement of pre-entry restrictions and the staggered withdrawal of asylum seekers from mainstream welfare provision that were apparent in the earlier legislation of 1993 and 1996, the 1999 legislation completely overhauled the reception and support services available to asylum seekers. In addition to the extension of carriers' liability, among the key innovations all new asylum seekers were to be separated from mainstream welfare provision. The Act introduced a centralised system of support through a voucher system (later withdrawn) and the dispersal of asylum seekers to designated areas of surplus housing to be operated by regional consortia under the supervision of the National Asylum Support Service (NASS). The rationale and principles of implementation for dispersal were further documented in a number of policy documents produced by the Home Office in 1999 (*Asylum seeker support* [1999a]; *Process manual* [1999b]; *Accommodation specification document* [1999c]).

Dispersal was to be introduced with the following aims in mind:

- to redistribute costs away from London and the south-east by "minimising the attractiveness of the UK for those whose application is unfounded" (Home Office, 1999a, para 1.1);
- to deter unfounded applications;
- to provide support to asylum seekers outside the benefits system;
- to avoid "adding to the problems of social exclusion" and racial tension (Home Office, 1999a, para 1.18);
- to avoid secondary migration.

In the 1950s and 1960s for example, the dominant assimilationist stance of government policy assumed that concentration was counter-productive to effective assimilation. Large numbers of a particular minority ethnic group congregating in one locality was automatically assumed to promote social problems and divisions. Deakin and Cohen (1970, quoted in Robinson et al, 2003, p 106), in their article 'Dispersal and choice: towards a strategy for ethnic minorities in Britain', succinctly stated the prevailing view that "the notion of dispersal of immigrants stands out as a clear cut policy goal". The basic assumption was that dispersal eased the burden on local services, reduced the possibilities of social friction and slowed down the tendency towards 'ghettoisation' in schools. The decline in assimilationist policies in the 1970s was accompanied by an emphasis on the importance of minority ethnic community clustering for effective integration. The evidence on whether ethnic concentration encourages or discourages integration remains unclear. Marcuse (1996, p 38), for example, has usefully distinguished between ethnic enclaves "as areas of spatial concentration" which are walled in socially if not physically, but which have positive consequences for their residents, as opposed to 'ghettos', which are entirely negative. The distinguishing feature relates to the permeability of the "walls that surround the cluster" (Marcuse, 1996, p 41): are these determined from the outside, operating to exclude participation in the mainstream, or created and maintained from within the enclave itself?

In relation to the current UK dispersal policy, the arguments marshalled in its favour tend to focus on the need for distributing social and financial costs equitably between different localities. Reducing social tensions arising from competition for scarce resources and the 'visibility' of minority ethnic groups are other strands of the argument advanced in favour of dispersal. As Robinson et al argue (2003, p 164), the basic premise of dispersal remains firmly assimilationist in character. From this perspective, dispersal as a form of enforced population control is primarily a means of reducing the social visibility of asylum seekers and their potential 'pollution' of social space. If the spatial concentration of asylum seekers and refugee communities is constructed as a problem for 'race relations', then their social dispersal is both a logical and desirable outcome. By contrast, there is ample evidence to suggest that clustering may on the contrary be a positive process that fosters community formation, ethnic networking and the long-term settlement of refugees (Robinson et al, 2003, pp 165-7). On the other hand, it is also clear that one of the unintended consequences of dispersal has been the introduction of minority ethnic groups into previously mono-cultural areas, with predictable results in terms of increased hostility and social friction.

Second, it should also be noted that dispersal policies feature in many EU member states (EUMS) including for example the Netherlands, Sweden and Germany (Boswell, 2001; Robinson et al, 2003) often as part of a more systematic process of decentralisation of the reception process (Pfohman and Amrute, 2004). Decentralisation in this case refers to the transfer of responsibility for asylum seekers from federal or central government to local authorities, while dispersal is more narrowly confined to "the physical allocation of asylum seekers to particular locations within a nation-state" (Pfohman and Amrute, 2004, p 19). Both decentralisation and dispersal are closely tied to the principle of 'burden sharing', which informs EU asylum policy. All three – decentralisation, dispersal and burden sharing – are part of the broader harmonisation of asylum policy which has accelerated since the Treaty of Amsterdam (Geddes, 2000), and in particular with the moving of asylum and immigration to the first, communitarian pillar of the EU. The Treaty of Amsterdam was signed in June 1997 and came into force in May 1999. It includes a positive commitment to the Geneva Convention and 1967 Protocol, which was confirmed in the Vienna action plan in 1998 and at the European Council Meeting in Tampere, Finland in October 1999. In this respect, the passing of Council Directive 2003/9/EC of 27 January 2003, laying down minimum standards for the reception of asylum seekers, has further consolidated a more uniform approach to the reception of asylum seekers across EUMS. For many advocates of refugee rights, the process of harmonisation has resulted in a 'lowest-common-denominator' approach, whereby nation states continue to operate national law below the level established within the community. As Christopher Hein (www.eurasylum.org) has argued:

> The subsequent process that began with the Seville Council and expanded after September 11th, appears to have been increasingly distant from the Tampere Conclusions … ultimately, national self interest has prevailed.

National differences between EUMS in the organisation of dispersal are clearly evident, depending on the political and geographical structures of the country in question. Federalism in Germany, for example, has resulted in a system of dispersal that is based upon the equalisation of costs between self-governing *Länder*, rather than the heavily centralised model that now operates in the UK. Nevertheless, the UK's convergence with EU policy is apparent in the restrictionism that continues to inform its approach to asylum. As Hassan (2000) has argued, asylum policy in the UK is based upon the twin pillars of restriction of entry and deterrence in relation to the withdrawal of in-country entitlements and rights.

Dispersal under the 1999 Immigration and Asylum Act

The principal changes to the support provisions for asylum seekers were included in Part VI of the 1999 Act, 'Support for Asylum Seekers'. Preliminary arrangements were developed in anticipation of the 1999 Act when the Home Secretary approached the Local Government Association (LGA) to formulate a strategic policy of dispersal, initially on a voluntary basis in collaboration with local authorities. This stage was superseded after the inception of the Asylum Support Directorate (ASD) – later to become the National Asylum Support Service (NASS) – and a three-phase roll out was implemented through continued voluntary interim arrangements with local authorities, a statutory basis from December 1999, and then with NASS becoming operational, an operational roll-out period of five months from April 2000. The last phase comprised first the dispersal of post-1 April port-of-entry applicants, then post-1 April in-country applicants and then pre-1 April applicants supported by local authorities under earlier procedures and statutes.

Regional consortia are the vehicles through which the public sector has been commissioned to deliver its input into the regional dispersal process. They were initially developed by local authorities, in anticipation of the centrally controlled statutory system, and coordinated by the LGA as a response to the government's proposals in the 1998 White Paper, *Fairer, faster and firmer* (Home Office, 1998). In November 1998, the LGA wrote to all local authorities requesting that they should consider setting up regional consortia on a voluntary basis prior to the formal commencement of dispersal in April 2000. The expectation was that these consortia would identify available accommodation and set up systems that would enable the process of dispersal to be implemented. At the end of 2002, there were nine regional consortia in operation:

- East of England;
- East Midlands;
- Greater London;
- North-East;
- North-West;
- South-East;
- South-West;
- West Midlands;
- Yorkshire and Humberside.

Northern Ireland, Scotland and Wales are also included in the dispersal arrangements (Home Office, 2002a).

In advance of the statutory system, a dispersal programme was implemented in response to the arrival of quota Kosovan refugees, with temporary leave to remain, in 1999, when a number of mainly northern local authorities played a major role in providing emergency accommodation. The requirement to deliver reception facilities and housing support within very short timescales helped develop the prototype for coordinated programming within localities. This formed the basis for the development of the more formalised consortia envisaged by the LGA and ASD. The approaches adopted and alliances developed at this stage, formed the basis for the structures that later emerged under the interim arrangements and subsequently became the basis for the contractual agreements with NASS from April 2000. In response to the government's dispersal timetable, regional consortia were formed towards the end of 1999 and early 2000, and a voluntary or interim dispersal scheme was introduced from 6 December 1999 underpinned by the Asylum Support (Interim Provisions) Regulations 1999, and coordinated by the ASD. This arrangement was effectively the precursor to the NASS-controlled dispersal programme and saw the inception of the resettlement of asylum seeker households away from London and the South East.

Box 3.2: The main principles of dispersal

In principal, dispersal was to be based upon the following features:

- the procurement of housing for dispersed asylum seekers by contracts between NASS and both the public and private providers in the regions;
- the dispersal of asylum seekers to language-based, multi-ethnic cluster areas where suitable housing and support services are available;
- a centralised management and funding of the dispersal of asylum seekers by a new agency, NASS;
- the coordinated provision of services and support (both public and voluntary sectors) through regional consortia of local authorities;
- an increased role for the voluntary sector in providing advice and support through One-Stop Services (OSSs) and emergency accommodation in the regions.

Evaluating dispersal

In practice, the implementation of dispersal has met with logistical and resource difficulties, which have continually hampered its effectiveness (Audit Commission, 2000a; Johnson, 2001; NASS, 2001; Wilson, 2001; Zetter et al, 2003b). The initial premise of the NASS dispersal programme for asylum seekers of April 2000 was language-based clustering in areas of ethnic community support, with access to social facilities and economic infrastructure in the regions outside London. Cluster areas would ideally have a suitable ethnic composition, good community relations and social networks in addition to an infrastructure of schools, translation and legal services and other subsidiary services. In the event, accommodation-led policy – the provision of affordable surplus housing has tended to prevail over language-based clustering and appropriate social and economic support for asylum seekers (Robinson et al, 2003). It is important to note that the quality of housing provision itself has also been variable (Carter and El-Hassan, 2003) both across locations and the different sectors involved in provision. In relation to the choice of cluster areas, the Audit Commission (2000) forcefully restated the principle that the assessment of suitable areas for asylum seekers should consider a number

Box 3.3: Deficiencies of the dispersal process

Commentators (Wilson, 2001; Carter and El-Hassan, 2003; Robinson et al, 2003) have consistently noted several deficiencies in the NASS dispersal arrangements. These are reinforced in our fieldwork and include:

- overcentralisation of the dispersal process;
- substantial shortcomings in the management, coordination, and sharing of data and information between NASS and the regional consortia;
- a procurement-and-contract-dominated model of dispersal which has worked against the development of comprehensive service provision strategies and the promotion of essential partnerships at the local level;
- severely limited delivery of the core principle of language-based clusters;
- inadequate resource provision: these shortcomings have severely impacted on core components such as the OSS. The level of resourcing was predicated on a projected demand which has proved to be a severe underestimate;
- the voluntary sector, including RCOs, has been inadequately resourced and supported.

of questions including ethnic composition and the existence of community networks. In many cases, it noted that this does not appear to have been effectively adhered to. Asylum seekers have been dispersed to areas in which there are no co-ethnics or available means of community support.

As several reports have suggested, in the practical implementation of the dispersal programme, NASS has adopted a strategy based on coordination and control rather than participation and dialogue. This has created tensions in relation to the regional consortia, which have consistently argued for the need for local sensitivity that a partnership model of policy implementation might offer.

As a response to growing criticisms of the dispersal programme, the NASS internal review in 2001 made a series of recommendations for reform. It underlined, in particular, a need to strengthen the regional management capacity of NASS. The review recognised that transferring some of the central functions that were carried out in Croydon to an enhanced regional manager's office could help to fill this role and could provide a proactive link between policy and implementation. However, the review was rather short on detail. Despite reforms brought in since the NASS internal review, including an enlarged role for NASS regional managers, the degree to which the regionalisation of NASS and a more transparent decision-making process has been achieved is open to question. The NASS internal review, while calling for the regionalisation of NASS management, stopped short of a more thoroughgoing regionalisation of authority and decision making in relation to dispersal. In this respect, the role of consortia, NGOs and the private and voluntary sectors is also uneven across the regions, with distinct organisational structures and degrees of coordination evident between the different actors and agencies involved in dispersal (Boswell, 2001).

Judged in its own terms as a means of 'spreading the burden' of financial and social costs, it is by no means clear that dispersal has been either particularly effective or efficient. Boswell (2001), for example, has cogently argued that while dispersal may have been effective in redistributing financial costs between London and the regions, this has not resulted in an overall reduction in spending. In addition, rather than reducing social tensions, dispersal, particularly in its early stages, has also tended to relocate social anxieties to areas with little previous history of minority settlement. Robinson et al (2003, p 166) go further in arguing that dispersal is actually more expensive and less efficient than other means of reception and settlement. In particular, dispersal is more costly than clustering because important economies of scale are lost in relation to the duplication of costs (administrative systems, staff and travel), which are spread across smaller numbers of asylum seekers dispersed to a larger number of regions.

From a review of the literature and our own fieldwork in the regions, an overall picture emerges of a centralised and regulatory structure that has struggled both to develop new systems and to embed the appropriate capacity to cope with the pressure to deliver precise but substantial targets for dispersal. The NASS, as the client and primary sponsor of the dispersal programme, is central to developing a culture of good practice. So far, however, it has not successfully done so. As a result, the operational aspects of dispersal are often delivered in an ad-hoc and erratic manner. Where performance is valued within NASS, it appears to be perceived within a narrow interpretation of contract compliance with a limited vision of the broader impacts or the wider policy objectives of dispersal. At the same time, a proliferation of agencies, actors and institutional structures has developed to implement the new legislation for dispersal. These outcomes raise important questions about the design of the policy model, its operationalisation and the sensitivity to local political, community and agency dynamics. In particular, in relation to asylum seekers and refugees, there is a need for dispersal to be undertaken within a more flexibly managed structure and process which better articulates the components of the dispersal system from the inception of asylum seekers to their eventual exit from the system. At the time of the fieldwork conducted for this book (during the course of 2002 to 2003), the logistics of dispersal would appear to have outweighed the requirements of effective refugee settlement in the regions.

Despite the considerable drawbacks to the dispersal system, it is clear that significant numbers of asylum seekers are choosing to remain in the regions upon receipt of a positive decision on their claim for asylum. Refugee communities are in the process of being formed outside London, in many cases for the first time. This has implications for the settlement of refugees in the regions and the role of RCOs, which are addressed throughout this book.

The 2002 Nationality, Immigration and Asylum Act

Before outlining the institutional framework for reception and settlement in more detail, it is necessary to briefly review the main changes introduced under the 2002 Nationality, Immigration and Asylum Act. These were substantially prefigured in the 2002 White Paper, *Secure borders, safe haven* (Home Office, 2002a), and include changes to citizenship rules under which applicants for British citizenship will now have to pass an English language test and attend a formal citizenship ceremony. The report of the 'Life in the United Kingdom' Advisory Group, chaired by Bernard Crick, *The new and the old* (Home Office, 2003b, p 11), concluded that, "Use of English language itself is possibly the most important means of diverse communities participating in a common culture with key values in common". The 2002 legislation was underpinned by a more general set of concerns around social cohesion and fragmentation, sparked by riots in inner-city areas of Northern England in 2001. The issues of citizenship, integration and social cohesion are central to the emerging public policy framework in the UK, with immigration and asylum often appearing to act as focal points for more generalised forms of social anxiety (Boswell, 2003). The broader ramifications of these issues are further addressed in the conclusions to this book.

In relation to asylum procedures, the main aim of the 2002 legislation was to instigate a managed system of 'end-to-end credibility', proceeding from induction and reception to increased reporting and surveillance procedures and terminating in either 'fast-track removal or integration' (Home Office, 2002b, p 14). One of the most controversial changes was the introduction of section 55 of the Act, which came into force on 8 January 2003. This prevented asylum seekers from receiving support from NASS if they had failed to apply for asylum "as soon as reasonably practicable". A number of judicial reviews were lodged resulting in a partial defeat for the government concerning its obligations under Article 3 of the European Convention on Human Rights (ECHR), which guarantees shelter as a 'basic amenity'. The government appeal against the decision on 18 March resulted in a further clarification of the "as soon as reasonably practicable" criteria that NASS were operating and an overhaul of NASS procedures as a result. In July 2003, a High Court judgment ruled that the failure of the Home Office to offer support to three asylum seekers amounted to a breach of its obligations under Article 3 of the ECHR. The Home Office was again given leave to appeal. The appeal, held on 21 May 2004, upheld the original ruling that section 55 was illegal and in contravention of Article 3 of the ECHR. At the time of writing, the Home Office was seeking leave to appeal to the House of Lords. Also of direct relevance to asylum seekers was the withdrawal of the right to seek employment and undertake vocational training until a positive decision has been made on their claim for asylum. This was introduced in July 2002 and did not require direct legislative change in order to be enacted. Before that date, asylum seekers could apply to the Home Office for permission to work six months after their claim for asylum had been made.

Refugee settlement

A detailed history of refugee settlement in Britain has yet to be written. Although there are ethnographic accounts of particular refugee groups, in some cases dating from the inter-war and post-war periods in the 20th century and covering nationalities such as the Armenians and Poles, there is no comprehensive history of refugee settlement, especially in relation to the period since the 1980s. More general historical accounts of refugee policy in Britain (Porter, 1979; Kushner and Knox; 1999; Schuster, 2003) provide insights into particular cases of refugee settlement and the shifting patterns of governmental and public response. A wealth of grey literature on the other hand has been produced, dating largely from the 1980s, which focuses on the policy issues affecting particular refugee groups, or on refugee groups within specific localities (Srinivasan, 1994). The work of local historian, Malcolm Dick (2002), on refugees in the West Midlands is a case in point, as is the oral history which has been conducted with particular groups such as the Vietnamese. Of the proliferating number of web-based organisations, the Information Centre about Asylum and Refugees in the UK (ICAR) provides a useful summary of current information on refugee settlement in its report on 'Patterns of Refugee Settlement Project' (www.icar.org.uk) and its recent publication, *The Somali community in the UK* (Harris, 2004). It is generally established that London is the primary location of refugee settlement in the UK. This is well documented, as is the concentration of refugees and asylum seekers in particular boroughs in London. In the absence of rigorous centralised data on the number and characteristics of refugees and asylum seekers, it is necessary to draw on anecdotal evidence concerning the size and characteristics of specific refugee groups. One central factor is the greater variety of nationalities and the size of refugee communities in London in comparison to the regions. In several cases, in the nationalities covered in this research, specific groups such as the Somalis, Tamils and Iranians, numbered over 10,000 in specific localities and up to 20,000 across London as a whole. According to a variety of estimates, there are in excess of 300,000 refugees and asylum seekers in London. The development of RCOs in London has reflected this general situation. It is important to note that our research does not reflect the formation of RCOs throughout the earlier part of the 20th century (Kushner and Knox, 1999). More recent refugee organisations, on the other hand, began to mushroom from the middle of the 1980s onwards. Current estimates are that there are between 500 and 600 refugee organisations, although again there are no reliable statistics on how many of these organisations are viable and functioning.

In terms of refugee settlement in the regions examined here, it is important to emphasise the mixed character of asylum seeker and refugee populations. In addition to the earlier inflows of refugees in the 19th century and the inter-war and post-war periods, this typically comprises a mixture of earlier programme refugees – Vietnamese and Kosovans, for example – and asylum seekers arriving during the 1980s, such as the significant number of Iraqi Kurds in Manchester. In Liverpool, for example, Somalis had arrived as migrants in the post-Second World War period and throughout the 1990s as asylum seekers as civil war intensified in the southern and central regions of the country. Asylum seekers and settled refugees in the regions consist therefore of these earlier groups, individuals dispersed by London boroughs prior to the NASS arrangements, asylum seekers under the interim arrangements and, from April 2000, the new NASS arrivals.

Refugee integration: the policy framework

The final section of the 2002 White Paper (Home Office, 2002a) is devoted to the theme of refugee integration. It is important to note that integration measures at present are only open to individuals recognised as refugees under the Geneva Convention. Individual asylum seekers currently making a claim to be recognised as a refugee have no integration rights or entitlements. The provisions relating to integration are not incorporated into the 2002 legislation but refer primarily to a number of administrative and organisational changes that have been set in train since the introduction of dispersal. In the UK, the NGO and voluntary sectors have traditionally taken a lead role in reception and settlement for quota and non-programme refugees. The term NGO here refers to organisations, which although formally independent from government, depend in large part upon Home Office funding and directly liaise with various government departments. The main examples here are the Refugee Council and Refugee Action, which are supported in practice by a range of smaller organisations including the Ockenden Venture and the Refugee Arrivals Project. The voluntary sector comprises a broader range of non refugee-specific organisations that are less directly linked to government funding or policy agendas, such as local church-based or welfare organisations. Refugee community organisations in this context may be regarded as

Box 3.4: The principal NGOs assisting refugees and asylum seekers

Refugee Action

This agency has been based in the regions since the early 1980s, working initially in Vietnamese settlement and later the Bosnian and Kosovan programmes. As an organisation, it prioritises the principle of self-activity among refugee groups and their own capacity for integration. Indeed, the emphasis is more upon maintaining home links and ties with the culture of origin, renewing and building communities under new settings, than it is with economic and functional integration in the receiving society. In the last four years, dispersal from London and the South East and the increase in refugees settling in the regions has impacted directly on the work of Refugee Action. The emphasis of its workload has correspondingly shifted from long-term settlement issues to day-to-day advice work for asylum seekers.

Refugee Council

The largest of the principal NGOs dealing with refugee and asylum seekers, the Refugee Council has traditionally been based in London and provides a range of advisory and advocacy services. Under the NASS arrangements, it also responsible for running the OSS in several of the regions. In common with the position of Refugee Action, under-resourcing and increasing numbers of asylum seekers have resulted in the neglect of community development and settlement work. The focus of the Refugee Council in the regions is on processing applications of those arriving in-region and the provision of emergency accommodation. The regional development team of the Refugee Council focuses on developing the participation of voluntary organisations rather than working with specific refugee groups.

local, ethnically based voluntary organisations with a specific remit in relation to refugees and asylum seekers.

In this context, it is interesting to note that, throughout the 1980s and most of the 1990s, 'settlement' was the preferred label to refer to general integration processes (Field, 1985; Refugee Council, 1987, 1997; Carey-Wood et al, 1995). Only since the 1999 Immigration and Asylum Act and the policy documents outlining a refugee integration strategy has there been a move to the term 'integration' in official policy discourse, a term which has only reluctantly been adopted by NGOs due to its suggestion of assimilation as the goal of refugee settlement.

Reception and settlement provision had tended to be uncoordinated and ad hoc in character for non-programme asylum seekers with no systematic national policy framework prior to the 1999 Immigration and Asylum Act. The lack of national intervention in refugee settlement and integration has led to significant local variations in coordination and provision for refugees throughout the UK (Robinson, 1998a). What is significant in this context is the development of new institutional arrangements for the reception and settlement of asylum seekers and refugees in the regions. There is above all a radically increased role for NGOs and the voluntary sector under the 1999 Act in the provision of the OSS. Refugee community organisations are also formally incorporated, albeit in a minor role, within the new arrangements. In addition, the local authority consortia, while charged with administering dispersal, are also responsible for developing regional integration strategies in order to encourage recognised refugees to remain in the regions.

Refugee integration is in the process of emerging as a distinctive policy area with its own rationale and administrative structure. According to Home Office (1999d, p 6) documents, the aim of integration is "to provide the opportunity for all refugees to be fully included in society and the opportunity to develop their full potential in their new host communities". Research teams concerned with integration have been established in the Immigration Research and Statistics Service (IRSS) of the Home Office, the Economic and Resource Analysis Unit, and the Research, Development and Statistics Directorate. The focus of some of this research is on the impacts of refugees on local economies and communities. The UK refugee integration strategy, which has developed in close conjunction with the dispersal system for asylum seekers since April 2000, is based upon a number of key policy documents. Chronologically these are:

- *Full and equal citizens: A policy and implementation model for the integration of refugees into UK society* (Home Office, 1999e);
- *A consultation paper on the integration of recognised refugees in the UK* (Home Office, 1999d);
- *Full and equal citizens: A strategy for the integration of refugees into the United Kingdom* (Home Office, 2000b).

Common to these is an emphasis on the formal incorporation of refugees in different spheres of development – social, economic, community, community safety and individual – in order for successful integration to occur.

Box 3.5: Refugee integration: a partnership model

The integration strategy is based upon a partnership model between NGOs, the voluntary and private sectors, local authority consortia and RCOs and proposes a division of labour between the national level and the regional level (Home Office, 2002b, p 70). Integration policy is set firmly within the framework of social inclusion and the promotion of harmonious community and race relations (Home Office, 1999e, p 5). The need for an inter-departmental governmental approach was emphasised with the development of the National Refugee Integration Forum (NRIF) and related sub-groups in education, housing, health, welfare, community safety, community development and employment. The NRIF was established in January 2001 and is chaired by the Minister of State for Citizenship and Immigration. It is a cross-departmental, consultative body (although with no formal policy-making powers) and operates through a number of designated sub-groups that are largely chaired by regional consortia managers. The NRIF is now located within the Asylum Appeals Policy Directorate rather than as before under the Race Equality Unit. This demonstrates its close connection with the work of NASS in distributing and supporting asylum seekers in the regions. According to *Full and equal citizens* (Home Office, 2000b, p 12) every "dispersal region in the country should have an integration policy in place by August 2001". The NRIF is the model for the regional integration strategies which should occur in conjunction with NASS regional managers and the consortia.

In August 2004, a draft consultation document, *Integration matters: A national refugee integration strategy*, was published by the Home Office (2004). The draft document acknowledges many of these difficulties while aiming to "take forward and amplify" the objectives of the earlier *Full and equal citizens* strategy document (Home Office, 2000b). Integration in the new document is believed to take place when refugees are empowered to "achieve their full potential as members of British society, to contribute fully to the community, and to become fully able to exercise their rights and responsibilities that they share with other residents" (Home Office, 2004, p 6). In relation to these three 'domains of integration', the document identifies a series of 'crosscutting challenges', including ensuring access to information, stability of service delivery and the provision of comprehensive and accurate data. 'New solutions' to integration are proposed, including:

- *local connections:* to encourage asylum seekers to remain in the region to which they have been dispersed by creating a local connection under the terms of the homelessness legislation;
- *the Sunrise (Strategic Uplift of National Refugee Integration SErvices) programme:* voluntary agencies will bid to carry out intensive work with refugees in the 28-day period after they have received a positive decision;
- *personal integration loans* which will cover all aspects of integration including employment, housing and English language tuition;
- *refugee integration loans:* available to all refugees wishing to take up vocational training or other items or activities that aid integration.

'Swift integration' and access to citizenship, including the mainstreaming of services to refugees, are the two dominant themes in the new integration strategy. These themes are very much in line with the government's broader social cohesion and race relations agendas, as we discuss further in Chapter Eight of this book.

Following the earlier integration document and the 2002 Nationality, Immigration and Asylum Act, there is a strong emphasis in the document upon the acquisition of the English language, both as an indicator of integration and as a practical marker of citizenship. Employment, retraining and re-accreditation are also key elements in the 2004 draft report. Significantly, RCOs are again explicitly acknowledged as key agents in mediating between the recipient society and refugee communities, although they "too often lack resources" (Home Office, 2004, p 6).

In line with earlier policy documents, the national integration strategy will be based upon a division of labour between the Home Office's Immigration and Nationality Directorate (IND), government departments, regional consortia, NGOs and local voluntary groups including RCOs. The NRIF remains, as before, the principal focal point for discussion of policy developments, although again without direct policy-making capacity. As before, the approach to refugee integration is primarily instrumental in nature, with a strong emphasis upon the mainstreaming of refugees through particular designated channels, bearing in mind their own specific circumstances and needs. While there is some acknowledgement of the complex character of integration as occurring in a number of different social spheres, there is less attention paid to the long timescales involved in integration – streamlining and 'swift integration' suggest a bureaucratic or managed approach to integration – or to the reciprocal relation between the receiving society and refugees. The integration domain of 'contributing to communities', for example, includes reporting racist attacks, improved media coverage of asylum seekers and refugees and capacity building for RCOs. This appears to go some way towards acknowledging the climate of hostility and fear towards asylum seekers and refugees and the difficulties that this poses to successful refugee integration. Yet the document also significantly fails to address how the broader asylum framework, based upon restrictionism, deterrence and control, adds to the climate of moral panic which the integration strategy subsequently attempts to alleviate. Differential processes of exclusion and inclusion underlie asylum and migration policy in the UK, as elsewhere in the EU (Boswell, 2003). The principle of non-integration in the reception phase (Joly, 1999) and the vast apparatus of deterrence wielded against asylum seekers necessarily sit uneasily alongside the aims of social inclusion and integration for refugees, which *Integration matters* (Home Office, 2004) proposes.

In practice, it would appear that the development of regional integration strategies has been delayed, with the logistical demands of dispersal outweighing settlement issues (Zetter et al, 2003b). At the national level there also remain key issues around the remit of the NRIF subgroups, particularly in terms of accountability and the absence of a clear programme of action. Although representatives from the different government departments are invited to attend the meetings of the various subgroups, this is voluntary and tends to be outside of regular working commitments rather than a part of designated roles. Without significant funding or policy-making capacity the subgroups and the NRIF as a whole occupy an ambiguous position.

A similar structural ambiguity marks the dispersal arrangements as a whole. Under the rubric of 'partnership', the consortia comprise a mix of central government, local authority, NGO, voluntary, RCO and private sector interests. The concept of partnership, as Ling (2000) has demonstrated, has its roots in the new managerialism that has permeated the public sector from the 1980s onwards. The restructuring of the welfare state was to be accomplished through organisational change and in particular the incorporation of partner organisations in "the pursuit of widely shared goals" (Ling, 2000, p 99). In similar terms, the new institutional framework for the reception and settlement of asylum seekers and refugees has redefined the relationship between different sectors and agencies along the lines of 'partnership' and 'participation' (Clarke and Newman, 1997; Newman, 2000). More critically, this process can be understood in terms of the development of a new type of governmentality, which involves the incorporation of hard-to-reach groups "into compliant collaborators in creating a more inclusive society" (Ling, 2000, p 90).

> Governmentality ... is concerned with making the voluntary sector, user groups and others fit to be partners within a new strategic arena ... prior to their participation in the partnership they must demonstrate their capacity to be good partners. (Ling 2000, p 89)

The implications of these statements for the incorporation of RCOs into the new institutional arrangements are further developed throughout this book.

There would also appear to be a fundamental tension between the aims of the integration strategy and the dispersal arrangements. Although there is a formal commitment in the integration strategy to refugee community formation and the role of RCOs in promoting the inclusion of refugees in the regions, it can be argued that dispersal violates the right of asylum seekers "to settle where they wish within national space, and therefore the right to congregate with co-ethnics, access specialist services, [and] create viable and self-supporting communities...." (Robinson et al, 2003, p 166). The issue of freedom of choice in relation to movement and settlement is crucial, with many commentators noting the rationale of dispersal in the redistribution of costs, rather than the safeguarding of the rights of asylum seekers (Pfohman and Amrute, 2004, p 54). The underpinning of dispersal in the logic of deterrence is another factor that may tend to militate against effective settlement. Dispersal may be viewed either as a policy instrument which intentionally encourages the increased marginalisation of asylum seekers and refugees, or as an attempt to manage the asylum process more efficiently by redistributing the social and economic costs caused by increasing numbers of asylum seekers. In either case, the focus on deterrence rather than the safeguarding of rights encourages a generally negative perception of asylum seekers and refugees. This is necessarily detrimental to the two-way relation between the society of reception and the 'newcomer', which is pivotal to the process of integration (Castles et al, 2003).

As we demonstrate in the next part of this chapter, the evidence to date suggests that despite the important resources which RCOs can offer, they are the least developed 'partner' in the integration arrangements (Zetter and Pearl, 2000). It is important to repeat that they are clearly specified as active agents in the integration process in various government publications, (Home Office, 1999d, 2000b). The Audit Commission

(2000a) in particular notes the importance of liaison with RCOs in order to provide more effective services to refugees and asylum seekers in the regions. The benefits of RCOs in adding value to service provision are continually underlined by the Audit Commission. Refugee community organisations, as they note, can relieve pressure on agencies by providing services themselves (Kelly and Joly, 1999), including interpreting services, support and assistance and in promoting 'positive images' and so on. The Audit Commission's recommendations include the formal recognition of RCOs in service provision for asylum seekers and refugees in the dispersal areas (Audit Commission, 2000a, para 63-8). The report strongly suggests that all consortia should seek funding to support RCO development outside London. The Audit Commission further notes that few local authorities had actually consulted refugee communities at the time of their fieldwork. Where this occurred it had tended not to be fully participatory in character and acted more as an information-gathering exercise than as a partnership mechanism. In general, RCOs occupy an ambiguous role as junior 'partners' in the reception and integration arrangements. The initial Home Office formulation of the role of RCOs was based upon community development models and partnership between central government, para-state and non-state actors (Home Office, 1999e). One of the key questions addressed in this book is how these formal partnership mechanisms work in practice.

Dispersal and RCOs

In order to orient our own research, it is necessary to briefly review the literature on dispersal and its impacts on RCOs. There is as yet little substantive research on the effects of dispersal on refugee communities and refugee organisations. What is available falls into four broad categories:

* London-based studies;
* regionally based research;
* comparative research between London and the regions;
* more general commentary on the implications of dispersal for RCOs.

Turning to the first type, the themes that have emerged for London-based organisations concern the increased workload which has been placed on RCOs as a result of dispersal. The Audit Commission (2000, p 43) notes that:

London-based RCOs are facing increasing demands on their time and resources from service providers in other parts of the country, often to meet a need for urgent interpretation services for new arrivals dispersed under voluntary arrangements.

Other research has similarly pointed to the need to support smaller RCOs in London that were often inadequately resourced and depended on volunteers. Increased workloads, and a general weakness in networking and infrastructure, and in access to funding and personnel were the principle features noted (Esa-Feka, 2001).

Outside London, there are to date only a small number of studies. Commissioned as part of the Home Office Foundation Reports in 2001, Fletcher (2002) outlines the distinctive character of the North East Consortium. This is distinctive in terms of the geographical characteristics of the area and its size. She also outlines the consequences for networking and refugee employment of the economic structure of the region. Fletcher (2002, p 1) argues that RCOs have a vital role to play in initiatives that "support and improve service provision and in terms of self-help through community development". The constraints facing RCOs and the emergence of new organisations in the North East are also extensively documented. Although RCOs have a unique role in supporting the integration process, and in defining integration strategies, their experience on the whole has been "typically of objectification, marginalisation and exclusion in the process of continued organisational vulnerability" (Fletcher, 2002, p 31). Her general recommendations are to increase the participation of RCOs in capacity building, the development of local strategic networks and in decision making in the region. Wilson's (2001) study of dispersal in West Yorkshire, although not specifically concerned with RCOs, similarly noted the weak development of RCOs and undeveloped networking in the region. Again, Stansfield (2001) writing for Nottingham Asylum Seekers focused largely on the failure of NASS to consult with local agencies, including RCOs. Zetter et al's (2003b) Home Office-commissioned research similarly pointed to the need for greater representation of RCOs at the local level given their role in providing services and assistance in the regions.

Comparative research between London and the regions is the least developed area in the existing literature. The one notable exception is a report produced for the Evelyn Oldfield Unit by Gameledin-Ashami et al (2002). The authors focused on a number of issues, including the capacity of RCOs to provide services; their contribution to settlement;

the impact of new legislation upon RCOs; and the effects of dispersal. The research drew upon earlier research in the UK on the importance of RCOs for settlement. It included a brief survey of dispersal areas, including Newcastle, Liverpool and Margate, and recounted the experience of arrival in the dispersal areas and the lack of preparedness of local service providers. The authors concluded that RCOs in the dispersal areas provided emotional support, practical assistance, awareness raising and expert knowledge that could potentially be utilised for regional policy development. On the downside, RCOs also suffered from a number of constraints, notably increasing demands made upon limited resources; weak organisational structures and poor working conditions. In sum, their role was largely defensive and undeveloped. On the whole, RCOs in the dispersal regions were found to be small in number and isolated from mainstream partnership arrangements.

By contrast, London was estimated to have 400 to 500 RCOs, many of which were the product of the refugee community which had settled from the late 1970s onwards and increasingly throughout the 1980s and 1990s. Institutional complexity had resulted in the formation of refugee consortia and borough-based refugee forums. From the middle of the 1980s, the Refugee Council had been instrumental in developing RCOs and resources. An increasing number of funders supporting RCOs had also entered the arena in this period. Organisations such as the Evelyn Oldfield Unit, for example, had cooperated with these agencies in providing training and support. Twenty-two RCOs were interviewed by Gameledin-Ashami et al (2002) in London, where higher levels of networking and funding than in the regions were apparent. Refugee community organisations provided three main types of advice: welfare advice, cultural maintenance and improving labour market access through English for Speakers of Other Languages (ESOL) provision. The London RCOs were heavily dependent upon funding from trusts and foundations. In general, there was poor monitoring of performance, a lack of accountability and weak management structures in RCOs. This meant that many RCOs in London continued to occupy a 'defensive role', as was the case in the regions. They could assist in refugee settlement but were poorly resourced to assist the long-term integration of refugees. Networking with other agencies was seen as a priority but again was in need of greater development in London.

Last in this review are the more general commentaries on the impacts of dispersal on RCOs. Zetter and Pearl (2000) provide a general analysis situating RCOs within the broader context of welfare restructuring and restrictive asylum policy and practice. This general orientation informs our approach to the fieldwork element in this research. The authors address the ways in which RCOs have responded to recent legislative changes, notably the 1996 Asylum and Immigration Act and the 1999 Immigration and Asylum Act. Positing the increased marginalisation and social exclusion of asylum seekers as a result of legislative changes to housing entitlements in particular, Zetter and Pearl argue that RCOs, like the "communities they serve" are likely to remain "on the margins". The authors note the explicit incorporation and co-option of RCOs within the new framework set up under the 1999 Immigration and Asylum Act but argue that this is not likely to improve the general position of RCOs. The changes introduced under the 1999 legislation have:

- reduced sources of community support and encouraged fragmentation of refugee communities by dispersal (although there is a formal commitment to language clustering);
- increased dependence on lower levels of state provision;
- reinforced a policy of non-integration of asylum seekers.

The authors point, therefore, to a growing role conflict for RCOs between sustaining service provision, as in the area of housing, and acting as advocates for asylum seekers in providing advice and support. This is an important empirical generalisation, which is further tested in the fieldwork as part of this research. More generally, the authors point to the undeveloped character of the RCO sector. Established NGO agencies, such as the Refugee Council and Refugee Action, have charitable status and operate at the national and local levels, whereas the RCO sector by and large is confined to the local level. Zetter and Pearl (2000, p 681) argue that:

> What is distinctive about RCOs at the local level is that they tend to be constituted as voluntary associations without formal legal status, and lack organisational structures and a professional core of staff. By contrast, agencies founded by non-refugees and asylum seekers tend to be formally constituted with charitable status.

While this is true there is also a need, as we further demonstrate in this research, to address inequalities and variation in the RCO sector itself.

Zetter and Pearl note two central trends among RCOs. The first is *consolidation*. Some groups, for example, have established networks, while other established groups have remained inward looking and have not networked effectively. The factors involved include variations in the politicisation of particular communities, internal divisions and varying educational levels in the community itself and in the personnel running RCOs. The second trend is the *emergence of newer groups*, particularly within the first few years of dispersal. Francophone Africans for example, are a notable minority in the two regional case studies in this research. Many individuals have arrived in areas without pre-existing forms of community support or ethnic networks. The length of time a group has been established in a particular locality, the presence or absence of established communities, the size of a community, their language base and the broader context of reception policies, are the crucial variables outlined by Zetter and Pearl in their analysis. Our research draws upon these variables in the fieldwork analysis.

Zetter and Pearl conclude by noting the persistent constraints on RCO survival, including:

- weak networking and coordination between RCOs and other actors;
- duplication of effort at the local level as a result of poor information exchange;
- undeveloped technical know-how and competition between groups over scarce local resources.

These structural limitations affect the ability of RCOs to break through into the mainstream. Invariably, 'partnership' arrangements favour the larger, longer-established groups, the charmed 'inner circle', and further marginalise the smaller RCOs. As they conclude (Zetter and Pearl, 2000, p 689), "rarely do smaller organisations, like RCOs, possess the skills and resources to access major funding or partnership opportunities". In effect, RCOs can expect to experience continued marginalisation while facing increased demands upon their personnel and resources.

Although the generally pessimistic tenor of these conclusions appears to be warranted by the evidence, it is also important to register the emergence of significant numbers of RCOs in the regions and the revival of networking processes within refugee communities and in their relations with the other actors involved in the dispersal arrangements. In this context, dispersal appears to have brought about a partial shift in the balance between London and the regions. For example, although many asylum seekers have chosen to remain in London and the South East on subsistence-only arrangements (Home Office, 2002b), both the West Midlands and North West consortia have significant numbers of new asylum seekers, at around 19% each of the total dispersed under the NASS arrangements. In addition, despite strong evidence of secondary migration to London from the regions there is also evidence in both of the areas covered here that around 50% of asylum seekers are choosing to remain in the regions upon receipt of a positive decision. There is, furthermore, a high incidence of secondary migration to the West Midlands, and Birmingham in particular, both from other regions in the country and also from other EU countries, notably in the case of Somalis (travelling as EU passport holders) coming from the Netherlands and Sweden. These factors suggest that there is a firm basis for the continued growth of refugee communities in the regions. In significant respects, therefore, these changes appear to be altering the parameters of refugee community formation in the UK. This is an important development that is more fully charted in the fieldwork chapters of this book.

Conclusions

This chapter has reviewed recent dispersal policy in the UK and the development of a new institutional framework for the reception and integration of asylum seekers and refugees. Institutional arrangements based upon partnership models have been devised between central government (NASS) and local authorities (organised as regional consortia) including NGOs, the voluntary sector, the private sector and RCOs. It was suggested that the partnership model, upon which the reception and integration arrangements are based, functions as a managerial response to the difficulty of coordinating different state and non-state agencies. On a formal level, at least, it also attempts to actively incorporate 'hard-to-reach' groups such as RCOs and refugees in the overall management of the reception and integration of asylum seekers and refugees. The specialist knowledge of RCOs and refugees is in this respect a vital component of 'value-added' expertise which policy makers have been quick to acknowledge and draw upon. Nevertheless, formal partnership mechanisms often appear to have fallen short in practice. Research evidence on the impact of dispersal on RCOs in London and the regions suggests a situation of continued marginalisation for RCOs. As we argued in Chapter One of this book, our research is oriented around a series of empirical questions relating to the impact of dispersal on refugee communities and RCOs. The following fieldwork chapters build upon and in some cases challenge the research findings that have been reviewed in this chapter. The more theoretical issues addressed in Chapter Two, concerning institutional constraints and the role of networks and social capital, are also developed within this framework.

FOUR

Refugee community organisations in London: consolidation and competition

This chapter begins by outlining the methodological issues underlining the fieldwork material presented here and in Chapter Six. The remainder of the chapter reviews the background to recent refugee settlement in London. In contrast to the regions, London is an established area of refugee settlement. The age and funding base of the refugee community organisations (RCOs) in the sample reflects, to some degree, the size and length of residence of many of the more recent refugee communities in London, particularly those dating from the 1980s and 1990s. Groups from earlier in the 20th century, on the other hand, such as refugees arriving in the inter-war and immediate post-war periods, have not been included in the sample.

The chapter also outlines the structural constraints affecting RCOs and the change in the rationale of refugee organisations as they progress from 'grass-roots' mobilisation to the consolidation of bureaucratic organisations. A number of important and more general theoretical themes are addressed in the chapter. A significant theme is the role played by competition over the symbolic and material resources conferred by the possession and control of refugee organisations. Other important themes are the construction of RCOs and the notion of community in relation to questions of gender and internal political divisions. The limitations of the dominant nationality-based model of refugee organisation are presented before turning to the importance of networks in refugee communities. The imbalances in the partnerships between RCOs and the better-developed and strategically more powerful agencies such as the leading refugee non-governmental organisations (NGOs) are a central feature of the chapter. The involvement of leading London RCOs in one particular network, the RCO development project, is discussed in detail, as this exemplifies some fundamental aspects of the relationship which RCOs have to the NGOs, statutory authorities and the Home Office bodies involved in the dispersal programme.

Methodology

Data sources

The data for this book is derived from a number of different sources. The principal primary data source is the sample of 40 RCOs that were interviewed across the three locations of London, the West Midlands and the North West. One of the main aims of the RCO sample was to collate basic information on organisational structures, resources and the operation of networks in refugee communities and in their relations with NGOs and the statutory authorities. In this case, rigorous sampling and the construction of a sampling frame are problematic where the nature of the population to be examined is ill defined. In particular, given the lack of clarity of the available data on refugees and asylum seekers in Britain (Robinson, 1998a; ICAR, 2003) there was a need to build from our existing understanding of refugee networks in the UK (Griffiths, 2002; Zetter and Pearl, 1998, 2000; Zetter et al, 2003b).

A clear rationale for the selection of RCOs was therefore fundamental to the research. Modifying Field (1985) and Carey-Wood et al (1995), we have focused on the following variables in the identification of relevant refugee community groups and RCOs:

- numbers and trends in asylum applications;
- pre-existing community and English language use;
- date of establishment of the RCO.

Contrasts in size and organisational capacity were also taken into consideration in selecting the particular RCOs which were to be included in the final sample.

Numbers and trends in asylum applications

Our earlier detailed examination of the asylum statistics for the UK (Zetter et al, 2003a, p 91) showed that the top five nationalities between 1991 and 2000 were from Somalia, Sri Lanka, the Former Republic of Yugoslavia (FRY), Pakistan and Turkey and accounted for some 30% of all asylum applications in that period. One aim of the sample of 40 RCOs across London and the two regions was to represent, as far as was possible, these principal nationalities. This is a broadly indicative measure, as it does not take account of recognition rates and therefore the number of asylum seekers granted leave to remain in the UK.

Somalis and Tamils are the two principal nationalities in the sample, closely followed by Sudanese and Congolese. Based upon our earlier fieldwork experience (Griffiths, 2002) the Somalis were intentionally singled out for analysis in the description of tendencies among RCOs. The inclusion of Sudanese RCOs reflects their preponderance on the ground rather than the incidence of asylum applications by this nationality. The number of Congolese claiming asylum in the UK doubled from 660 to 1,240 in 1999, dropping slightly to 1,030 in 2000. Again, the number of Congolese RCOs included reflects their organisational capacity and prevalence rather than their significance in the asylum statistics as a whole. However, they are important as examples of the increasing number of Francophone Central African groups arriving in the UK with little or no history of settlement in London or the regions. Their specific problems are also addressed in the main body of the text. Bosnian and Albanian RCOs were included, although in smaller numbers in the sample. In none of the locations was there evidence of any Pakistani-based RCO in operation, individuals from this nationality appearing to be catered for by existing networks and alternative forms of ethnic organisation. A small number of Turkish/Kurdish organisations was also interviewed to reflect the overall trend in asylum applications throughout the period 1991–2000.

While not representative of all of the main nationalities claiming asylum throughout the 1990s, the sample does give an indication of organisational activity among two of the principal nationalities, Somalis and Tamils, and also a flavour of some of the newer groups arriving in increasing numbers towards the end of the decade, notably Iraqis (including individuals of Kurdish origin) and Congolese. In several cases, the selection of RCOs depended upon the incidence of particular refugee groups on the ground and their degree of accessibility. Illustrations from particular RCOs in London and the regions are used to clarify essential points in the argument in the fieldwork chapters.

Pre-existing community and English language use

A few states, Sri Lanka, Somalia, India, Pakistan and Nigeria (all of which have former colonial links to the UK) consistently supplied the steady flow of asylum applications throughout the 1990s. This is not to deny the significance of increases from particular regions such as eastern Europe…. Applications from Europe increased from 8 per

cent of total applications to 23 per cent of applications
from 1991-96. (Zetter et al, 2003a, pp 89-90)

Regarding the core sending states throughout the 1990s, we further
observed (Zetter et al, 2003a, p 90) that all of the core sending states
had established or growing communities in the UK and that all of
these states were at one time colonies of the British Empire. In the
case of Somalis and Tamils, both had pre-existing although small
communities in place before the increase in asylum applications from
the late 1980s onwards. Both had knowledge of the English language,
although again this was not uniform in the two cases. The degree to
which these factors have aided organisation in the two groups requires
further detailed examination. The available evidence suggests that in
the case of the Somalis, organisational proliferation has taken place
along the lines of clan and regional divisions. As new groups of Somalis
arrived during the 1990s, more organisations developed which reflected
the divergences within Somalia itself (Griffiths, 2002). The Tamils at
first glance appear to be less prone to factionalism based upon home
divisions. The three London-based Tamil organisations in the sample
had no explicit political affiliation or identification. By way of contrast,
the recently arrived Francophone groups have encountered a situation
of language difference and the absence of any settled communities of
co-ethnics or co-nationals, particularly in the dispersal regions. Despite
these impediments and their relatively small size, the Congolese in the
fieldwork locations are among the most active in terms of organisational
development. The evidence on Turkish/Kurdish and Iraqi settlement
in London also suggests a highly uneven process of settlement (Al-
Rasheed, 1994; Griffiths, 2002), with isolated footholds of Turkish
Cypriots, Turks and Iraqi students and intellectuals from the 1950s
onwards providing a bridgehead for the more intensive asylum
migration of the 1990s.

Date of establishment of the RCO

A critical distinction in the RCO sample is between the longer-
established organisations, such as the Vietnamese, Somali, Tamil and
Ethiopian, which were founded from the early 1980s onwards, and
the emergence of recent organisations such as the Central African.
This basic contrast provides useful pointers to the role of historical
and contextual factors in the formation of RCOs. In terms of the
comparison of the date of establishment of RCOs in London and the
regions, concerning the 40 organisations as a whole the spectrum

ranges from the earliest founded in 1982 to several organisations formed in 2003.

The contrast between the locations is clearer if we briefly examine each case study area in turn. The oldest organisation in the sample of West Midlands RCOs was founded in 1990. The majority, nearly two thirds, have been established only since 1999. An even more contemporary feel characterises the small number of RCOs interviewed in the North West. In this case the earliest date of establishment is 1997, while over half of the sample has been established since 2001. By contrast, the majority in the total sample of 40 RCOs (13 out of 14) established between 1982 and 1990 are based in London. The sample of London RCOs divides equally between those established up to 1988 and those established after that date. The inclusion of Vietnamese, Ethiopian, Somali and Tamil organisations explains the significant number of organisations founded prior to 1988 in the sample of London RCOs.

It is important to emphasise that these differences in the sample between locations are not representative of the distribution and character of RCOs in the different areas as a whole. The small numbers involved and the principles of selection of RCOs in the three areas mean that the differences noted here are indicative only. More large-scale quantitative analysis of RCOs in the UK is certainly required, along the lines of McLeod et al's (2001) examination of black and minority ethnic (BME) organisations. The principle aims of the research conducted here have been qualitative, and in particular have related to exploring the organisational rationales of RCOs and the impacts of legislation upon refugee organisations and refugee communities.

Turning to the other primary data sources used in the research, a limited number of semi-structured interviews with NGO personnel involved with refugee community development and with representatives of statutory authorities were undertaken in the three locations. Here, the aim was to elicit information on the involvement of the different actors in the institutional arrangements for the reception and settlement of asylum seekers and refugees. The main institutional actors interviewed were from the Refugee Council, Refugee Action, representatives from regional refugee councils, and local authority and consortia personnel in London and the regions.

The secondary data drawn upon for the research consists of the limited amount of academic literature and more extensive grey literature on RCOs located in the Refugee Council archive, which is now housed at the University of East London. Resources from the burgeoning number of migration websites in the UK were also drawn upon. In both cases it should be noted that much of the grey literature is unpublished and is of variable quality and scope. Reports produced by local authorities, non-governmental organisations, refugee consultancies and specialist organisations and RCOs are also cited in the text where appropriate. A significant deficiency in much of the secondary data is the limited basis of the samples used and the policy-driven character of the research aims and objectives.

Methods

The interviews with RCOs were based upon semi-structured questionnaires that combined a series of questions about organisational structure, resources and networks with open-ended questions that aimed to elicit more general responses. These were typically with representatives of RCOs (coordinators or directors of the organisation) and were supplemented in a few cases by participant observation with staff and clients involved in refugee organisations. The views of RCO users were not examined in detail in the fieldwork, as this would have required considerably more in-depth treatment of particular RCOs than was possible within the scope and aims of the research. These were, as we have indicated, to examine the effects of dispersal upon RCOs in London and selected locations in the regions. The comparative themes developed within this general framework are the primary focus of the research, rather than the detailed analysis of specific RCOs and their relationship with their particular community base. What we intend is that our analysis will provide the basis for further examination on the micro level of the dynamics and processes occurring within refugee communities and organisations.

In all cases, the interviews, which lasted between one to two hours, were taped and transcribed. Participant observation was used in a limited number of cases, particularly in relation to the Somali and Sudanese organisations where more extensive commentary is made in the text on some of their organisational practices and characteristics. Access to the refugee groups was facilitated by key contacts in the NGO sector and statutory authorities in London and the cities of Birmingham, Manchester and Liverpool which had been developed from our earlier research in those cities (Griffiths, 2002; Zetter and Pearl, 1998; Zetter et al, 2003b). The qualitative material was analysed by using conventional thematic analysis, which operates through a process of identification of themes and regularities in interview transcripts. Translators were not required for the interviews with RCOs, as the educational level, professional background and language ability of the coordinators of organisations were generally high.

The choice of locations outside London

The choice of case study locations outside London was determined by a number of factors, including the size of refugee communities; the scale of development of RCOs; and the settlement history of refugee groups. Concerning the dispersal areas, in 2002 the top dispersal regions in the UK were in the North West, the West Midlands and Yorkshire and Humberside at 19% each of the total (Home Office, 2002b). Statistics for 2002 indicate a total of 54,045 supported in NASS accommodation and 37,815 in receipt of subsistence only (Home Office, 2002b). The top five nationalities applying for both support and subsistence under NASS in 2002 were:

(1) Iraq (12,955)
(2) Afghanistan (6,805)
(3) Somalia (5,620)
(4) Zimbabwe (5,280)
(5) Sri Lanka (3,380) (Home Office, 2002b).

This strongly reflects the principal countries of origin of asylum applications throughout 2002. The choice of the West Midlands and the North West for closer examination was therefore well grounded. In addition, the three case study cities of Birmingham, Manchester and Liverpool also have the added advantage of being familiar to the research team from our earlier research in those cities (Zetter et al, 2003b).

The presentation of the material in the case studies is organised around a number of themes relating to aspects of RCO: the significance of competition in contrast to processes of cooperation; the emergence of new organisations and the consolidation of older, better-established RCOs; and, finally, the alternation between fragmentation and unity in refugee communities. The fieldwork chapters proceed from an examination of the organisational and resource issues affecting RCOs, to a discussion of the thematic material generated from the interviews. For purposes of comparison the thematic material focuses on questions of community, networks and social capital and the impact of dispersal and legislative change upon RCOs. These sections address theoretical issues that are also a core component of this research.

Refugee settlement in London

There is a long-standing history of refugee settlement in London although there is considerable variation in patterns across London boroughs (Haringey Council, 1997; ELCHA, 1999; Audit Commission, 2000b; MORI, 2000, 2001). In relation to the earliest group in the RCOs interviewed, evidence from the settlement of Vietnamese refugees had suggested high levels of concentration in and around London. Robinson and Hale (1989) had found that 46% of all Vietnamese quota refugees were living in London by 1988. Carey-Wood et al (1995) found that 85% of asylum seekers who applied for asylum between 1983 and 1991 did so from addresses in London. The Audit Commission (2000b) estimated that between 240,000 and 280,000 asylum seekers and refugees were living in London in 1997. The distribution of asylum seekers and refugees between London boroughs was not even. Newham, with an asylum seeker and refugee population of around 20,000, and Hackney and Haringey with asylum seeker and refugee populations of 16,000 and 20,000 respectively, were among the highest, while Havering and the City had fewer than 1,000 asylum seekers and refugees each. The Local Government Association (LGA, 2000) found that 90% of all destitute asylum seekers who were being supported by local authorities in the UK in March 2000 lived in London and the South East.

The East London and City Health Authority (ELCHA, 1999) provided comprehensive estimates of the distribution of refugees and asylum seekers in London. Its report estimated the total refugee population (defined as those with refugee status, asylum seekers, individuals with lesser forms of status and refusals) between 1983 and 1997 as approximately 280,000 to 330,000 (higher estimate) and 240,000 to 280,000 (lower estimate). This research has been updated to include the years 1998-99, in the 2001 baseline mapping study conducted by MORI for the Renewal Project in West London (MORI, 2001). The total number of refuges in London calculated for the years 1983-99 is estimated to be between 322,000 and 370,000. The report again confirms high concentrations of refugees in Newham (20,900-24,200), Haringey (21,900-25,300), Ealing (13,500-15,600) and Hackney (13,400-15,500). It is important to note that the ELCHA report estimates are based upon averaging results from five different sources, including Home Office data and a variety of local sources including social services and schools registers (ELCHA, 1999, p 26). The key methodological limitation concerns the assumption of those remaining in London which is based upon the estimates of 85% in

Carey-Wood et al (1995) for the period up to 1997 and in the research conducted by MORI a reduced figure of 75% to account for the effects of dispersal since that date. None of these estimates is totally reliable and are based upon a number of key assumptions, all of which are open to challenge (MORI, 2000, p 51).

The concentration of refugees and asylum seekers in London reflects the more general population characteristics for the UK as a whole (Home Office, 2001, p 39). London has the UK's largest labour market (Home Office, 2001) and hosts a high concentration of migrants in key inner-city boroughs. Over 60% of Newham's population and 54% of Brent's population are of minority ethnic background (Census, 2001). More generally, within the regions it would also appear that asylum seekers and refugees concentrate in the principal cities, such as Birmingham in the West Midlands and Manchester in the North West (Zetter et al, 2003b). Overall, the concentration of refugees in London and the South East is undergoing a process of gradual change due to the asylum seeker dispersal policy introduced in April 2000. It is important to recall, however, that a significant number of asylum seekers has chosen to remain in London on subsistence-only arrangements, without accommodation supplied by the National Asylum Support Service (NASS). At the end of 2002, 76% of individuals in receipt of subsistence-only support from NASS were living in London (Home Office, 2002b), suggesting the continuing significance of refugee networks in London.

Corresponding to the concentration of refugees and asylum seekers in London and the South East is the overwhelming presence of NGO resources and personnel in the capital. At the same time, the picture is characterised by a proliferation of small, specialist NGOs and voluntary sector agencies that support asylum seekers and refugees. This is aside from the Refugee Council, which operates across London and has two regional offices, and Refugee Action and the regional refugee councils that operate across the regions and in Scotland and Wales. In London, there is a wide-ranging network of refugee-related NGOs and voluntary bodies, including the World University Service (WUS), the Refugee Education and Training Advisory Service (of the WUS), the Refugee Council, the Medical Foundation for victims of torture, Asylum Aid, the Refugee Legal Centre, and the Refugee Assessment and Guidance Unit of the University of North London. In addition, there is a broad spectrum of advisory bodies, campaigning groups and web-based groups, including the Information Centre about Asylum and Refugees in the UK based at King's College, London.

RCOs in London

There are several different estimates of the total number of RCOs in London. Gameledin-Ashami et al (2002) estimate between 400 and 500 RCOs in London, whereas the Refugee Council database suggests 600+. The Renewal Project in West London has a database of nearly 300 RCOs for the boroughs of Brent, Ealing, Hammersmith and Fulham, Harrow, Hillingdon and Hounslow alone. The research produced from the project noted that a significant proportion of RCOs in these boroughs described their funding as under immediate threat (15%-18%) or as generally insecure (29%-36%). On the other hand, there was evidence that "significant parts of the refugee community sector in West London are now mature, developed organisations" (Michael Bell Associates, 2002, p 12). In terms of the internal differentiation of the RCO sector, it is important to note that Esa-Feka (2001) calculated that there were over 200 small RCOs across London that were struggling to survive on a daily basis. Although there has clearly been a proliferation of organisational development in London since the mid-1990s, when the Refugee Council estimated slightly over 300 RCOs in the capital (Zetter and Pearl, 2000), there are no clear estimates as to the proportion of organisations that are secure and well established. Anecdotal evidence would suggest that the high incidence of new organisations forming is matched by a significant number of organisations either losing funding or otherwise ceasing to function as viable entities. A fairly rapid turnover of organisations at the peripheries appears to be accompanied by the persistence of a solid core of established RCOs in London.

In terms of the general trends in the development of refugee organisations, Gameledin-Ashami et al (2002) note that, since the mid-1980s, 'refugee consortia' have been formed, followed by 'generic refugee organisations' and 'refugee forums' in the early 1990s. This process of organisational consolidation and diversification had led to the development of borough-based networks in the late 1990s. Many of these initiatives were prompted by the funders and key agencies supporting refugees, including the community development team of the Refugee Council and the Evelyn Oldfield Unit. The Evelyn Oldfield Unit was formed in the mid-1990s by a coalition of the large funding bodies in London – City Parochial Foundation, London Borough Grants and the Refugee Council – to provide technical support for the development of RCOs. The Renewal Project of West London is a significant example of cross-borough collaboration. It is funded by the Single Regeneration Budget and represents an alliance between statutory service providers and RCOs across West London.

The sample of 20 London-based RCOs obtained for this research has been selected according to nationality (or other basis of group identity), the date of arrival of the group and the history of settlement of groups in particular parts of London. Hackney, for example, is a significant area of settlement for both Turkish/Kurdish and Vietnamese refugees.

Resource base and organisational issues

As Table 4.1 indicates, the sample of RCOs in London is dominated by nationality-based organisations. Two women's organisations were included and also a specialist mental health project, a refugee housing association and a refugee youth project.

Distribution of nationalities

Four Somali, three Tamil and two Turkish/Kurdish organisations are included in the sample. This distribution, in part, is intended to reflect the principal nationalities claiming asylum throughout the 1990s (Zetter et al, 2003a). In addition, two Vietnamese organisations were selected as they provide a useful point of contrast to later refugee groups arriving under different conditions in the 1980s and 1990s. Afghan, Ethiopian, Iranian, Iraqi, Kurdish and Sudanese groups make up the remainder. Concerning the newer groups, the Roma had proven difficult to contact and appeared to be weakly organised while the Congolese and other Central African groups are represented in the sample of RCOs from the West Midlands. In general, the newer arrivals are underrepresented in the sample, a factor which may reflect weak organisation, or a lack of visibility due to alternative forms of networking outside mainstream channels.

Dates of establishment

The Vietnamese and Afghan organisations are the oldest in the sample, both dating from 1982. The majority of organisations, 12 out of 20, were established in the 1980s, specifically between 1982 and 1989. Seven organisations were established in the 1990s and only one since 2000. The sample, therefore, is skewed towards the longer-established organisations, many of which have been in existence for over 10 years and in some cases for nearly 20 years.

Table 4.1: Summary of RCOs interviewed in London

Nationality/group represented	Date begun	Charity	Paid worker	Funding	Community size	Location
Afghan	1982	Y	N	N	6,000	Ealing
Ethiopian	1984	Y	Y	Y	6,000	Camden
Iranian	1984	Y	Y	Y	10,000	West London
Iraqi	1986	Y	Y	Y	10,000	West London
Kurdish (Iraqi)	1985	Y	Y	Y	8,000	West London
Single women's organisation	1999	Limited company	Y	Y	NA	Tower Hamlets
Somali	1990	Y	Y	Y	10,000	Lambeth
Somali	1993	Y	Y	Y	5,000	Kensington and Chelsea
Somali	1986	Y	Y	Y	3,000	Shepherd's Bush
Somali	2003	N	N	Y	5,000	Harrow
South London	1991	Y	Y	Y	NA	Merton
Sudanese	1992				5,000	Hounslow
Tamil	1986	Y	Y	Y	10,000	North London
Tamil	1985	Y	Y	Y	12,000-15,000	South London
Tamil	1986	Y	Y	Y	10,000	North London
Turkish/Kurdish	1999	Y	Y	Y	NA	Hackney
Turkish/Kurdish	1989	Y	Y	Y	7,000	Hackney
Vietnamese	1982	Y	Y	Y	15,000	Hackney
Vietnamese	1988	Company with charitable aims	Y	Y	15,000	Hackney
Women's Association	1993	Y	Y	Y	NA	Hackney

Legal status

All of the organisations apart from a Somali mental health project which had been formed in the spring of 2003 had charity status or were limited companies with a charitable purpose.

Membership

In contrast to the regions, where membership in organisations was limited by the size of the RCO and the refugee community, most of the organisations in London reported large memberships. One Kurdish organisation reported over 6,000 registered members across London, while more typically membership was in the hundreds. Some organisations were not membership organisations, as in the case of the specialist mental health organisation and youth and arts project. Again, in contrast to the regions, on the whole, records of membership were more carefully maintained in the RCOs in London. Concerning the size of the organisations, Gameledin-Ashami et al (2002), for example, note that membership in their sample of 22 London-based RCOs was 1,048 on average, with several organisations reporting membership in the high thousands.

Funding: amounts and sources

Another pointed contrast with the regions was the amount of funding which the London RCOs had secured. Sixty per cent of the London RCOs were medium-sized organisations (with funding of £50,000-£250,000 per year), while 20% were small (<£50,000) and large (£250,000+) respectively. These broad distinctions, as in earlier chapters, are taken from McLeod et al (2001, pp 36-7). The smallest amount was just over £4,000 while the largest was in excess of £500,000. The two biggest organisations in terms of funding had managed to tap into European sources (the European Refugee Fund and EQUAL (europa.eu.int/comm/employment_social/equal/index_en.cfm) – and other large funders in the UK, such as the Learning and Skills Council. In both instances, these were refugee women's organisations that had been formed relatively recently (within the last 10 years). More typically, funding levels were between £70,000 and £200,000 for the current financial year in most organisations. In the case of one Somali mental health project, there was a small 'start-up' grant from the Home Office Community Development Fund. Again, confirming other research on RCOs in London (Esa-Feka,

2001; Gameledin-Ashami et al, 2002), the main funders were the Association of London Government, the National Lottery Community Fund, local councils, a variety of trusts and Comic Relief. Voluntary monetary contributions formed a negligible and rather ad-hoc source of additional funding. In the one case where funding had been withdrawn from an organisation, it was kept running purely by voluntary support. Indeed, there were several cases where funding had not been continuous throughout the existence of a particular organisation. Most organisations had started as voluntary networks, which only later, after several years, had gained funding.

Paid workers and staffing

The number of paid staff reflects the generally higher level of funding in the London RCOs. One of the largest organisations had 11 full-time staff and two part time. Several had eight full-time members of staff. The majority had over four members of staff, either on a full- or part-time basis. The smallest organisations had at least one full-time member of staff. While this allows for greater continuity and the development of professional skills in an organisation, there was a recurrent problem in maintaining staff. One well-established Iranian organisation noted that once an individual had been 'trained up' in a certain area of expertise they were attracted by the higher salary levels outside the voluntary sector. A relatively high turnover of staff was noted in several of the organisations.

Services provided

In contrast to the regions, there was considerably greater diversity in the range of services provided by RCOs in London. Advice and sign posting were the dominant activities in all of the organisations. As Gameledin-Ashami et al (2002) note, advice work tends to fall into the categories of welfare and legal advice (accessing benefits and clarifying immigration status) and accessing the labour market. All of the organisations provided welfare and legal advice, although to varying levels according to whether the organisation had the Community Legal Service 'Quality Mark'. Under the 1999 Immigration and Asylum Act, new legal requirements had been introduced for organisations to qualify for providing immigration advice. The 'Quality Mark' is the recognised standard indicating that an organisation is qualified to provide immigration advice. Half of the sample had the mark at the time of fieldwork, although acquiring this had been time-consuming for the organisations concerned. One organisation in particular had chosen to specialise in legal advice by going into partnership with a local law firm which provided a member of staff for several days a week. Housing, welfare and legal advice were the main activities undertaken in this general category.

It is important to note that two of the longer-established RCOs in the sample had been subcontracted to the Refugee Council to undertake the functions of the One-Stop Service (OSS), providing advice and arranging support for NASS asylum seekers in London. For the organisations concerned, this was seen as a chance to develop organisationally and also to show that they could provide services outside their immediate national or ethnic community. The complexity of the relationship between RCOs and the Refugee Council is discussed more fully later in this chapter.

Only half of the organisations provided direct services relating to education, employment and training. These ranged from sophisticated employment and training schemes, information technology and English for Speakers of Other Languages (ESOL) to self-employment schemes in different sectors of the local economy. One Turkish/Kurdish organisation in Hackney had specialised in the field of secondary education, providing Turkish-speaking co-educationalists to work in schools alongside pupils. On the whole, these types of services were provided by the larger, better-funded organisations that had built up expertise in particular areas. Again, the refugee women's organisations stood out as exemplary in the range of services they provided. A minority of organisations were specialist in the sense of providing services to particular groups or for particular needs such as mental health and youth. The services in these cases were finely tuned to the requirements of these particular groups.

In addition to services relating to general welfare and legal advice on the one hand, and education, employment and training on the other, around three quarters of the organisations provided a range of cultural services relating to general aspects of well-being in their communities. These included supplementary classes, mother-tongue instruction, drama and folk dancing, the production of newsletters and general social activities and cultural events. The extent and sophistication of these services varied considerably across organisations depending upon their financial and human resources.

Organisational aims and rationale

A common theme in the interviews was the gradual change that had occurred in the structure and rationale of organisations, particularly for those RCOs that had been established for over 10 years. Initially, many RCOs reported that their aims had been to provide informal support to their communities but that after a period of time the formal requirements of accountability and responsibility to funders in particular had assumed more significance. One Sudanese coordinator explained the transition from an informal network to more formalised bureaucratic structures:

> "People need a sense of belongingness, somewhere to turn to. Especially from our background. There was the extended family making your backing for you. When you are coming here you are just on your own. So you start to look for other Sudanese and then other people come together. It will become like a necessity if you have young children.... As time goes on ... part of settling there is a lot of requirements ... to be effective you need to be structured in one way or another. Also because you will be responsible.... If you do translation ... the Home Office need to have it from a reliable source. Also that you can be reliable and questioned and monitored in terms of funding.... You are going to administer money properly and so on...."

Gameledin-Ashami et al (2002) have characterised this in terms of the differences in the *types of accountability* that affect RCOs, either towards their community or the funders which allow the organisations to remain economically viable. In the transition from self-help group to established bureaucratic organisation, there is a tendency to lose sight of the initial aims of the organisation. As one community activist from Sudan commented:

> "You find this organisation has developed [names a particular RCO] got a management committee and funding.... But when I go to the management committee and say how many women are coming ... and deciding what they want? No, she said it is difficult to get them. *This is the model of the RCO which is more responsive to the funder than their community group, their supposed service users....* So

they're not leading a sort of grass-roots movement. If I provide a
service it's to legitimise my status and the money that I am
getting... It's about accountability.... Accountability is a
big issue." (Emphasis added)

The conflict between the opposing rationalities of grass-roots
community development and the bureaucratic requirements of public
accountability were sometimes at play within a particular organisation,
or otherwise represented by what appear to be different types of
organisational models in RCOs. The one clear example of an
entrepreneurial model of RCO development in the sample was of a
small one-woman organisation which was established in the late 1990s
and had grown to a complex organisation with an annual turnover in
excess of £450,000 by 2003. This development was based upon the
identification of a distinctive 'market niche' in the RCO sector, the
needs of single refugee women living in hostels in Tower Hamlets.
The organisation now extends to all single women in London and
clearly fills an important gap in the market. This business model is not
necessarily opposed to the requirements of grass-roots representation,
but there is certainly a difference in emphasis between this and the
needs-based model of RCOs, which tended to predominate in the sample.
As one Somali worker noted of her relationship to funding
organisations:

> "Organisations like me, we put more importance on clients
> in need. And some organisations they put more importance
> on attending their [the funders'] meetings, training they
> provide.... So, if I feel myself that training is not much
> useful or ... I have to go on something which is useful.
> Because I feel to help the client in need better than
> anything."

How specific organisations managed this conflict depended on a
number of factors. For many organisations, there was a continual tension
between the requirements of 'form filling' and monitoring by funding
and regulatory bodies – including the Office of the Immigration
Service Commissioner which awards the Quality Mark – and the
need to be responsive to the requirements of their own communities.
Very often the balance between the two was felt to be inappropriate.
As one Somali coordinator remarked, "All your work is preparing
procedures and policies which are often not really necessary....To get
the balance is difficult".

Alongside this conflict and also related to the passage of time was evidence of *organisational diversification* as a result of the changing composition of particular refugee communities in London. Many of the RCOs noted that, although their organisational aims had not substantially changed (they remained fundamentally committed to helping new arrivals to settle and adapt to the UK), the fact that refugees had settled and established families brought a series of new issues in its train. One of these problems was an ageing population. Another key issue was the schooling and education of children. Organisations had responded to these changes by developing new projects for the elderly, youth and schoolchildren. Regarding the change in organisational focus, an Ethiopian worker noted:

> "It has changed a lot. The basic objective of establishing a community is still carried on. That is serving asylum seekers and new arrivees. To provide information and what not.... Besides we have different services. Those people who arrived in the 1980s now have different needs. Most of them are away from home. They need support. So we have an elderly project to provide services ... but also women's project and youth project."

This was a common theme among the more established groups, many of which were approaching or had reached their 20th year, such as the Tamils, Vietnamese and Iranian organisations. In another case where rapid growth had occurred in a refugee women's association, the organisation had to create additional managerial layers to cope with the new needs and levels of demand.

Funding: issues and problems

Although the majority of organisations in the sample were medium sized and had been in existence for over 10 years, most of them continued to regard funding as the key issue impeding sustainability and continuity of provision. There were several factors in operation that made funding into a fundamental issue for RCOs. The first concerned the dwindling money pot that was available for RCOs to draw from. By way of illustration, the National Lottery Community Fund was one of the main sources of funding for the RCOs in the sample. It provides development funding for up to three years for projects rather than the majority of core costs (administration and personnel). Three funding streams are available:

- awards for all projects (up to £5,000);
- medium-sized grants (up to £60,000);
- large grants (up to £250,000).

The general climate, according to representatives of the Community Fund, is of increasing competition in the black and minority ethnic (BME) sector. This is within a context of a declining budget for the Community Fund from £45 million in 2000 to £26 million in 2003. The percentage of BME grants has remained constant (although declining in absolute terms) at around 27% of the total Community Fund budget. Increased competition over a declining amount of funding is therefore one of the factors currently affecting RCOs.

The difficulty in funding core administrative costs is the second factor that appeared to adversely affect the sustainability of many RCOs in the sample. As one Somali coordinator remarked:

> "A lot of the funders want to fund projects but the sustainability of an organisation they can't fund because their money also, they're accountable as well….They need to be sustainable. There are those kinds of issues. They don't want to fund an admin officer. They like to see outputs … the office manager, what can they say? … *They're more interested in outputs, something they can measure….*" (Emphasis added)

The question of measurable outputs is closely related to the labour-intensive character of the work performed by RCOs. On the face of it, the outputs of RCOs may appear to be quite meagre. The Somali coordinator above noted that, "I think a week we see about 50 people. Our clients are illiterate. They come in with Housing Benefit forms … just doing one can take four hours". One corollary of this is that in the absence of substantial funding for core costs many RCOs fail to grow in size over the years. They remain static and vulnerable to the changing conditions imposed by funding bodies.

Conditionality of funding is a third factor affecting RCOs in London. In particular, the European Refugee Fund administered by the Home Office is conditional upon 50% match funding by organisations. This tends to rule out the smaller RCOs and favour the larger organisations and NGOs that dominate the refugee sector. This is related to the fourth factor impeding RCOs: the inequities which RCOs face in competing for funding against much larger institutions. A Sudanese coordinator noted that:

"It's the main problem for all organisations. You have to struggle against the big cats on the ... even within the voluntary sector people are not equal. With one paid worker you do the advice work, you do the one-to-one work, to do networking.... To do funding application in itself is not an easy thing.... You have to find the means a year in advance. You may apply three or four funders, only one if you are lucky enough will come off. Because you are competing against all the voluntary organisations, refugee organisations, most of them properly staffed with fundraisers.... For us, I'm the fundraiser, I'm the administrator, I'm the advice provider [laughter]."

A lack of organisational specialisation and expertise constantly plagued RCOs in their relationships to the larger organisations which dominated the field:

"Just take an example. This is an Ethiopian organisation. A foreigner for whom English is a second language. A very small organisation. Comparing my committee's application against let's say the Refugee Council's application, has so many more experts, so many resources, fluent language.... Putting that on the same table and making us compete for a small pot of money won't be fair. It's not intentional but we work with that handicap for which we cannot blame anybody. Like I told you, there are some organisations, if they have to attend a meeting outside of their office they have to close the office or miss the meeting because of a shortage of manpower." (Ethiopian chair)

The more general perception of pervasive power imbalances between the RCOs and NGOs in the refugee sector is addressed more fully later in this chapter.

The limitations of 'community'

The dominance of nationality-based organisations among RCOs is commonly noted in the literature (Gameledin-Ashami et al, 2002). There are, however, important exceptions to this rule. A broad spectrum of RCOs organise on a variety of different bases, including special needs (disability, the elderly, youth and schoolchildren); multinational affiliation as in the growing number of refugee consortia in London boroughs; organisations based upon locality as in the South London refugee association; and organisations which are exclusively aimed at meeting the needs of refugee women. All of these distinctive grounds for refugee organisation cut across any simple notion of the 'refugee community' as the sole basis of organisation and mobilisation. The continued dominance of the nationality-based organisation is therefore in need of some qualification, particularly regarding the politicisation of refugee communities and the problematic relationship between national communal identities and gender relationships. These qualifying factors are discussed later in this chapter.

The politicisation of community

One of the distinguishing features of refugee communities is their relation to the political situation in the country of origin (Kunz, 1973, 1981; Al-Rasheed, 1993; Joly, 1996). In general, political factors play an important role in defining refugees as a distinctive category of forced migrant (Zolberg et al, 1989). This is despite the fact that there are often tangled relationships between economic and political factors in the determinants of 'refugee flight' (Richmond, 1993). Within academic discourse, the attempt to enforce a rigid distinction between refugees and other categories of migrant, other than in terms of legally encoded forms of protection, is becoming increasingly untenable. The asylum–migration nexus is now a firmly established area of academic investigation (Koser, 2001, 2002) and to some extent undercuts any simple division between refugees and other migrants, either in conceptual or pragmatic terms. Nevertheless, political factors are often primary considerations in the analysis of refugee communities in exile. There is, for example, a rich literature on the effects of politicisation and the selective construction of national and communal identities upon refugee communities living in the diaspora (Kay, 1987; Vasquez, 1989; Bousquet, 1991; Eastmond, 1993, 1998; Wahlbeck, 1998; Griffiths, 2000; Kelly, 2003).

In this research, our discussion of the regions focused on the role of newly emerging RCOs in defining, building and representing refugee communities. The issues raised by the sample of London RCOs are somewhat different. Most of the organisations in the sample are well established and have passed through the stage of struggling to define their identities. Griffiths (2002, p 60) for example, following Reilly (1991) and Wahlbeck (1998), has charted the ways in which in the early 1990s the Partîya Karkarên Kürdistan (PKK) or Kurdistan Workers' Party gained ascendancy in the Turkish/Kurdish organisations in Hackney and Haringey. Communal identities have typically been defined by the major PKK-affiliated organisations in a way which has tended to exclude or marginalise minority positions or interests in the Turkish/Kurdish community (Wahlbeck, 1998). In this respect, it is important to note that the politicisation of community remains a central feature of refugee organisations in London.

There was one clear example in the sample of a Sudanese organisation that was at the centre of a number of contending political factions. It is important to recall that the Sudanese community as a whole is divided according to whether an individual comes from the Muslim-dominated north of the country or the Christian south. While these distinctions were often of no importance on a personal level, the north–south distinction has a more ready political significance. As the coordinator of the Sudanese organisation in question remarked:

> "War created mistrust between people. So they [individuals from the south] will come to you as individuals....We used to socialise [but] if it's an official platform, they tend to identify themselves as 'southerners'."

In the early stages of organisational development, the organisation had been heavily politicised and identified with a number of contending political factions. As the coordinator stated, regarding the organisation, "People tend to come with their own differences. So each political party they will put it as their end to manipulate it". Her own appointment as coordinator had brought about a significant change in the organisation, away from the dominance of the politically appointed management committee to a more structured approach that was directly accountable to funding bodies. Personal manipulation of funds by various sections of the management committee was a recurrent problem for the new coordinator. As she remarked, "They thought that they were above the law, because they are related to this political party or something". The tension between her role and the politicisation of the organisation was still being played out at the time of interview. It was a conflict of interests that was also compounded by the gender dynamics at play in the organisation, as the majority of the management committee were men and reportedly tended to treat Sudanese women as secretaries or adjuncts to their own interests.

As the comparison of Somali and Kurdish refugees in London has suggested (Griffiths, 2002), in the absence of a hegemonic leadership in the refugee community, politicisation tends to result in fragmentation and a loss of impetus for refugee organisations. In the case of the

Sudanese organisation in this sample, research commissioned by the organisation itself (Ashami and Dumper, 2003, p 19) concluded that:

> The organisation does not appear to be accessible to its users. There seems to be a perception among many, that it is concerned mainly with organising festive events, and primarily serves those of a particular political orientation.... The management committee lacks members with UK voluntary sector and seems to be linked to political positions. There is no sense of a common purpose linked to the ability to deliver services. When members of the management committee visit the Centre, they appear to be there for reasons other than service delivery.

Politicised communities may therefore result in a dissociation of organisations from the communities they are assumed to represent. In this respect, the principle of nationality-based organisations (and the assumptions of common identities in refugee communities) may tend to conceal the conflicting interpretations of the community and of its diverse needs which occur in reality.

Gender and the construction of community

There is an extensive literature on the gender dynamics of refugee organisations (Page, nd; Evelyn Oldfield Unit, 2003a) and of the relationship between gendered and national identities in diasporic and refugee communities (Kay, 1987; Al-Rasheed, 1993; Buijs, 1993; Yuval-Davis, 1997; Camino and Krulfeld, 1994). Two of the RCOs in the sample of London organisations were for refugee women. In both cases, the rationale of the organisations was connected to the perceived inability of nationality-based organisations to cater for the specific needs of refugee women. These included issues around the asylum determination process (Crawley, 1997), domestic violence in refugee communities, employment (Dumper, 2002), and health-related issues.

One of the main reasons given for setting up women–only organisations was the issue of confidentiality. Women were potentially more at risk of retaliation in cases of reported domestic violence if they remained within their own communities and community organisations. As Yuval-Davis (1997) has suggested, gender relations are an inherent part of how the national community is imagined. Both biological and cultural continuity are effectively embodied in women. The issue of 'honour' relating to the preservation of sexual and familial codes is therefore paramount in many diasporic communities (Yuval-Davis, 1997, p 143). In this respect also, it was argued that nationality-based organisations were less likely to be as sensitive to the importance of gender-based persecution as women-only organisations. Multinational or gender-based organisations were perceived as a positive advantage for refugee women, as opposed to the dominant nationality/community-based model of refugee organisations. In particular, there was the ever-present question of the dominance of men in the public sphere which was replicated in the majority of RCOs interviewed in London. This was despite the fact that women were involved as management committee members or as workers or volunteers in refugee organisations. Most of the organisations had equal opportunities policies in place, yet only in a minority of cases were women employed in the key positions of authority in the organisation.

One generic refugee women's organisation that had only been in existence for 10 years had mushroomed in activities and size since the mid-1990s. With an annual turnover in excess of £500,000, it was also the largest RCO in the sample. It was the focus of intensive networking practices between women's organisations across London, involving capacity building and the establishment of new women's organisations. Its networking activities involved participating in a variety of organisations including the Hackney Domestic Violence Forum and the Refugee Women's Domestic Violence Network that operates across all of the London boroughs. It also participated in the national Refugee Women's Network that addresses such issues as 'honour killing', domestic violence and female genital mutilation. Forms of bridging social capital would therefore appear to be particularly strong in the networks formed by refugee women's organisations in London. The success of women's networks requires further independent analysis, particularly concerning the degree to which they offer an alternative to the competitive ethos that often appears to dominate in the refugee sector as a whole.

Competition, resources and social capital

Competition is one of the central factors affecting the political economy of refugee organisations. This occurs at several levels: between factions within a particular refugee group and over the symbolic and material resources which refugee organisations offer, their potential as sources of social capital.

Organisational proliferation is a pronounced feature of specific refugee communities. The Somalis are notable for the large number of organisations across London (Somali Conference, 1998). Originally confined to Tower Hamlets and Isle of Dogs where the earlier generation of Somali seamen had settled (El-Solh, 1991), Somali refugees settled in different areas of London in increasing numbers from 1992 onwards in response to the burgeoning civil war in the southern and central regions of the country (Griffiths, 2003). Typically, settlement occurred on the basis of clan and sub-clan affiliation (Griffiths, 2002, p 104). The transmission of information via networks was an essential part of Somali settlement across London. One example in the sample is of an organisation that was set up by second-generation Somalis in Shepherd's Bush in 1986. This changed from being a social club for the children of the original seamen to a vital lifeline for Somali asylum seekers from the late 1980s and early 1990s. As the coordinator observed:

> "This organisation is actually the reasons they came to this
> area. There was no other way they could actually come.
> They came and got the advice. The news travelled – word
> of mouth. So they would come straight away from the
> airport and know there was an organisation there who
> could help them."

With rising numbers from different parts of Somalia, organisational proliferation occurred throughout West London. The same representative from the Shepherd's Bush organisation noted that, "Initially even community organisations, they did tend to transfer tribal issues from back home. *They say this community is for this tribe so we'll have to form our own*" (emphasis added). Reference to the Somali community of 'this tribe' was commonplace during interviews and suggested that home affiliations continued to fracture Somali RCOs in London. Refugee organisations in this sense may act as symbolic markers, defining a sense of belonging to a specific sub-group within the larger Somali community. It is important to recall here that processes of recognition and 'status' are essential aspects of the formation of social capital (Bourdieu, 1986). The institutionalisation of networks in the form of an organisation or association allows for the further development of social capital within the specific sub-group. This process is conflictual, as specific sub-groups carve out turf and areas of control, rather than naively normative as is suggested in Putnam's account of social capital.

Organisational proliferation, again taking the example of the Somalis, would also appear to be connected to the potential acquisition of material resources and benefits. Research has consistently suggested that refugees experience significant downward mobility in Britain and higher levels of unemployment than other ethnic groups (Bloch, 2002; Carey-Wood et al, 1995). This broader context of material and social inequalities directly impinges upon the formation of refugee organisations. The rationale for refugee organisations is not simply to respond to needs within the community that are not being met by the statutory authorities. More fundamentally, it can be seen as a response to the obstacles that prevent refugees from accessing the mainstream labour market. Refugee community organisations are quite simply one of the few means of employment available to refugees. As the above Somali coordinator observed in relation to the proliferation of organisations in refugee communities more generally:

> "The RCOs feel that that's the only way they can get funding and it's the only route to employment. A lot of refugees they think that this is their only chance of getting off unemployment.... A lot of them set them up because they've exhausted other avenues of getting employment. A lot of communities they look to their own community for employment. They cannot infiltrate, they find it hard to get employment outside...."

Competition over organisations as material assets may be more associated with their role in providing employment than any direct access to funding that they offer. Indeed, it is commonplace in the literature to point to this aspect of RCOs as one of their principal integrative benefits for refugees. This is, however, more often asserted than fully demonstrated. In practice, employment and training is available only to a minority of individuals engaged in RCOs. The significance of RCOs for integration is therefore unclear. Employment when it does occur through RCOs tends to remain within the closed world of the ethnic economy. As another coordinator of an RCO observed, "You're just staying within your sector. You're not going outside". The barriers to employment that often act as spurs to the formation of RCOs also act, on the whole, to keep employment firmly within the ethnic enclave or refugee sector.

Equally important to the control of material resources and access to employment is the symbolic significance of organisations. The legitimacy conferred by institutional belonging is closely connected to forms of symbolic recognition; that is, being recognised as a specific community organisation, or assuming a 'name' in the public arena, a factor which in turn provides the basis for the future development of social capital. Putnam's analysis of associations as forms of social capital had suggested that they play a key role in cementing collective norms and in promoting social integration. The analysis presented here indicates rather that organisations can be viewed as one of the few means for refugees to secure material and symbolic resources. Competition and conflict over control of organisations is therefore endemic to this situation, rather than aberrant or dysfunctional.

Building networks

Competition is not the whole of the story, as sustained collaborative efforts between RCOs are commonplace across many parts of London. The building of this type of bridging social capital is an important part of the work of RCOs. As indicated earlier in this chapter, refugee consortia became increasingly popular from the mid-1980s onwards, often developing in tandem with local authority refugee forums and other forms of refugee networking sponsored by the community development team of the Refugee Council, among others. The majority of RCOs in the sample had participated in refugee forums in their borough and broader-based coalitions of voluntary agencies in the borough area. The time spent on cultivating networks depended upon the resources available to the organisation. Too often, limited resources meant that organisations had to batten down and focus on their own immediate interests. One Tamil organisation in Newham, which had recently experienced a drastic cut in its funding, had been forced to take a rather sceptical view of the value of networking. As the chair of the organisation remarked:

> "Sometimes we think that we gain more knowledge by sitting here and focusing on our own work ... but we are still attending a few meetings if it is worthwhile."

He later added that, "if there's no resources these networks are only paper-talk". Lack of resources in RCOs typically meant that, in the words of one Somali organiser, "we're all of us chasing our own interests".

In some cases, it was felt that informal networks rather than formally constituted ones had been more effective in building bridges between refugee organisations. Again, for the Somalis the problems of disunity could be overcome in practice by informal networking between organisations. As the coordinator of a Somali organisation in south London noted:

> "We tried to set up a Somali forum a long time ago and it never succeeded. Some had a hidden agenda. Some were after the resources. Indirectly now there is a link but once we say that we want to formalise it, it doesn't work. So now I just pick up a phone and tell other community organisations I've got this-and-this problems, how can I solve them? Straightaway I'll get the help and support that I need. I want to formalise it … I don't know, maybe we're not a formal society…."

Certain scepticism also marked the development of formal networks and partnerships with agencies outside the refugee community. Networks with statutory authorities and funders, although generally positive, were occasionally seen as modes of excluding outsiders rather than as a means of encouraging participation. Another Somali coordinator remarked of the funding bodies and statutory agencies:

> "They want, you know, a kind of partnership, they want a kind of networking, but the network itself is not an honest network…. If there is a group of people who come together and meet together the funding is divided between certain groups, things like that. That's the reality I have seen myself."

An extreme example of the perils of partnership was the case of a Vietnamese organisation, An Viet, which had established its own housing association in 1987. This was the first Vietnamese association to register with The Housing Corporation and had a proven track record of success, having expanded its activities outside London to the regions. By the early 1990s, it appears that the relationship between the two wings of the Vietnamese organisation were seen as problematic by The Housing Corporation, in particular that too much control was being exercised by certain members of the executive committee. At the time, The Housing Corporation had also introduced the notion of 'group structure' that encouraged the formation of partnerships with larger housing organisations. Encouraged by The Housing Corporation, An Viet put out tenders for partnership collaboration, which was won by the BME organisation, Ujima (Swahili for 'Working together'). As a representative of the Vietnamese housing association, now reconstituted as a subsidiary of Ujima, remarked:

> "And that's when the problems really started in some
> respects....The expectation of how the partnership would
> work were somewhat different from the reality, in that Ujima
> exercised and I think were asked to exercise by the Housing
> Corporation, quite a significant amount of control. And
> that meant they could hire and fire board members. In fact,
> they replaced virtually the whole board in 1993-1994."

Legal battles ensued between An Viet and Ujima and continued for
the remainder of the decade. For the current chair of the organisation,
the 'take-over' was a clear case of asset stripping by a more powerful
BME 'partner'. More neutrally perhaps, the incident reveals the
vulnerability of RCOs to the agenda setting of their more powerful
partners, whether these are from within the BME sector or quasi-
governmental bodies (Zetter and Pearl, 1998).

Although most of the RCOs reported 'good' relations with their
immediate borough authority, the gap between the rhetoric of
partnership and the reality was a consistent theme in the interviews.
Recounting a story of her troubled relationship with the local housing
department, one Somali worker raised a series of questions regarding
the status of RCOs:

> "The problem is also really are you recognised as a
> profession? The refugee community organisations, in real
> terms are you seen as a professional body, that's what I have
> to ask myself. I don't think you are.... As soon as you say
> you work for a refugee community, 'What is that, what do
> you do?' So you're not seen as a professional person. Is it
> about power? Is it because you're not powerful? I don't
> know what it is."

The sense of 'not being taken seriously' by local authority professionals
had also been noted in the sample of RCOs from Birmingham (see
Chapter Six). Arguably, this is a question of training within local
authorities and statutory agencies concerning the role of RCOs that
needs to be comprehensively addressed.

Cross-borough collaboration of RCOs with statutory authorities
and agencies has nevertheless occurred successfully over the years, as
the Renewal Project of West London illustrates. The most significant
example of London-wide collaboration between RCOs is the Refugee
Working Party (RWP), now called London Refugee Voice (LRV).
This was founded in the middle of the 1980s by a combination of

leading RCOs and agencies and was initially more of an informal network than an established organisation. The RWP was funded by the then London Borough Grants Unit (now the Association of London Government) and was facilitated by the Westminster Diocese Refugee Service (WDRS). It was essentially a policy forum for developing ideas and strategies and gaining a higher profile for RCOs in London.

One organisation that had participated in the RWP from the outset suggested that participation in the RWP also had more immediate benefits for organisations:

> "It was prestigious to become a member of RWP because that meant you could get funding. Everyone wanted to join. I remember we wanted to join at that time because it was like a guarantee of you getting funding or like a way into funding.... So when we first got our funding from LBG [London Borough Grants] we joined straight away, because we thought that's a good way of ensuring that our funding will continue."

The decline of the RWP had been accompanied by a more inclusive role for the organisation as increasing numbers of RCOs lacking funding joined it. Interestingly, its value for participants appeared to decrease as a result of its broadened appeal. Several of the RCOs interviewed in the sample had participated in the RWP and were now involved in its replacement body, the LRV. The original RWP had ceased to function as a viable organisation by the end of the 1990s. When the WDRS withdrew support for the project (as part of a general restructuring of its work) it was replaced by LRV in November 2002. The LRV is still a fledgling organisation, with limited funding and with a membership of 82 RCOs across London. Fifteen 'big agencies', including the Refugee Council, Refugee Action and Asylum Aid, are co-members, although their role in the organisation is currently unclear. Over half of the RCOs joining the LRV are newly established, according to the recently appointed chair of the organisation. The narrative of the RWP and its transformation into the LRV requires further unravelling, as it bears closely upon the involvement of London RCOs with refugee communities in the dispersal areas, which is addressed in the next part of this chapter.

The impacts of dispersal

The impact of dispersal on London-based RCOs has been complex and consists of a series of ad-hoc, uncoordinated responses as well as more collaborative approaches to addressing the needs of newly emerging refugee communities in the regions. The history of the RWP is tied to the unfolding story of dispersal and to the relation between the different agencies and partners involved in its implementation.

The RCO Development Project

Prior to the implementation of dispersal, a series of consultative meetings was held between the RWP and the Coordinators Training and Support Scheme (COTASS) of the Evelyn Oldfield Unit, which acts as a "voice of RCO managers and coordinators". These meetings were focused on the issues raised by dispersal and the role of RCOs in the new arrangements. Coming out of these debates was the formation of the RCOs Development Project (RCODP). The RWP and COTASS were on the steering committee of the RCODP but because of financial constraints they were unable to manage it directly. This role was given to WDRS.

The RCODP was only one of the joint ventures between the RCO sector and the key agencies that took place at the time. With the implementation of dispersal, five RCOs were subcontracted to the Refugee Council (working under contract to the Home Office) to provide support to NASS asylum applicants, both within their own communities and to other nationalities. The RCODP was funded by the Refugee Council and Refugee Action and other agencies through the Interagency Partnership (IAP), which consists of the key NGOs supplying support under the NASS arrangements. In the words of a former employee of the RWP:

> "The project came about through negotiation with the big agencies, the big boys, when they were negotiating with the government, just pre-NASS. The agencies were trying to secure contracts for themselves being involved with the NASS. These networks were part of the negotiations. And in the end the agencies secured contracts with the Home Office and all RCOs got this very tiny project [RCODP]. And there was this issue of the management and because they couldn't host it, WDRS has become the legal employer but the steering committee

comprised Refugee Working Party and COTASS. It wasn't really part of those networks. It was really complicated ... this structure created loads of problems for everyone...."

Complexities in management structure and disagreement between the different networks involved, including the role of the agencies that were funding the project, meant that the RCODP did not work as well as planned. Some useful work was done before the demise of the RWP, including the development of a consortium for extending outreach to the regions (RWP, 2001). The consortium at the time consisted of Albanian Youth Action; Halkevi Kurdish and Turkish Community Centre; South London Tamil Welfare Group; Community of Congolese Refugees in Britain; Carila Latin American Welfare Group; Ethiopian Community in Britain; Karin Housing Association and the Eritrean Community in UK. In the words of the individual quoted above:

> "We facilitated eight RCOs to form something like a consortium, initially more informal, and all sort of well-established RCOs representing different communities, especially dispersal communities, that they have these communities in several cities but mainly in Liverpool and Manchester. They facilitated meetings where they came together to discuss how they could help their communities outside London. And we organised a fieldtrip to Liverpool and Manchester, where for example in the morning they offered advice to their communities in those areas. What happened is that through other organisations in the areas, voluntary and statutory agencies and then a working lunch and then a visit to hostels ... a real sort of exchange of information. A lot of people didn't realise in the regions these RCOs are so well established.... The project really aimed to have advice delivery in those cities."

Disagreements on the steering committee about the aims of the project and the withdrawal of support from the WDRS led to RCOs in London being asked if they wished to tender to run the project. What happened next is a bone of contention between RCOs and the agencies that funded the RCODP. The facts are clear: several RCOs put in bids to host the project, including the Ethiopian Community in Britain (ECB) and a Tamil and Kurdish organisation. The steering committee voted in favour of the Ethiopian organisation. In the event, the contract was given to Praxis, which is not an RCO but an umbrella organisation providing a range of services to refugees and migrants in East London. The majority opinion among the RCOs involved was that undue influence had been placed by the agencies, in particular the Refugee Council and Refugee Action, in arriving at this outcome. In the words of the former employee of the RWP:

> "Again, it is like there is no faith in RCOs. OK, the idea was that even if we were not an independent project an RCO could host the project, because Westminster Diocese were not going to.... So we said an RCO is more than capable of hosting this project, still with the involvement of other RCOs and networks. And two organisations volunteered, including the ECB and a Kurdish group.... The recommendation from the staff was for the ECB.... And later someone just turned up and they wouldn't give it to the RCO, it had to be Praxis, which is not an RCO. It just has to be again a big brother agency.... Loads of RCOs they were very suspicious in the consortium. They were really annoyed about it. They said they haven't been consulted.... It was definitely agency preference, we think...."

Reconstructing past events of this sort is necessarily problematic. What is clear is the perception on the ground among RCOs that partner agencies had wielded their influence to arrive at an outcome they preferred. The common perception was that this was due to the agencies' commitment to developing their presence in the regions. A London-led RCO may well have had different priorities. As the chair of the key Tamil organisation involved in the RWP and later LRV remarked of the RCOs relation to the agencies:

> "They all know us. They know that we are very powerful as refugee communities. I don't say that they neglect us. Because RA [Refugee Action], RC [Refugee Council] they're all interested in getting funding in order to make the dispersal area work. And in establishing regional offices. We are not that big. So our confinement to London has two main objectives. To empower established organisations and to help un-established organisations to come to a certain level. To share this expertise, to develop community organisations in the dispersal areas.... I also support the

point that community organisations must be established in the dispersal areas. The difference comes in whether this can be achieved without London Voice and making use of the London expertise. Or whether you can go on your own…."

Differences in organisational priorities and perspectives underlay this fairly open breach between the RCOs and agencies involved in the RCODP. The agencies were plainly perceived to be 'going it alone' by failing to appoint an RCO organisation to run the project in the regions.

A number of issues are raised here. First is the economic dependence of RCOs on the main agencies involved. The RCODP was funded through the IAP, as part of general Home Office funding for dispersal. Of the differences between the agencies and RCOs, the Tamil spokesperson again remarked:

"The point is that they [the agencies] are driven by funding policy. We are far away from the funding policy. We are driven by local needs. That is the difference."

Second is the imbalance in power that necessarily results from this. Agenda setting and institutional bias that favours the preferences of the large NGOs and state institutions are the key factors involved. At a subjective level, the sense of being underestimated, of a lack of faith in the capacity of RCOs to run projects impartially and competently was commonly expressed by those interviewed. Third is the broader question of the difference in rationales between the refugee agencies, with their close ties to the Home Office and the needs-led dynamic of RCOs. As we shall see in the case of Birmingham, there is a pervasive sense of distrust of the Refugee Council among a broad spectrum of organisations, and particularly among RCOs in the city. Under-resourcing of the Refugee Council had been one of the main factors involved in this situation. At the level of perception however, the Refugee Council is often seen as an adjunct of the Home Office and consequently tarred with the same brush.

The involvement of the agencies in the dispersal programme had also led to a perceived gap between their resulting organisational growth and the needs of refugees on the ground. As the Tamil chair remarked of the growing disjuncture between the agencies and the refugee communities:

"There's a general drawback in all of this thing. When you grow larger and larger you ignore the grassroots level. We want bottom up activities…. If you see the history, the Tamils who are here, somewhere they have connections with older Tamils. They're not coming from the sky. So why don't you plan to incorporate the expertise, the experience, the relationship to develop? To do the same thing. You get funding and you have your own plan and you think, we may be a hindrance to your plan. I don't know! … What I say is all these organisations have less contact with the grass-roots level. So their thinking may not reflect, or may not match with the thinking of the local communities. This is what I suspect."

These are highly significant comments. From this perspective, the accumulated social capital of refugee communities, the expertise deriving from networks established over decades is in danger of being sidelined by imposed policy directives and imperatives emanating from the centre and the organisational requirements of the large NGOs. The more general concern is that the agencies may also be failing in their traditional role of advocating for refugee rights. As the same Tamil individual joked, "Now it is partly they [the agencies] don't want to antagonise them [the Home Office], partly they want to please us, so the policy lies in between".

Despite the tangled history of the RCODP, it is now based at Praxis and has been running effectively for several months. At the time of the fieldwork, the RCODP had undertaken consultation visits to seven regions, had contact with 26 RCOs, established a working relationship with the Community Development sub-group of the National Refugee Integration Forum (NRIF) and undertaken various types of research into the regions and RCO development. The LRV, which replaced the RWP in November 2002, is also beginning to grow. It has recently (October 2003) withdrawn from participating in the advisory committee of the RCODP due to a conflict of interests between developing its London-based activities and the focus of the RCODP on the regions. London Refugee Voice is currently under-resourced and unable to undertake any significant activities in the regions. At a meeting of the LRV held in August 2003, there was also a concern expressed that the LRV should dissociate itself from Praxis, as it might be made to 'take the blame' if things went wrong later on.

Ad-hoc responses to dispersal

In addition to these coordinated initiatives, individual RCOs have attempted to respond to the changes brought about by dispersal. A typical response was the following from the coordinator of an Ethiopian organisation:

> "We had very calls from the regions before dispersal started. There were very few Ethiopians outside London. Now we have to run here and there and we have financial and human resource limitations. Now most of it is done by telephone. But the telephone cannot be as effective as when we are with a client. But still we try to cope...."

Lack of facilities in the dispersal areas and the hostility of local populations were also routine complaints that RCOs had to deal with. In a number of cases this had resulted in a 'drift back' to London. A Somali worker observed that:

> "[M]any clients they call us from outside and say, 'We cannot live here'. Some of them say they don't feel happy because people are looking at us or throwing stones and some people they left and they say they're not going back. And I don't have any help for them. If I go to the local authority they say, 'OK, this person is intentionally homeless'.... Sometimes we try to make them calm where they are. Sometimes they come to us."

In addition to individuals returning from the regions there are the large number who choose to live on subsistence-only assistance and to remain in London. In either case, additional burdens have been placed upon the existing community resources in London. As one Somali coordinator remarked, "We try to find people they can stay with. But you know nobody will accept someone for one year". The difficulty in the view of many of the RCOs interviewed lay in the lack of established refugee communities in the regions. London was the preferred destination for asylum seekers precisely because of the existence of settled refugee communities:

> "After coming here I have seen that it would be better to be settled here [in London] – most Ethiopians are living here. If you're dispersed outside of London to any corner

of the UK, probably you will have a communication problem, cultural conflict you know if you're the only black person around that area...." (Ethiopian association)

Granted that dispersal was now a fact of life, there was still some debate over exactly what form community organisations should take in the regions. As we note in the case of the West Midlands, there is a tendency (although no explicit policy) for the agencies to support multinational models of refugee organisation. In particular, it is believed that organisational proliferation and competition can be avoided by this means. The opinion among the RCOs interviewed in London was that there was still a strong case for nationality-based organisations. This was forcefully expressed by the chair of a Tamil association that had pioneered collaborative work with Tamils in Liverpool and had been actively involved in the RCODP and its outreach work in Liverpool and Manchester. Referring to the case of the Tamils, he argued:

> "If you can give them the confidence that there is a small group which they can link, so they won't be determined that we should live in London. The main disadvantage of refugees to move down to dispersal areas to the best of my knowledge, employment. In London the opportunities are more. Why they are reluctant, another thing is insecurity, because the community is not there, the community organisations are not there. Even now I am fighting with so many agencies [Refugee Council and Refugee Action] when they are planning multi-based community organisations. I said on principle this is right. But as a Tamil family, you'd be happy to visit a Tamil organisation. I don't say you must have 700 organisations for 700 communities. But depending on your number, if you come and you have your friend, you will be happy."

The move to multinational organisations in the regions may be a positive development in respect of avoiding duplication and increasing information sharing and the pooling of resources. Yet the desire to organise on ethnic and national grounds among refugee groups remains. The force of ethnic bonds and the sense of trust engendered by these were common themes in the interviews. It was also the case that more immediate institutional self-interest was at stake for some of the RCOs in the sample. A Kurdish organisation, for example, had developed individual initiatives to assist their co-ethnics in the dispersal areas. This was seen as both a form of solidarity and as a response to the declining number of Iraqi asylum applications that had occurred since the Gulf War of 2003. The decline in the number of Kurds arriving in London meant that the organisation had to broaden its base in order to expand in future. In the words of the coordinator of the Kurdish organisation:

> "Communities outside London were not nearly so well organised as in London. Therefore, I thought that if we could, they could set up organisations and we could help out. We had two meetings with RA [Refugee Action] in Sheffield....We've now got in £19,000 for that project.... We've got the money for Sheffield. They're setting up their own organisation. We're sending a part-time worker. When we give them support from here, sending up our advisors.... Because of declining numbers, we're now beginning to concentrate more on the dispersal and integration."

At present, the jury is out concerning the optimal model of organisational development for RCOs in the regions. Whatever the outcomes, they are certain to reflect the different priorities and institutional interests of the main actors involved in the dispersal and settlement arrangements.

Conclusions

This chapter has reviewed the recent settlement of refugees in London and the development of RCOs, in particular since the mid-1980s. This provides the essential backdrop to the more recent developments, which have occurred in the regions since the introduction of dispersal. Chapter Five, then, outlines the institutional and policy background to the situation in the regions, which is developed through the fieldwork material presented in Chapter Six.

To summarise the argument presented in this chapter, we have noted the concentration of refugees and asylum seekers in particular areas of London. There are an estimated 500-600 RCOs in London, although a significant number of these are small scale and have insecure funding. Most have developed since the mid-1980s. Since that time, refugee consortia, refugee fora and the cross-borough collaboration of RCOs have grown at an increasing rate.

The sample in London consisted of 20 RCOs, selected principally according to nationality and date of establishment. There was a bias in the sample towards well-established organisations, the majority of which were founded in the 1980s. The size of membership in the organisations reflected the scale of the refugee communities in London. Over half of the organisations were medium sized (with funding of £50,000-£250,000 per year), while one fifth were large in terms of their funding base (£250,000+). The main funding sources were the Association of London Government, the Community Fund, local authorities and a variety of trusts. Staffing levels and services were well developed in the majority of RCOs, although only half had sufficient resources to offer services relating to education, employment and training. The majority of services consisted of signposting and advice and guidance.

The aims of the older organisations had changed over time as new needs arose in the communities. There was also a tension between maintaining the grass-roots dynamics of the organisations while satisfying the requirements of bureaucratisation and accountability to funders. Funding remained a key issue for the organisations in an increasingly restrictive and competitive environment. Although the majority of the sample was nationality-based organisations, several of the RCOs organised on different bases, including special needs and gender. The notion of the homogenous refugee community underpinning nationality-based organisations was questioned on two particular counts: the politicisation of community, which resulted in different 'visions' of the collectivity, and the significance of gender relationships. The central factor here was the antagonism between the interests of refugee women and those of the putative national/refugee community. Refugee organisation on the basis of gender appeared to have been particularly successful in the two women's groups in the sample.

Competition was noted as a central feature of the political economy of refugee organisations. This took two primary and interdependent forms, relating to the material and symbolic resources which RCOs offer. Refugee organisations in this light are both a means of securing employment and other material benefits and of gaining forms of symbolic recognition. The institutionalisation of networks in organisations consolidates social capital and allows for the future development and acquisition of social capital. Rather than conceived of in normative terms as the development of networks of norms and trust, this process may be regarded as inherently conflictual in nature and driven by competition over resources of both a material and symbolic character.

This chapter also reviewed the very real processes of collaborative working, both between RCOs and between RCOs and other agencies. Here the evidence was mixed as RCOs encountered unequal partnerships in their networking activities. The history of the RWP and the RCO Development Project was described in some detail as this exemplifies a number of dilemmas facing RCOs. Issues of control and agenda setting in collaborative working, particularly with the key refugee agencies, were highlighted in relation to the institutional arrangements for the representation of RCO interests developed as part of the dispersal programme. Ad-hoc responses to dispersal have also taken place by London-based RCOs, although currently with little effect due to limited resources.

In contrast to the normative model of voluntary associations developed by Putnam, this chapter, to use Bourdieu's terminology, has emphasised the conflictual fields affecting refugee organisations. This applies both to their internal workings and their relation to the "agents who have an interest in the game that is played in the field in question" (Siissiänen, 2000, p 22). These agents include other RCOs and voluntary organisations, the key NGOs and the state institutions responsible for the specific policy area of reception and refugee settlement. The following two chapters apply this analysis to the actors and agencies operating in the regions.

FIVE

The institutional and policy framework in the regions

This chapter reviews the institutional and policy framework in the West Midlands and the North West. It begins by contrasting the socioeconomic characteristics of the two regions before proceeding to examine the structure of the consortia and the current integration arrangements for refugees in the regions. In the case of the West Midlands, the principal focus is on Birmingham. As the largest city in the region, it also has the highest number of asylum seekers and a growing and diverse refugee population. After outlining the history of refugee settlement in the city, a profile of the main refugee groups is presented.

In the case of the North West, the main focus is on Liverpool and Manchester and the surrounding localities. Again, they are the largest cities in the region and also have the highest number of dispersed asylum seekers and an increasing and diverse population of refugees.

The chapter also explores local authorities' strategy, policy and practice in coping with new arrivals and the more recent settled communities. The chapter concludes by reviewing the recent history of asylum seeker and refugee settlement in the regions and in particular the cities of Birmingham, Liverpool and Manchester. The principal focus of the chapter therefore is to provide a comparative framework for the examination of refugee community organisations (RCOs) in the two regions that follows in Chapter Six.

Socioeconomic characteristics of the regions

Overview of the West Midlands

The West Midlands region consists of seven metropolitan districts, three unitary authorities, four shire counties and 24 district councils. With a population of approximately one million, Birmingham is the regional centre and largest recipient of asylum seekers under the National Asylum Support Service (NASS) in the region. The other principal cities are Coventry and Wolverhampton. The West Midlands region as a whole has a population of 5.3 million (Census, 2001). In terms of its general economic characteristics, Advantage West Midlands (AWM, 2001) notes that in the West Midlands region, GDP per head was 6% below the national average in 1996. On the Index of Local Deprivation, the West Midlands has two districts in the top 10 and six in the top 50 most-deprived areas (AWM, 2001, p 13). According to the regional consortium, West Midlands Consortium for Asylum Seeker and Refugee Support (WMCARS, 2003, p 8), "the west midlands metropolitan area has a significant concentration of deprivation and poverty and this has been recognised through the use of Single Regeneration Budget and associated Government programmes and through the allocation of European and Structural Funds". There is considerable internal variation in the region, with outlying areas such as Stoke-on-Trent having a high concentration of poverty and reported racial incidents. Several districts in the West Midlands rank high on the Index of Local Deprivation and all of the metropolitan areas apart from Solihull are deprived according to the criteria set out in the Social Exclusion White Paper.

Overview of the North West

The North West region is dominated by two large cities: Manchester and Liverpool. The region has an overall population of 6,729,764 with a relatively small minority ethnic population (5.6%). Greater Manchester is an urban conurbation comprised of Manchester in addition to a number of other towns: Bolton, Bury, Oldham, Rochdale, Salford, Stockport, Tameside, Trafford and Wigan (Census, 2001). According to the 2001 Census, Manchester has a total population of 392,819 people, with Greater Manchester having a population of 2,482,328. The minority ethnic portion of the population in Greater Manchester is 9%, with Pakistani (3%) and Indian (1. 5%) as major groups. The city of Manchester has a significant higher percentage of minority ethnic population (19%) with Pakistani (5.9%), Black Caribbean (2.3%) and Black African (1.7%) as major communities.

Liverpool's population is 439,473, with the Merseyside conurbation (including: Knowsley, St Helens, Sefton, and Wirral) totalling a population of 1,362,026. The conurbation of Liverpool has a largely 'white' population (97%). The Chinese community is the largest minority ethnic group (0.6%). Both Liverpool and Manchester have established minority ethnic communities, while Merseyside and some parts of Greater Manchester do not. Liverpool and Manchester, according to the 1998 Index of Local Deprivation, are respectively the first and the third most deprived local authorities in the country.

The North West has experienced considerable depopulation in the last 20 years. As a result, there are many empty properties that are available on the market at very low prices: a recognised incentive for dispersing asylum seekers into the region. "Liverpool", one interviewee stated, "is a very old, cold and sick city, with many empty houses". Interestingly, a new factor emerged while fieldwork was being undertaken: Liverpool's nomination as the European Capital of Culture in 2008. According to some interviewees, the extensive programme of urban regeneration in the city is likely to impact negatively upon asylum seekers, leading to their expulsion from the city centre where many of them are now settled.

Structure of the consortia

The West Midlands

The West Midlands Consortium for Asylum Seeker and Refugee Support (WMCARS) was established on 8 November 2000 under the general control of the consortium regional manager. Birmingham City Council (BCC), as the lead local authority in the consortium, directly negotiated the contract with the NASS. The first phase of the contract included Birmingham, Wolverhampton and Coventry city authorities and the metropolitan districts of Dudley, Walsall, Sandwell and Solihull. Stoke-on-Trent joined the consortium in February 2001. According to its Business Plan for 2001, the WMCARS consists of four main elements (WMCARS, 2001):

(1) an *executive group:* its role is the overall management and monitoring of the Consortium in order to reflect national policy;
(2) a *regional stakeholder group*[1]: this will enable the executive to fulfil its roles, and recommend systems to improve service provision across the region;
(3) *the wider community:* a number of interest groups are involved here, although they are spelt out in less detail than the executive and stakeholder groups;
(4) *local groups:* these include local voluntary groups and refugee community-based groups (RCOs).

This document further states that, "the work of the Stakeholding Group will be achieved through local groups and community networking" (WMCARS, 2001, p 10); that is, components three and four above. It is implicitly assumed that information will move freely from the local to the executive levels. Research conducted in the West Midlands has suggested that this model has not worked fully in practice, with several non-governmental organisations (NGOs) in the region noting a lack of consultation between the different actors involved (Zetter et al, 2003b).

The WMCARS, nevertheless, has been active in promoting debate around the issues of refugee integration. For example, the conference, 'Dispersal or Disposal? Retrieving Refugees' Skills for Our Society', was held under the auspices of the WMCARS and the Midlands Refugee Council in January 2001. In addition, the role of RCOs and the issue of refugee integration are significant elements of the WMCARS Business Plan of 2003-04. It is important to recall that under the Home Office National Integration Strategy (Home Office, 2000b), the regional consortia are required to have regional integration strategies in place to aid the integration of refugees in the regions. The WMCARS in its Business Plan for 2003-04 states that its aim "is to continue to develop and implement resources to prevent the social marginalisation of refugees by dealing effectively with the legal, cultural and language obstacles and empowering refugees to make positive decisions about their future" (WMCARS, 2003, p 10). As members of the consortium acknowledge, the current Business Plan does not constitute a formal integration strategy but rather a statement of aims in relation to the key areas affecting refugee settlement. It should be noted that RCOs are formally represented in the WMCARS as part of the 'stakeholder group'. The degree to which this type of formal incorporation reflects the social and economic issues faced by refugees and their specific organisational problems is open to question, as the fieldwork evidence in this chapter suggests.

Although there was no regional integration strategy in place during 2003, the manager of the consortium had been working in collaboration with the Centre for Urban and Regional Studies (CURS) at Birmingham University to develop a regional integration strategy. The WMCARS successfully secured funding under the Home Office Purposeful Activities Programme for 31 projects aimed at offering outlets for social activities for asylum seekers and refugees (WMCARS, 2002). The overall aim is to encourage interaction between asylum seekers, refugees and local communities. The WMCARS has also been granted funding under the Challenge Fund (2002-03) for mental health (social and cultural support) and for Roselodge Housing for a project designed to assist refugees to set up commercial enterprises (*Full and equal citizens: the newsletter of the Home Office Refugee Integration Unit,* June 2002). In terms of the general coordinating role of the consortium, the opinion expressed by NGOs and voluntary groups in Birmingham was that more work needed to be done to provide a clear, strategic direction for the integration of refugees in the city. Lack of independent decision making under the NASS arrangements was consistently cited as one of the principal reasons for the late development of a regional integration strategy, while firmer regional control of reception and settlement was seen more generally as a key issue by many of those active in the WMCARS (Zetter et al, 2003b).

The North West

The North West region as a whole received asylum seekers during the Kosovan crisis in 1999 and this formed the basis for the structure that later emerged under the interim arrangements and then with NASS from April 2000. Some of the towns of Greater Manchester received asylum seekers during this period, while, on the West side of the region, only Liverpool hosted any significant number of asylum seekers during the Kosovan crisis and the interim phase. The region has always been divided into two halves, with the West and East having separate NASS offices in Liverpool and Manchester respectively. However, the consortium extended across and included the whole region until May 2001 when Manchester City Council, the lead authority on the East side of the region, signed a supported accommodation contract with the Home Office. Liverpool, to date, has still not signed such a contract. From May 2001, the region contained two separate consortia, each with its own structure, executive and associated administration. This division of the North West region into the East and West sub-regions is a fundamental feature of the dispersal process in the region. The different responses of the lead local authorities on each side of the region have made a very significant difference as regards statutory provision, the role of the voluntary sector and private sector providers and the function and influence of refugee community groups.

It is problematic to speak of effective coordination in relation to the regional dispersal of asylum seekers. Up until relatively recently, there was only one regional representative of NASS, the NASS regional manager. The coordination that does occur is largely as a result of initiatives taken by the regional consortium and ad-hoc arrangements between the principal NGOs and RCOs. Other significant contractual relationships are between the individual private providers and NASS. The content of these latter contracts has generally been kept secret and is subject to rules of financial confidentiality. This has caused some resentment among members of the consortium in that the modus operandi of the latter has been, and is, one of openness and information sharing.

Information flows between NASS and the consortium, and other actors, are equally problematic. Individuals interviewed as part of this research frequently referred to difficulties in contacting the appropriate person within NASS in relation to a particular query. They also reported a very high turnover of staff at NASS and a resulting lack of continuity in operational activity. There was universal agreement that communication with NASS was extremely fraught. It was also commonplace for individuals to refer to the inaccuracy of the information passed on by NASS concerning the number and nationality of asylum seekers that were being dispersed to the region. One of the most common complaints was that the consortium members had received no information whatsoever about asylum seekers being dispersed into privately provided accommodation. In practice, it is clear in the North West that certain locations should be considered as 'no go' areas for asylum seekers due to local hostility. Nevertheless, the placement of asylum seekers in precisely those areas appears to be occurring, often without the consortium's knowledge.

Since May 2001, the East sub-region has operated as a separate entity. It is comprised of 11 local authorities: Manchester, Bolton, Bury, Oldham, Rochdale, Salford, Stockport, Tameside, Trafford, Wigan (the authorities that comprise Greater Manchester), plus Blackburn with Darwen. In the East sub-region, Manchester performs the role of lead authority. The Association of Greater Manchester Authorities has played a key role in the process of overall coordination. The consortium is structured on the basis of multi-agency fora, with each of the local authorities adopting this structure based upon the Audit Commission's recommendations in its publication, *Another country* (Audit Commission, 2000a)[2].

Reception of dispersed asylum seekers into consortium accommodation is the responsibility of the asylum teams of the local authorities. As regards asylum seekers being dispersed into private sector accommodation, it is their role to receive asylum seekers and take them to their accommodation. In-region, and out-of-region, dispersal is slightly more complex. This occurs when Refugee Action has placed asylum seekers who have claimed asylum in the North West in emergency accommodation. It is then Refugee Action's responsibility to organise and coordinate their dispersal either within the North West or outside it.

As mentioned earlier in the chapter, Liverpool City Council has not yet agreed a contract to receive asylum seekers with the Home Office. It appears that the main obstacle has been a failure to agree over the appropriate level of financial resources, although some interviewees referred also to political tensions between the central Labour government and the local Liberal Democrats-led council. The lack of a formal agreement has affected the shape taken by dispersal on this side of the region producing, in general, poor coordination and coherence in public intervention.

During the interim arrangements, Liverpool managed its incoming flow of asylum seekers by accommodating them in a reception centre located at Greenbank Court. After very protracted negotiations, the city council finally agreed on the terms of a contract with the Home Office at the end of February 2001. However, the lease on the reception centre ran out two weeks later and the local authority was unable to negotiate an extension of the lease. The result was that the local authority decommissioned its asylum accommodation services and, to date, no longer receives asylum seekers. The consortium formally continues to exist on the West side of the region and Liverpool still performs the role of lead authority. However, the absence of the contract dominates the situation. The consortium formally includes 21 local authorities, two of which are county authorities. Other than Liverpool, two other authorities have received only a handful of asylum seekers (Zetter et al, 2003b).

The functioning and viability of the North West Consortium [West] was strongly criticised by several individuals during the course of interviews. Albeit in a rhetorical vein, some individuals even went so far as to question the very existence of the consortium. As one respondent said, "To my knowledge, the North West Consortium [West] is a ghost".

NASS and the impacts of dispersal

The West Midlands

In relation to the responsibilities of NASS in the West Midlands, the NASS regional manager's role is to oversee:

- NASS's arrangements with local authorities and private providers for the reception of asylum seekers dispersed to the West Midlands;
- the dispersal from the West Midlands of some asylum seekers presenting themselves within the region;

- the transfer of unaccompanied minors from the care of local social services departments to the NASS arrangements for support when they reach the age of 18;
- the management of NASS's contracts with the Refugee Council and the West Midlands Local Government Association (LGA).

New asylum seekers presenting themselves within the West Midlands are referred to the Immigration and Nationality Department's Enquiry Unit in Solihull, where they are given a Form IS96 granting them limited leave to remain in the UK. They are then referred to the Refugee Council's regional office, to complete a NASS form applying for support, and to be placed in emergency accommodation while their NASS claim is assessed. Then, they may be dispersed. The former regional manager conceded that there have been delays in moving new applicants on from emergency accommodation because NASS has not been able to cope with the volume of applications. Also, some application forms have had to be returned to the Refugee Council because they were incomplete or incorrectly completed.

From April 2000, NASS began dispersing new asylum seekers to Birmingham and the West Midlands, and from 29 August 2000 all new applicants for asylum became the responsibility of NASS. Their accommodation, before NASS signed contracts with the West Midlands local authorities, was often in private small hotels or hostels, either with meals provided or self-catering under the voucher scheme. Under their contracts with NASS, the private landlords are supposed also to provide information on access to schools, the health service, legal services and 'community support'.

One of the former NASS regional managers estimated that, as at 30 October 2000, there were 1,300 asylum seekers placed by NASS in the West Midlands region with private accommodation providers. For the numbers placed by local authorities in London and the South East, there is no clear evidence; he suggested an approximate figure of 10,000 asylum seekers in the West Midlands. In November 2000, NASS expected that after 4 December, when contracts were signed with local authorities, there would be around 15 people per day being sent by NASS to the West Midlands. This forecast was based on the then-current rate of applications for asylum projected forward. The contracts were supposed to come into action on 4 December 2000, but by the beginning of January 2001, Birmingham City Council had still not received any asylum seekers referred from NASS for accommodation, although other West Midlands councils had received a small number. By mid-January, there had been 172 'bookings' (of families or, mostly, single people) from NASS for the West Midland county, but only 72 at most had actually arrived.

In 2001, under pressure from an increasing housing crisis in London the original principle of language-based clustering of asylum seekers had been deferred by NASS in favour of dispersal according to the availability of housing. As in-region arrivals had been increasing dramatically in the West Midlands throughout 2001, Birmingham City Council, the lead authority in the WMCARS, negotiated for a system of in-region dispersal. Consequently, in-region dispersal, under agreement with NASS, has been in operation in the West Midlands since April 2001. According to the Refugee Council (which runs the One-Stop Service [OSS] for the West Midlands), in-region applications account for about one half of all NASS-supported asylum seekers in the region. The large number of secondary migrants arriving in Birmingham has been documented by Robinson (2002).

The estimates for the total number of asylum seekers (including dependants) supported by NASS in the West Midlands at the end of 2002 was 10,255; of that, the majority were in Birmingham, Coventry, Stoke and Wolverhampton. The top five nationalities dispersed to the West Midlands at the end of 2002 were from Iraq, Afghanistan, Iran, Pakistan and Somalia (see Table 5.1).

There were also significant numbers of asylum seekers from the Czech Republic (480); the Former Republic of Yugoslavia (FRY) (435); the Democratic Republic of Congo (250); Romania (240); and the Congo (235) (Home Office, 2002b). Significantly, not all of these nationalities are represented by a relevant nationality-based RCO, especially in the case of Iran, Pakistan, Romania and the Czech Republic. Nationals from Somalia, Afghanistan and Iraq have well-established RCOs in the region, notably in Birmingham, Coventry and Wolverhampton. It is important to emphasise that the above statistics are provisional and do not provide an estimate of the total numbers of the asylum seeker and refugee population as a whole.

Table 5.1: Top five nationalities dispersed by NASS in the West Midlands as at the end of 2002

Country of origin	Number
Iraq	2,795
Afghanistan	1,260
Iran	995
Pakistan	500
Somalia	500

The North West

Boswell (2001, p iii), in her critical review of dispersal policy, has argued that:

> The increased social marginalization of asylum seekers resulting from dispersal may [also] have negative repercussions for race relations in general.

On the surface, this prophecy appears to have been confirmed by events, the most alarming of that has been the significant increase in support for the British National Party (BNP) in the North West. However, it may be misleading to assume a direct relationship between dispersal and any assumed deterioration in 'race relations'. As many individuals noted during interviews, not all communities where asylum seekers have been dispersed are affected by increasing social tensions. This, they suggested, depended upon the interplay of several factors, inter alia: a lack of previous experience of settled migrant communities in dispersal areas, pre-existing poor and under-resourced services, and a lack of preparation and proactive approach to community participation on the part of the Home Office and local authorities.

The government response, as several respondents noted, has been consistently shortsighted. The decision to react to an increase in racial incidents by blocking the allocation of asylum seekers to specific areas clearly fails to address the root causes of increasing social tensions in dispersal areas. The absence of a coherent public education campaign on dispersal is a central factor here (Robinson et al, 2003). As suggested by Moran, for example (2003, p 21):

> There had been no associated attempts on the part of national or local government to explain, and therefore help local people to understand why these people are here, how little they actually receive from the state and the fact that what may be hundred[s] of thousands of them receive nothing at all.

Local authorities have dealt with the inflow of newcomers dispersed by NASS to their wards in different ways. As one respondent argued, it is hard to provide a general judgement on the impact of dispersal. "It is patchy," he remarked, "although I certainly don't think there has been enough work with the local population or enough investment from the central government to the local services to make the transition

Table 5.2: Top five nationalities dispersed by NASS in the North West as at the end of 2002

Country of origin	Number
Iraq	1,720
Czech Republic	1,035
Iran	1,025
Pakistan	795
Afghanistan	790

neat or more sustainable". A key area of concern is the capacity of public services to deal with the needs of the new arrivals.

According to Home Office statistics, as at the end of 2002, the top five countries of origin dispersed in the North West were Iraq, Czech Republic, Iran, Pakistan and Afghanistan (see Table 5.2).

Africa is the most significant continent of origin, with an overall number of applicants of 3,210, coming from more than 17 nations.

Such a variety of countries of origin has a number of implications for public services, in particular relating to the need for interpreting and translation services as well as information translated into several languages. In an area with no previous experience of multi-lingualism, this has been a major problem, particularly given the lack in some already deprived boroughs of resources for 'mainstream' services. In this respect, NGOs and refugees have helped local services to cover huge gaps in their interpreting and translation needs. This is an important job that, as stressed by a development officer of the Multi-Agency for Refugee Integration in Manchester (MARIM), "is rarely recognised and never adequately paid". A spokesperson for the North West Consortium (East) expressed a similar concern, noting of service providers that "nowadays they have a statistically significant population speaking foreign languages and the needs of this population have to be addressed at statutory level".

A central factor in the interviews with statutory authorities was the lack of a coordinated and strategic approach, both at regional level and also at the local level in relation to Liverpool. According to previous research (Zetter et al, 2003b), given the absence of a consortium-wide contractual relationship with NASS, there is generally weak coordination and a poor strategic response to the dispersal of asylum seekers to Liverpool in particular. In this situation, various voluntary agencies are forced to 'pick up the pieces' created by the lack of overall coordination. The main NGO that appears to operate a coordinated and strategic response is Refugee Action. The only other coordinating agency is the regional NASS office. This covers the whole of the North West with only a limited number of staff and has therefore found it virtually impossible to play a strategic role within Liverpool. The other voluntary agencies and refugee organisations have been compelled to operate on a response basis as problems and needs arise.

In the East sub-region, the regional consortium operates with the support of active multi-agency partners. This guarantees better coordination and use of resources, although the strategic coordination does not extend to the private rented sector, that covers 70% of the asylum seekers in the East sub-region, and 100% in the Western sub-region[3] (Zetter et al, 2003b). In the Greater Manchester conurbation, Salford and Bolton are the two largest recipients of asylum seekers after Manchester.

In the spring of 2002, in response to the forced dispersal over the previous 18 months of upwards of 1,200 asylum seeking people from 63 different countries into the overwhelmingly white, working-class city of Salford (effectively doubling the city's black and minority ethnic [BME] population), a project about refugees and asylum seekers was presented to the Central Government Single Regeneration Budget 5 Social Inclusion stream by the University of Salford. The project was subsequently funded, resulting in the formation of the Salford Refugee and Asylum Seekers Participatory Action Research project (RAPAR) in September 2002. The project has the core aim of developing evidence about the needs of asylum seekers, refugees, the indigenous community and the service delivery sector, with the overall aim of improving participation and service provision. According to Moran (2003, p 10) the project, "centralizes the asylum seeker's perspective about their experience. The issues that it is prioritising within its research programme are those brought to it by the city's asylum seeking population".

A factor to consider in these predominantly 'white' areas is the visibility of asylum seekers. As an officer from the North West Consortium argued, previous to 1999 in places like Bolton there were only a small number of asylum seekers. A significant increase in numbers, however, occurred from 2000. The key question was the increased use of public space by asylum seekers. With time on their hands and "very little money ... any form of recreational activity free and reasonable is very attractive". Asylum seekers therefore had become more conspicuous and subject to criticism and attack.

Apart from some Somalis, there were few asylum seekers or refugees in Liverpool until the beginnings of dispersal introduced under the Immigration and Asylum Act 1999 (IAA99). Preceding this, in 1999 there was an intake of 320 refugees from Kosovo. Research conducted early in the life of the IAA99 emphasised the enormous changes wrought by the legislation in areas such as Liverpool, where the number of asylum seekers increased exponentially. The report stresses that:

> The speed with which legislative changes have had to be implemented has meant that asylum seekers were settled into localities where few agencies had experience of hosting them and where networks of support are absent or underdeveloped. (Gameledin-Ashami et al, 2002, p 23)

To cope with such changes, new arrangements were needed, including:

- new contracting arrangements between local authorities and NASS;
- innovative responses to demands for statutory services from a new and diverse client group;
- adjustments by voluntary and community organisations to include new residents within their activities and support framework.

According to the chair of the Liverpool Network for Change[4]:

> "Asylum seekers and refugees are a partisan issue in the city. The leading political party and its constituency are largely Conservative, although there is no Conservative Party in Liverpool. They don't want to be seen as welcoming towards asylum seekers and, instrumentally, used to blame the Home Office for any problem."

A concern expressed by interviewees when asked about the role of Liverpool City Council in the management of dispersed asylum seekers was that, considering the lack of the contract with NASS and the major role played by private landlords, it was not very clear what local authorities could actually do and what their role was in the dispersal arrangements. There was, it was suggested, a lack of structural coordination with NASS and the Home Office in Merseyside. By way of contrast, in Manchester the situation appears slightly better. Multi-agency fora meet regularly in different boroughs and help to better coordinate services and to better use resources.

A final factor to be considered in the evaluation of the impact on the dispersal in the region is the role of the media. To Liverpool Network for Change, in general the local media are quite sympathetic towards asylum seekers. In part, however, this is due to the intensive advocacy work performed by NGOs. Far less sympathetic is the national press that is seen as one of the main factors fuelling prejudice and racism in the area. The media, according to several respondents, rarely articulated the relationship between dispersal policy, the demonisation of asylum seekers and the steady rise of the BNP on 'sink estates'.

As suggested in a number of sources (Wollenschläger, 2003; Pfohman and Amrute, 2004), the management of the 'move on' stage – from the reception and asylum determination phase to settlement – is a major problem in the integration of refugees in a number of European Union (EU) states. In this respect, the coordination of different agencies and bureaucratic practices are key missing elements that need to be more fully addressed. For example, the development officer of the North West Consortium stressed that:

> "Asylum teams in local authorities are based in very different departments and, as a consequence, they tend to have also very different theoretical approaches. It is a huge problem to define procedures and understand who does what. Besides, many tasks that once were covered by housing departments are now transferred to the private sector."

In relation to Liverpool, the City Council has a strategic group on asylum seekers and refugees that meets on a monthly basis, the Liverpool City Council Refugee Strategic Planning Committee (LCCRSPC). In interviews, concern was raised about the effectiveness of the group. One interviewee summed this up by noting that "at every meeting you have different people from very different agencies of very different levels that speak of very broad issues there. There is no focus on refugee organisations or empowerment and I have never seen a refugee representative there. It's quite alarming".

In Manchester, with its diverse and settled communities, local authorities have been able to develop a better understanding of the practical work that is necessary for capacity building. By contrast, Liverpool has a more mono-cultural population and a much less diverse community. As a result, new communities may find it that much harder to settle and access resources. The refugee voluntary sector in Liverpool has set up a 'shadow statutory provision' to attempt to 'fill the gaps' but the efficacy of this is very much dependent upon the goodwill of individuals. Also, because of the emergency situation in Liverpool, NGOs and voluntary agencies have adopted a 'helping mode', rather than doing capacity building and community development. As noted by a Refugee Action officer, in Manchester:

"Nothing happens when an asylum seeker gets a positive decision. The North West Consortium should ask for paper to move rather than people. At the moment, there is no mechanism for helping a smoother transition."

The problem, however, is not just the lack of proper counselling. "Advice is poor," he argues, "because the opportunities for refugees are poor". To address this issue, MARIM is lobbying the city council trying to raise attention to the refugee integration issue in the context of the discussion of the Agenda 2010[5].

Asylum seekers and refugees in the regions

The West Midlands

According to the WMCARS, as of May 2003, estimates for the total number of asylum seekers in the West Midlands indicate an approximate figure of between 25,000 and 30,000 (see Table 5.3).

There are no reliable statistics for refugees in the region although their number has been estimated at over 50,000 (WMCARS, 2003). Data from Stoke-on-Trent, Wolverhampton and Coventry (CAB, 2001; Phillimore and Goodson 2001; Coventry City Council, 2003) suggest that a significant number of asylum seekers are choosing to settle in the localities once they have been recognised as refugees. According

Table 5.3: Numbers of asylum seekers in the West Midlands as at March 2003

Local authority[1]	Number
Coventry	3,500
Birmingham	6,000
Dudley	1,400
Walsall	1,300
Sandwell	3,000
Wolverhampton	2,500
Stoke-on-Trent	750
Solihull	100
Total	18,650

Notes: [1] The figures include: local authority placements and interim measures. The figures exclude the following: (1) Those placed by local authorities from the South-East and London. (2) Figures for Shropshire, Worcestershire, Herefordshire and Staffordshire. (3) Those asylum seekers who have arrived through secondary migratory patterns, ie on subsistence only. (4) 2,500 individuals who are currently in emergency accommodation. Estimates would then raise the total number of asylum seekers (those awaiting outcomes on their applications for asylum) to between 25,000 and 30,000.

Source: WMCARS (2003)

to the WMCARS, it is reasonable to assume that around 50% of asylum seekers who receive a positive decision will remain within the region. This means that a continuing stream of refugees will need to be settled in the region in the foreseeable future. In the fieldwork, Birmingham was selected as the primary source of information concerning refugee communities and RCOs in the West Midlands. Its central political and administrative importance in the region, in addition to its significance as an area of refugee settlement, is discussed below.

Birmingham

Birmingham has struggled with its legacy as the one-time 'workshop of the world' since the decline of industrial production in the 1970s. From the 1980s onwards, the city has attempted to re-invent itself around prestige retail projects, business tourism and the development of service industries. The £530 million overhaul of Birmingham's Bullring shopping centre is the latest in a line of 'makeovers' for the city centre ('Ghost town fear as shops flock to Bullring', *Birmingham Post*, 3 September 2003). Running alongside these prestige projects has been a process of continuing social polarisation and the neglect of basic social and physical infrastructure in the city (Loftman and Nevin, 1996). The official packaging of Birmingham as the 'meeting place of Europe' belies another history of 'globalisation from below' (Henry et al, 2000) in the transnational ethnic and economic linkages that interlace the city.

Birmingham has a population of 977,087 people and of that, 29.6% are from minority ethnic backgrounds (Census, 2001). Asian and African Caribbean migrants in the post-war period joined existing Irish communities and a diverse array of nationalities, including Chinese, Italian, Hungarian and Yemeni migrants (Henry et al, 2000). Particular areas of Birmingham, notably Sparkbrook and Handsworth, occupy a central place in the race relations literature produced from the 1960s onwards (Rex and Moore, 1967; CCCS, 1982). It is notable that these areas have continued to house new migrants, in particular the signficant number of Somali asylum seekers, refugees and EU citizens who have come to Birmingham since the late 1990s.

Reviewing the history of refugee settlement in Birmingham, as local historian Malcolm Dick has carefully documented (Dick, 2002), Jewish refugees escaping persecution in Tsarist Russia had been arriving in the city from the 18th century. By the late 19th century, their numbers had increased significantly. Initially poor and lacking networks, by 1914 a strand of Jewish entrepreneurs had emerged and the social position of Jews in Birmingham (numbering some 6,000) was more firmly established. The principal post-Second World War refugees were the Poles and Serbs. Most Poles arrived as ex-servicemen or survivors of the concentration camps. The Catholic Church played a significant role in maintaining identity and social networks among the approximately 6,000 Poles living in the West Midlands. Similarly, in the case of the Serbs (numbering only a few hundred), the Serbian Orthodox Church that was built in 1968 has acted as a lynchpin of cultural and social solidarity. In contrast to many of the later refugee arrivals from the 1960s onwards, the Poles and Serbs were 'European' in origin, had clear routes into employment, a Church-based form of social solidarity and established business and professional backgrounds prior to arrival (interview with Malcolm Dick, May 2003).

Ugandan Asians in the 1960s and Vietnamese in the 1970s and 1980s also settled in the West Midlands under government dispersal schemes for programme and quota refugees. The diverging fates of these latter groups has been well documented in the literature (Robinson and Hale, 1989; Joly, 1996; Robinson et al, 2003), with the Vietnamese generally experiencing high levels of unemployment and the Ugandan Asians significant upward social mobility (Robinson, 1993b). Compared to earlier quota and programme refugees, asylum seekers in the 1990s arrived at a time of increasing public hostility. Of the refugee groups arriving in the 1990s, there is as yet little primary research concerning their characteristics and experience of settlement.

Outside London, Birmingham has arguably one of the fastest growing asylum seeker and refugee populations in Britain. There are a number of factors involved in Birmingham's attractiveness as an area of refugee settlement, including the existence of established ethnic and refugee groups, the city's proximity to London and the relative development of economic and social facilities. Robinson (Zetter et al, 2003b, p 81) has pointed to the following factors:

> ... the presence of fellow nationals, the presence of nationalities from the same part of the world and the fact that Birmingham was thought to be a safe city.

The popular conception of Birmingham as 'Europe's most Islamic city' may be another factor in encouraging refugee settlement in the city. Yet the city stands in marked contrast to London as an area of only recent settlement for significant numbers of refugees. The refugee infrastructure of statutory, voluntary, NGO and RCO provision is significantly less developed than is the case in London. In general,

Birmingham is responding to the increasing numbers of asylum seekers arriving in the city by developing new institutional arrangements and solutions to the issues posed by the long-term settlement of refugees.

For example, the asylum team in Birmingham City Council (*Report to the director of housing*, January 2001) has begun to develop the integration component of the WMCARS's role in providing assistance and advice to individuals who have been granted status. The integration and settlement of refugees is to be based upon 'interagency partnership' involving the development of English language skills, employment, housing and the promotion of new refugee community organisations (*Report*, January 2001, p 5). Small grants are being awarded to facilitate the setting up and development of RCOs under the discretion of the lead officer of the asylum team.

The 'take-off' in the number of refugees and asylum seekers in the city has occurred since 1996, as a result of ad-hoc dispersal from London boroughs, organised dispersal under the NASS arrangements and the 'spontaneous' in-region arrivals of asylum seekers. Recognised refugees have also come to the city in increasing numbers in this period, after they have received status in the UK or in other EU countries such as Sweden, Denmark and the Netherlands (Bang Niesen, 2004). In-region arrivals and dispersal have been significant features in the West Midlands. By the middle of 2002, for example, 80 asylum seekers were 'self-presenting' per week in Birmingham. The increase in arrivals has raised pressing issues around 'exit' or 'move-on' from the NASS system, as positive decisions result in more refugees seeking to settle in the region.

In terms of the principal nationalities and numbers involved, statistics supplied by NASS in February 2002 for postcodes that housed significant numbers of asylum seekers in Birmingham indicated that Iraqis, Iranians, Afghans and Somalis were among the main nationalities[6]. This corresponds closely to the principal nationalities for the West Midlands as a whole. Since that time there has been an increasing number of Zimbabwean and Central African asylum seekers dispersed to the West Midlands. As indicated earlier in this chapter, there are an estimated 6,000 asylum seekers supported under a variety of measures in Birmingham. There are no reliable statistics on the number of refugees in Birmingham. Community estimates suggest between 10,000 and 15,000 refugees in the city. According to the NGOs working with refugee organisations in the city, the five main refugee groups are Afghans, Ethnic Albanians, Kurds (Iraqi), Somalis and Iranians. Smaller nationalities include the Sudanese who first arrived as students in the 1980s then in increasing numbers as asylum seekers after 1992. In the last few years, there has also been an increase in the number of Congolese and other Francophone asylum seekers and refugees. None of these nationalities, with the possible exception of the Somalis, Sudanese and Iraqis has had significant historical links to the UK. Knowledge of the English language will have been present at least in part in these nationalities. In other cases there were no pre-existing networks or linguistic ties. Here community networks have been built up from scratch or mobilised through the churches, as in the case of some of the Central African organisations and the Ethnic Albanians.

It is also important to note that not all of the nationalities that figure in the asylum seeker applications are represented by community organisations. Iranians, for example, have no organisational representation. The large number of Pakistani asylum seekers in the West Midlands and individuals from the Czech Republic are not represented by community organisations. The reasons for non-representation are complex but may include the existence of strong community networks and migrant organisations that 'absorb' asylum seekers and the educational and professional background of specific groups, that again obviates the need for formal community organisation. There is some anecdotal evidence, for example, of professional backgrounds among many Iraqi Kurds, and significant educational qualifications among Iranians in particular (interview with Malcolm Dick, May 2003). There are also strong indications of self-employment among Iranians (restaurants and painting and decorating firms) while certain sections of the Somali population have been active in the proliferating number of small shops and internet cafes that have mushroomed in particular areas of Sparkbrook and Balsall Heath in the last few years.

The North West

At the beginnings of dispersal in April 2000, the North West was the second largest recipient of asylum seekers, with 3,420 distributed to the region. By 2001, the number of asylum seekers in NASS accommodation in the North West had increased significantly by over 139%, reaching a total of 8,160 asylum seekers dispersed to the region. Asylum seekers allocated voucher-only support at this time numbered 450. As at the end of December 2002, the North West was the region with the highest population of asylum seekers in NASS accommodation with 10,325 dispersed asylum claimants. This figure was only slightly in excess of the West Midlands at 10,255 dispersed asylum seekers, as indicated in Chapter Three of this book. A significant increase of asylum seekers receiving voucher-only support (925) was also recorded. According to the latest Home Office statistics, at the end of September 2003, the number of asylum seekers allocated in the North West was 9,755. Table 5.4 shows the distribution of asylum seekers in Merseyside and Greater Manchester conurbations as at September 2003.

As at the end of September 2003, the top five nationalities dispersed by NASS in Liverpool were Sri Lanka, Lithuania, Somalia, Iraq and Czech Republic. In Manchester, they were Pakistan, Iraq, Iran, Czech Republic and Somalia.

An interesting point emerges from the statistics on the distribution of voucher-only asylum seekers in the region. As the data indicates (Home Office, 2003a), asylum seekers not in need of accommodation support, and who choose the North West as their location, have preferred to settle in Manchester rather than in Liverpool. The data also highlights the gradual increase of asylum seekers voluntarily settling in the North West that can be regarded as a sign of an ongoing process of settlement within the asylum seeker and refugee communities.

Although no reliable statistics on move-on and secondary migration from dispersal areas are available at the moment, a Refugee Action officer estimates that around 50% of those who receive status tend to

Table 5.4: Numbers of asylum seekers in the North West as at the end of September 2003

Local authority[1]	Dispersed	Disbenefitted[2]	Total
Manchester	1,610	10	1,620
Bolton	1,025		1,025
Bury	590		590
Oldham	680		680
Rochdale	465		465
Salford	1,195	5	1,200
Stockport	255		255
Tameside	285		285
Trafford	130	5	135
Wigan	915		915
Greater Manchester	7,150	20	7,170
Liverpool	1,880		1,880
Sefton	125		125
St Helens	5		5
Merseyside	2,010		2,010
TOTAL M & GM[3]	9,160	20	9,180
TOTAL North West	9,720	30	9,750

Notes: [1] Only those local authorities in Greater Manchester and Merseyside where NASS dispersed or disbenefitted cases are resident are shown.
[2] Disbenefitted cases are cases which were previously supported under the main UK benefit system and have been moved onto NASS.
[3] M = Merseyside; GM = Greater Manchester.

Source: Home Office (2003a)

remain in Greater Manchester. As mentioned earlier in this chapter, local authorities in the region have only recently started to consider the phenomenon seriously and to work on long-term integration strategies for the new arrivals. Major changes in service delivery, school provision and health support are at stake. Despite the efforts already taken, integration strategies are still in the early stages of development. The lack of coordination at regional level does not assist the work of local authorities and the circulation and dissemination of good practice, which is often left to NGOs and ad-hoc initiatives.

There were many asylum seekers in Manchester before NASS started dispersing individuals under the IAA99. Manchester has had a tradition of welcoming refugee arrivals, particularly over the last 30 years, from Eastern Europe, Latin America and Vietnam. The city also has a history of campaigning on issues related to asylum, and remains a centre of the anti-deportation and sanctuary movements in the UK (Cohen, 1994). Manchester hosted a large number of Irish and Jewish refugees throughout the 19th century. Significant proportions of these earlier arrivals and their descendants had settled in the city centre, mainly in the university district, where an important academic centre attracted refugee students and intellectuals. Earlier ad-hoc dispersal of asylum seekers in response to the 1996 Asylum and Immigration Act and the IAA99 in particular has changed the situation in Manchester considerably, in relation to the size, composition and number of refugee communities. Before 1999, there were large Somali, Sudanese, Sri Lankan, Indonesian Vietnamese, Kurdish, Bosnian and Kosovan communities. Organised dispersal has brought asylum seekers from a diverse range of countries to the city. Moreover, Manchester has also been the focal point for people dispersed to the Greater Manchester area. Better-informed and more culturally sensitive service provision, a cosmopolitan environment and the possibility of becoming 'invisible' or 'blending into' the local environment also appear to have attracted asylum seekers to the area. With the greater preponderance of asylum seekers and refugees in cities such as Bolton and Salford this situation is necessarily beginning to change. The overall refugee population in Greater Manchester area is estimated at around 15,000.

In Liverpool, many asylum seekers are placed within or near the L8 postcode area (Toxteth, Granby and Dingle), which has a long multicultural tradition. Other large contingents of asylum seekers have been dispersed to L4 (Everton), L6 (Anfield) and L7 (Kensington) postcode areas. In these areas there have been numerous reported cases of tension and conflict with the local 'white' community.

Liverpool has some established ethnic communities who had started to arrive in the aftermath of the Second World War. They were mainly ship and port workers coming from Somalia and Yemen. Since the late 1980s, a number of refugees from these two countries have joined the pre-existing migrant communities. In some cases, the newcomers have founded their own organisations, while in other instances they have collaborated with the established organisations and transformed them according to their needs (Bulle, 1995). In terms of Liverpool's response to newcomers, although it has a long history as a port and a firm reputation as a multi-ethnic city, as one interviewee remarked, "Liverpool is still a largely mono-cultural city with a strong Irish flavour".

Conclusions

This chapter has reviewed the institutional and policy framework in the regions. The socioeconomic characteristics of the regions, the structure of the consortia, the role of NASS and the character of asylum seekers and refugees in the two regions have been outlined. The North West, with its slightly larger population size and broader geographical spread, has a history of political divisions that impact upon current dispersal arrangements. Birmingham, on the other hand, occupies a central position in the West Midlands in economic and administrative terms. The structure of the consortia reflect these differences, with the WMCARS, led by Birmingham City Council, showing more effective centralised coordination than appears to be the case in relation to the divided consortium in the North West with its history of political factionalism. The involvement of NASS in the regions has also been distinctive, with a slow uptake of asylum seekers by NASS in the West Midlands leading to a form of locally coordinated in-region dispersal as more asylum seekers arrived in the region from 1999 onwards. The response of NASS in the North West appeared to have been similarly ad hoc in character, with many respondents reporting a lack of a coordinated or strategic approach to dispersal in the region. In particular, the division between Western and Eastern sub-regions has consistently impeded cross-regional operations. While Birmingham City Council had made some headway in implementing integration and settlement packages for refugees, the picture in the North West was far more mixed. Liverpool, for example, with its largely monocultural background, had been less successful in initiating a successful response to the needs of asylum seekers and refugees. Manchester on the other hand, with its greater diversity, had begun to develop the groundwork for effective refugee settlement. Both the

West Midlands and the North West are two of the highest recipients of asylum seekers under the NASS arrangements. Both also have a significant history of minority ethnic settlement prior to dispersal, including refugees and asylum seekers. Nevertheless, it is clear that the specific configuration of local factors, including demographic composition and socioeconomic characteristics in the regions has impacted upon the structure and capacity of the consortia arrangements. Chapter Six, which follows, focuses in detail on the impacts of dispersal upon RCOs in the two regions.

Notes

[1] The regional stakeholder group consists of translation and interpreting services, accommodation/housing provision; health care; mental health; social services provision; education services; legal services; elected members group: refugee representative group; community relations; communications group; voluntary sector group; financial resources group; employment/leisure issues group.

[2] The consortium office is comprised of the following staff: regional manager; finance officer; development officer; a senior placements officer; two placements officers, and two administrative staff. A development officer has been recently appointed following up the action plan for integration discussed in a seminar on 2 July 2002.

[3] On 26 November 2003, the Home Office announced that the contract with housing firm Landmark to provide homes for asylum seekers is to be terminated. A six-month review concluded that the company was in breach of the contract. Campaigners greeted the decision, which affected 600 asylum seekers in Liverpool, Wirral and Wigan.

[4] Liverpool Network for Change is a charitable company which exists to support voluntary and community groups in Liverpool and its neighbourhood, many of whom are faced with major challenges of social exclusion and working within deprived areas.

[5] Agenda 2010, a partnership led by Manchester City Council, Manchester Council for Community Relations, the Progress Trust and AAAPT Community Agency, will tackle racism and racial discrimination in the city over the next 10 years. It is helping Manchester's BME communities identify vital issues and priorities for action. By engaging the BME voluntary sector, Agenda 2010 will

link regeneration initiatives and local service provision. The council is working with all sorts of agencies towards a community strategy to promote the economic, social and environmental well-being of the city. Agenda 2010 gives Manchester's BME communities an opportunity to shape and influence that strategy.

[6] The Immigration Research and Statistics Service (IRSS) was requested to generate a sample of asylum seekers in NASS accommodation in Birmingham. This sample was to have the following structure: 10 cases with postcode beginning B11; 10 cases with postcode beginning B12; 10 cases with postcode beginning B16; and 10 cases with postcode beginning B29. The population was taken from the confirmed arrivals report generated from ASYS (the NASS asylum seeker database) on 11 February 2002. This gave the following population sizes: 52 cases with postcode beginning B11; 37 cases with postcode beginning B12; 293 cases with postcode beginning B16; 283 cases with postcode beginning B29. Cases were initially selected randomly from each group by sorting on name and then using systematic random sampling. These cases were then tested to check their representation of the population. The top five nationalities in the population of all four postcode areas were Iraq (38%), Iran (20%), Afghanistan (15%), Somalia (2%) and Kosovo (2%). (Information supplied by NASS, February 2002.)

SIX

The development of RCOs
in the regions

This chapter outlines the results of interviews conducted with the principal refugee community organisations (RCOs) in Birmingham, Liverpool and Manchester. The key themes addressed are organisational resources, the development of communities, the networking process and the impacts of dispersal and recent legislative change on refugee groups and RCOs. The discussion of the West Midlands is framed within the issues raised by the literature reviewed in Chapter Two, particularly relating to the usefulness of social capital as an explanatory framework. The chapter goes on to present a profile of the main refugee communities in the North West and their social and political involvement at local and regional level. In both the West Midlands and the North West, the main issue addressed concerns the interplay between refugee communities, the voluntary and NGO sectors and local authorities. While the examination of the North West follows a parallel structure to the case of the West Midlands, both the common ground and points of comparison with that region are also brought out. A thematic treatment is applied to both regions: the West Midlands is viewed in terms of emerging organisational forms (Zetter and Pearl, 2000), while the fieldwork from the North West highlights issues of fragmentation and unity in refugee communities (Griffiths, 2000). Chapter Seven further develops the comparative framework to include both London and the regions.

RCOs in the West Midlands: emerging organisational forms

In the West Midlands as a whole, but particularly in Birmingham, the key issue concerns the growth in the number of RCOs that has occurred over the last few years. Estimates by non-governmental organisations (NGOs) working in Birmingham suggest that prior to 1999 there were only three or four functioning RCOs in the city. As of October 2003, there were estimated to be over 30 RCOs in Birmingham. Not all of these are viable and functioning organisations. Many of the newer organisations, for example, are competing for the same limited space, notably in the case of the Somali and Central African organisations. On the other hand, several of the older organisations have experienced periodic crises over funding and management problems that have impeded their overall development.

A total of 12 organisations in Birmingham were interviewed as part of this research (see Appendix). The choice of RCOs was based upon a number of factors including prior knowledge of the principal refugee groups in the city; the prevalence on the ground of particular nationality-based RCOs and the availability for interview of the different groups. Overall, as indicated in Chapter Four, representation of the principal sending countries of the 1990s was an important underlying factor in the selection of the sample. Given the limited numbers involved, it is important to note that quantitative analysis was not considered appropriate, although some tentative attempts at generalisation are made from the sample. The following analysis combines the structured and unstructured elements of the interview schedule.

Resource base and organisational issues affecting RCOs in Birmingham

Table 6.1 gives a general indication of the date of establishment, legal and financial status and approximate size of the refugee group.

Distribution of nationalities

Information supplied by a variety of sources in Birmingham (Midland Refugee Council, Refugee Council and Refugee Action) indicated over 30 RCOs in the city, with seven Somali organisations and an equal number of Central African and Congolese-based RCOs. Two Kurdish (Iraqi) organisations were operating at the time of the fieldwork, a third having stopped working sometime during 2002. The RCOs interviewed therefore reflect the principal nationalities in the city – Afghan, Albanian, Somali and Kurdish and other African groups, in particular the proliferating number of Central African organisations that had developed since 2001.

Dates of establishment

Of the 12 RCOs interviewed, 10 had been established in the period since 1999. Only one Sudanese and one Kurdish organisation had been in existence for more than 10 years and even here there was

Table 6.1: Summary of RCOs interviewed in the West Midlands

Nationality/group represented	Date established	Charity	Paid worker	Funding	Approximate size of community
Afghan	1999	Y	N	N	4,000
African (general)	2001	Y	Y	Y	NA
Albanian	1999	N	Y	Y	3,000
Bosnian	1996	Y	Y	Y	1,000
Central African (Congolese)	2001	N	N	N	NA
Congolese	2002	N	N	N	NA
Kurdish (Iraqi)	1992-99	N	Y	Y	5,000
Somali	1997	Y	Y	N	6,000
Somali	2001	Y	N	Y	NA
Sudanese	1990	Y	Y	Y	1500
Sudanese	1999	Y	Y	Y	NA
Women's organisation	2003	N	N	Y	NA

evidence in one case of organisational stagnation followed by a resurgence of activity in the period after 1999. Five of the organisations had been established between 2001 and 2003, indicating the extremely rapid character of organisational activity in the city particularly among some of the recent African groups. The Albanian and Afghan associations formed in 1999 reflect the changing pattern of asylum applications in that period. It is interesting to note that both organisations had experienced fluctuations in fortune in the period to 2003, largely due to the effects of funding shortages.

Legal status

Six of the organisations had charity status. Charity status was difficult to obtain for several of the organisations due to the stringent requirements involved.

Membership

As the majority of RCOs were newly formed the membership base was quite small, on average between 50 and 100. In many cases no formal records were kept of membership, which tended to be ad hoc and informal.

Funding: amounts and sources

In general, there would appear to be a positive link between legal status and funding: all of those with organisations with charity status had funding for example, although there were significant differences in the amount of funding obtained. With one exception, all of the organisations were 'small' organisations (McLeod et al, 2001) with funding up to £50,000 for the year 2002-03. The one exception was an organisation that was part funded by the Department of Health. Of the eight organisations receiving funding, the majority were within the range of £10,000 to £20,000 per year. The amount of funding did not appear to be related to the length of time an organisation had been in existence. Some of the newer organisations had been the most successful in terms of securing funding. The main funders included: Awards for All; Birmingham City Council start-up grants; Housing Association Charitable Trust; Comic Relief; Community Fund; the Home Office; the Department of Health; the Midland Refugee Council; a variety of trusts including the Digbeth and Cadbury Trusts and the European Social Fund.

Paid workers and staffing

Seven of the organisations had paid workers on their staff. The employment of paid staff allowed for greater 'professionalisation' of organisations, although here it should be noted that many of these posts were part time. Organisations, even with paid staff, continued to rely heavily upon volunteers to provide services.

Services provided

Advice and signposting were the main services provided by RCOs. Limited resources meant that the majority of RCOs were unable to provide direct training relating to employment and education. Most of the RCOs were engaged in cultural activities such as mother-tongue instruction and supplementary classes for children. Only in the one case was specialised health advice being given: this was by one of the better-funded organisations that had a long-term contract with the Department of Health to assist refugee and asylum seekers relating to health issues, particularly HIV and AIDS.

A number of other themes relating to organisational issues were raised in the interviews. The most significant are addressed here.

Organisational aims and rationale

In common with the literature on RCOs, the main reason given for setting up organisations was to fill the gaps left in service provision by the statutory authorities. Most often, the problems encountered by refugees and asylum seekers attempting to access services hinged on the question of language barriers:

> "We saw that there were real problems in the community, first of all due to the language barriers. They might know where to go but because they cannot express themselves ... you have to take them to job centres, GPs.... Let's set up a group where they can come to see us because there are people you cannot reach because you don't know they exist." (Congolese coordinator, Birmingham)

Filling in gaps in service provision, identifying problems and unknown sections of the refugee population were some of the main organisational aims. This was particularly the case in relation to 'weaker' groups, women and children and individuals with specific health needs, who were less vocal than other sections of the population. While providing advice and assistance to co-nationals, acting as a bridge to the receiving society was often the immediate aim of the organisation. This could also be framed in more general terms as helping to build the resources of the community:

> "We wanted to create something that would exist forever.... Why I am doing this is to support my community. There is a gap between the people who come from Somalia, their education, their background and in Europe. So they need a line, a bridge in between them. The way they are here they don't understand what's going on.... My purpose is to learn something. To learn how to handle a community.... I have been here four years. Maybe when I am 55 years I will be going back to Somalia so I will know how to create something. Learning is the best. And the second thing is my children are here. If I don't build something for them now they will face the same problems that I have myself now.... So when they finish their education here to come and handle it. *You need to put something in front of them so later on they can handle it.*" (Somali coordinator, emphasis added)

Building a resource for the future that could be utilised for development in Somalia and for future generations of Somalis in the UK (a form of collective social capital where benefits directly accrue from participation in networks) was an explicit aim of the organisation for this Somalian. Indeed, in several other cases the same link was made between building organisational capacity and the broader processes of community development, both at home and in the new settlement context. Somali, Sudanese, Central African and African organisations shared a similar goal in this respect, premised upon building community capacity in the UK and at home. Several organisations had formal links with development projects in their home countries and actively encouraged communication between community members in Birmingham and at home. Associational activity as a means of generating collective resources in the community was therefore an explicit aim of many of the organisations. Providing services and assisting with adaptation to British society were seen as necessary immediate goals but with the longer-term aim of developing communal resources clearly in view. In practice, however, this ideal encountered a number of obstacles, the most pronounced of which was funding.

Funding: issues and problems

Funding was raised as a key issue throughout the interviews conducted. There were a number of themes here, including the sheer difficulty in obtaining funding:

> "We are struggling with funding. We have small funding for training and bits and bobs of things but we are struggling with funding. And one of the biggest drawbacks is the big funders tend to ask the question that, 'Oh, you don't have a track record'....They want to see that you have managed a certain amount of money for a certain period of time. Other funders talk about you. So it's quite difficult being a newly set-up organisation.... Filling in the forms because some of the questions are not straightforward. Even when we read it as a straightforward question when we answer they say, 'No, we wanted this....'. We were struggling to understand what is the outcome, output, input, you see.... Most of them offer help. You can ring up and say what did you mean here and they will explain what they meant. Then you will answer but still you will not get the funding. Sometimes we don't know what they want." (Sudanese organisation)

There are a number of issues here, notably a perception of increasing bureaucratisation on the part of funders and the difficulty in obtaining a track record, particularly for the new organisations emerging in Birmingham. If obtaining funds was difficult in most cases, then there were also problems attaching to the acquisition of funds. Money in many cases was seen as the primary reason for many groups setting up as organisations. As one Congolese volunteer noted, "People – they set up an organisation because money is there. I think you have come across that – because the money is there". Conforming to the worst prejudices of the popular press, this has to be taken seriously as a commonly expressed viewpoint in the majority of RCOs interviewed. It was for this reason that many of the newly emerging organisations, although they recognised the importance of funding, were cautious about applying for funds:

> "We know very well that we need money to do our work. The main thing for us is to understand what our aims and objectives are basically. To share it with all our members.

When we are convinced that everyone is fully convinced about that then we can start. We can start applying for money. Because money is very ... money is dangerous. To get money from someone is very easy. But to work to fulfil your goal without a good organisation is very difficult. Our priority is to understand what is the plan, the programme, our objective, to share this and then after that we can apply for money." (Central African organisation)

For the newly emerging organisations interviewed here, money was necessary, difficult to obtain and also difficult to manage. Many of them were aware of the pitfalls of organisational development based upon a ready supply of money, rather than clear-cut objectives. Despite this, there was some evidence of incipient competition for turf and identity between newly emerging groups in Birmingham. Several of these were from the same nationality, in particular the Congolese and Somalis. For those organisations with funding, there was a high level of dependency upon small-scale, short-term funding, often from a variety of sources. Some of the largest and well-established nationalities, including Somalis and Albanians, had experienced organisational stagnation and collapse as a result of fluctuations in funding. Although structural instability can be said to characterise most of the RCOs interviewed in Birmingham, there was one example at least of an organisation that had consolidated its position through establishing a 'market niche' by specialising in health issues for refugees and asylum seekers.

Defining RCOs

One of the first questions that had to be addressed when initiating the fieldwork was what the research team meant by the term 'RCO'. As we argued in Chapter Two, the definition of RCO in the policy and academic literature is ambiguous and, to some extent, contested. Taking a prescriptive definition as our starting point would have pre-empted the acknowledgement of precisely this conceptual ambiguity. In addition, considering that the respondents – representatives of statutory authorities, NGOs and refugee organisations – participate in the process of policy development and its implementation, it was vital to gauge their perceptions on this issue. What was most notable was the broad variety of responses that reflected predispositions and interests that the different actors brought to the field. The self-definition of 'RCO' by those actively involved in the organisation concerned would typically hinge on the notion of building community resources and providing services, as indicated in the section on organisational aims and rationale earlier in this chapter. In other cases, where the definition was introduced from the outside, more formal criteria were involved:

> "What we expect is a certain level of organisational coherence, transparency and visible community involvement. There are too many people, particularly in certain communities, who want to set themselves up as refugee organisations without the knowledge or backing to do so. It's in everyone's interest to have a bit more formality in the proceedings." (Asylum team member, Birmingham City Council)

As we discuss in the following part of this chapter, for several of the newly emerging organisations in the city, it was precisely the level of formal, bureaucratic commitment required by the statutory authorities and funding bodies that had appeared to alienate significant numbers of individuals in particular refugee communities.

Defining and representing communities

Although there was a strong commitment to building community resources, there was also a tendency among RCOs to refer to their particular 'community' rather unproblematically. But as representatives of RCOs were also aware, communities had to be both defined and built. Defining the community was a particular issue for the newly emerging Congolese organisations, who saw themselves alternately in national, geographical, linguistic or cultural terms. One Congolese organisation, for example, highlighted their pan-African identity, while also emphasising the French language as a common bond:

> "We tend to see ourselves as Africans instead of being Congolese ... so they become an African community. As a whole it's much more stronger because they share experiences from different countries and you know more about Africa than your own country.... Diversity creates another experience we are going through. I think, there's much more into a multinational community than only one nationality.... You can reach everyone. Everyone is coming to us regardless.... They know it's French speaking. It's not

about Congolese. We don't give priority to anybody. Everyone is equal." (Congolese organisation)

Other predominantly Congolese organisations defined themselves more in geographical terms as 'Central African', or as belonging to the 'Great Lakes' region, for example. The high degree of organisational activity among the Congolese groups in Birmingham appeared at the same time to be accompanied by a process of defining the boundaries and character of the particular community they were aiming to represent.

If defining a community is one of the first stages in establishing a viable community organisation, then for the more established organisations there was a continual issue around the process of building the community. The Kurds, one of the largest refugee groups in Birmingham, were well aware of the importance of community work:

> "Some of the RCOs, they do specific things like just advice and I don't think you can get the confidence and trust of all your members through just advice. So we do other things like advice and help and support. Build our relationships, do cultural events and some meeting and gathering. Do something for families and children … should do all of these together so that we can say we are leading a community or representing the community. You've got confidence and trust from the people, your people, so you have support … I believe we can get 2,000 people on the street just one single day…." (Kurdish association)

The degree to which organisations succeed in building and representing their communities is of course contingent upon a number of factors. As the literature reviewed in Chapter Two indicates, the level of skill, expertise and motivation in the leadership of organisations is a crucial variable. However, the character of the group in question is also highly significant. Educational levels and prior experience of bureaucratic organisational models and volunteering in the country of origin were noted on several occasions as highly significant in explaining the degree of participation in community organisations. As the Kurdish organiser quoted earlier indicated:

> "But still they [Kurds] don't understand what the organisation is for. Because when we say an organisation or association, directly they're going to think about the

political parties and there should be some benefit for them. And it's hard for you to explain for one client in a first contact. So, usually I ignore this question when they ask, 'What's your association doing?'. I say nothing, 'Just some people who are gathering together, you can come to next meeting'. And when they came they see us that we are working and helping, they will come again. And later when they find out that they all volunteer without any payment, some of them they will appreciate, some of them they say you are crazy...." (Kurdish association)

Dissonance between organisational norms in the country of origin and those in the receiving society could therefore be significant in explaining low rates of participation in particular refugee groups. In other instances, prior historical connections had fostered expectations of state patronage, which again encouraged passivity in the group. As one Somali coordinator remarked:

"Two things. They believe that Somaliland has a connection with Britain. They think that if we say something to the government they will listen us.... They normally come when they need. If I ask them to come, 'Oh, I don't have time'.... When I need to see them I almost say, 'Let's have a festival'.... They don't understand the meaning of this. They never have before. Nobody knows what an organisation means. What the community means. They understand this office only supports them. They don't understand what it means. So they need more understanding of what the community means."

Despite active volunteering in associations, low participation rates and passivity were noted by several of the RCOs interviewed. Here the claim often made by RCOs to directly represent their communities appears problematic. The role of the leadership in the organisations, although not explicitly examined in this research, is an important variable (Werbner and Anwar, 1991). In most cases the lead personnel in organisations were university educated and had occupied professional occupations in their home countries. This could sometimes lead to a noticeable gap between the personnel of the organisation and the population they served, as in the case of some of the Somali organisations. The Somali organisation referred to earlier, for example, was headed by educated individuals from the north of the country who served a population consisting largely of single mothers from the south. In general the women were uneducated and illiterate in both Somali and English. The representation of women within organisations and in women-only organisations was an area of increasing importance in Birmingham at the time of the fieldwork. The gender dimension of RCOs is a highly significant variable, as we have noted in greater length in Chapter Four.

Becoming a community and developing community organisations are by no means straightforward processes. As one representative of the Refugee Council in Birmingham caustically remarked, "We force an idea of something that they don't really understand" on refugees. The opportunity structures in place encourage refugees to mobilise to defend their interests through recognised forms of organisational activity. These are the only means of securing legitimacy and credibility in the local political and policy environment. Defining, building and representing a community are a necessary part of this process. It is important to note here that the assumption of community unity and identity that informs policy making and funding regimes can be a particular stumbling block for certain groups.

The community development worker in one Somali organisation remarked that Birmingham City Council and the West Midlands Consortium perceived Somali disunity as a problem, and that both of them had tried to bring Somalis together in the past. As he remarked, "Because of these divisions no funder was able to help them". Although there is a great deal of organisational activity, the Somalis "will not be seen to be doing something for the community". As noted earlier, there are currently at least seven Somali organisations in Birmingham, many of which are apparently based upon family networks or other relatives and friends. Competition for funding would appear to be one element here, although home divisions based upon clanship and regional affiliations are also important (Griffiths, 2002). It is important to note that the Somali population in Birmingham is a complex mix of individuals who have arrived largely from 1997 onwards, either as EU citizens (recognised refugees) from the Netherlands, Denmark and Sweden (many of whom are single mothers) or as asylum seekers under a variety of arrangements including ad-hoc dispersal from London boroughs, the interim arrangements and NASS dispersal.

Representation and accountability were indeed central issues for RCOs in Birmingham. A few groups were singled out as exemplary but it was commonplace for the Midland Refugee Council (MRC) to receive complaints about RCOs in Birmingham that they were seen by refugees and asylum seekers as not to be doing their job effectively. One East African group had received charity status and a small working grant from the MRC that was used entirely on telephone bills and renting office space. Within a few months the group collapsed due to a lack of participation by members. The chair of the group was also a trustee of the MRC.

Negative instances of this sort have to be balanced by the fact that the majority of RCOs in Birmingham are in the very early stages of organisational development. Of the 12 RCOs interviewed, 10 had been established in the last four years. Only the Kurdish, Somali, Afghan and Ethnic Albanian have populations that were of any significant size (that is, in excess of 3,000). The absence of a broader institutional infrastructure and framework, the dense network of NGO and voluntary organisations that are characteristic of areas of London, for example, has also been an obstacle to RCO development in the city. Representatives of RCOs were keenly aware of the importance of networking, both within their own communities, between refugee groups in the city and with the NGO and statutory sectors. However, networking, as the next part of this chapter illustrates, could also be seen in more ambivalent terms.

Building networks

As noted in Chapter Two of this book, the concept of social capital suffers from a number of shortcomings, not least of which is terminological vagueness and difficulty in operationalisation. Several accounts that have attempted to use the framework suggested by Putnam have come up against the circularity of argument that has been noted by Portes (1998), for example. Serra (1999) argued that participation in political activities in India, one of the central measures of social capital in Putnam, depended crucially upon levels of literacy. As a consequence (Serra, 1999, p 18):

> The line of causation from social capital to state performance
> is not proved in the case of Indian states, since, if literacy is
> a fundamental intervening variable, it is itself a product of
> public policy.

Political activity does not directly generate social capital but is itself a product of pre-existing forms of social solidarity and commitment.

Putnam's distinction between bonding, bridging and linking forms of social capital, as noted in Chapter Two, is an attempt to concretise the different types of network involved in the formation of social capital. Numerous publications under the aegis of the World Bank (1999) have further attempted to develop Putnam's initial distinctions into a more sophisticated conceptual framework, distinguishing between micro and macro levels of analysis and structural and cognitive forms of social capital. The result is to further promote social capital as an explanatory 'catch-all' for a variety of unconnected phenomena. The development of a concrete methodology, the social capital assessment tool (SOCAT), aims to combine qualitative and quantitative data, incorporating the relevant structural and cognitive elements of social capital. In practice, there are considerable difficulties in generating a general methodology, as social capital is fundamentally contextual in character and inheres in particular networks and relationships between individuals. Networks have different meanings for the actors involved according to the context. Above all, there is the need as Fine (1999, p 7), following Bourdieu, insists, to construct social capital "in terms of its content as meaning". Strict notions of measurement and quantification are particularly problematic when applied to the concept of social capital, as they necessarily tend to objectify social relationships and context-specific levels of meaning. More often, the attempt to distinguish levels or domains of social capital results in further compounding the circularity and tautology in the argument (for example, see Lynch, 2001).

The focus here is on relationships and networks between refugee groups (bridging social capital) and between refugee groups and official channels at both the NGO and statutory levels (linking social capital). As noted in Chapter Two of this book, the approach here is essentially critical. In particular, we ask whether the concept of linking social capital adequately addresses the question of power relations and structured inequalities that affect refugee groups. With these caveats in mind it is clear that the formation of networks between refugee groups was regarded as important by most of the RCOs interviewed in Birmingham. There were examples of effective networking organisations that had been in place for several years. The Bosnia Herzegovina UK (BHUK) Network, for example, had been in existence since 1996:

> "The committee of the network – each member organisation sends a representative to the committee. So the committee actually decides on the future of the network. The chairman is from London, the treasurer is from Derby, the secretary is from Hartford.... Usually they send people who have experience. That's why the network is so

successful. Because the people already have the knowledge of it, how it should work and how to push it forward.... With a network it gets easier because people already know, they have some background....That was the purpose of it, just to exchange the information and make life easy." (BHUK Network)

Another generalist African organisation had been built up from representatives of the different African organisations in the city:

"This organisation ... when we started from representatives, first Sudanese they sent one representative, then Somali they sent one representative, then Nigerian. If we want to discuss anything related we wanted them to attend the meeting so that they can take it back to their own community."

The benefits of networking across groups were clear in both cases: building upon prior stocks of experience and expertise, facilitating communication and the exchange of information. The process of networking had to some degree been eased in the case of the Bosnians who had arrived as part of an organised programme of reception and settlement.The coordinator of the BHUK Network observed that the existence of a programme created a ready-made set of networks that individuals could draw upon (Kelly, 2003). For many of the other nationalities, networking across groups has been difficult to organise. There are significant obstacles to building bridges between groups, particularly for the newly emerging RCOs in Birmingham.The issue of competition, particularly within specific nationalities, was highlighted as an impediment to effective networking across groups:

"It is very difficult, very, very difficult to organise such things. Because you can have a community want to compete.Very big problem, because people are competing for resource.The same pool people go to. Even one country but there are different organisations.We are pressing them that the resources are limited. It is better a country will have one organisation. So that when there is money it will go to that organisation. Each and everyone will benefit...." (African organisation)

Newly establishing RCOs often had a different set of priorities. As a worker at the Kurdish Association indicated, "'Cos most of them is new, not just Kurdish, as new they are focusing too much on what to do to develop themselves. First how to establish their community, how to get funds, how to maintain their name and their activities. That's their priority first". The majority of newly emerging organisations in Birmingham confirmed these limitations. Despite this, within a few months significant advances had been made in Birmingham in forging links across the different groups. The history of this is worth recounting in some detail.

Birmingham Refugee Network

Birmingham Refugee Network (established during the Summer of 2003) grew out of focus groups and a consultation process held between Refugee Action, the Refugee Council, the MRC and RCOs in Birmingham in May and June 2002.

Eight community development officers working with RCOs in the city were interviewed in focus groups by a student volunteer from Refugee Action. The nationalities were Afghan, Albanian, Congolese, Kurdish, Sudanese and Algerian. The questionnaire used for this research was supplemented by action research with RCO and Voluntary Services Organisation (VSO) members of the Birmingham Refugee Forum (BRF) that principally consists of service providers from the various local authority departments in the city. A number of themes were identified in the focus groups, including:

- the role of RCOs as service providers, that is not sufficiently recognised by statutory authorities or by their own communities;
- the difficulty in sustaining organisations based largely upon volunteering;
- the isolation of RCOs, hence the need for more effective external networking with agencies, other BME groups and official (Home Office) recognition of the services performed by RCOs;
- problems of funding and sustainability.

Of these, the issue of consultation was felt by RCOs to be the most pressing. In particular, it was felt that the issues facing RCOs had changed since dispersal and that there was a need for these changes to be registered at a broader level. Initially, the BRF was to be the vehicle for articulating the viewpoint of RCOs. In practice, a small number of RCOs in Birmingham have developed closer collaboration and begun to develop their own RCO network.

This earlier initiative, supported by Refugee Action, the MRC and the Refugee Council, resulted in the April 2003 conference, 'Between two worlds: refugee communities in Birmingham', that was hosted by the RCOs involved. According to a Sudanese representative at the conference, the main issue identified in the earlier research was the need for refugees to 'represent themselves'. As she argued:

> "Through that research from that student we felt that refugees must represent themselves.... We have the ability to stand and say what is our problem."

The results of the workshops held at the conference suggested a number of priorities: networking needed to be improved both among RCOs and in their relationships to service providers. There was a need for a two-way communication process that engaged cultural meanings on both sides and for these issues to be built into training programmes for service providers. In general, more 'proactive working partnerships' were needed between the RCOs and statutory authorities. A range of other factors was identified including increased representation of RCOs on the BRF and the need for improved service provision and training in RCOs.

Box 6.1: The Midlands Refugee Council

This is a community-based charity founded in 1987 as a voluntary association of refugee groups. It provides a free service to refugees and asylum seekers, offering advice, counselling, advocacy and support in the fields of immigration, welfare rights, employment and training and a variety of related fields. The MRC is principally concerned with refugees but works with asylum seekers as volunteers at the Council, particularly in the areas of self-employment and training (MRC, 2001). The MRC is likely to play an increasingly important role in longer-term plans for the integration of asylum seekers and refugees in the region, through skills-matching and other work in the fields of employment and education. In terms of employment, the MRC has a good track record of getting refugees into employment, particularly in the shortage areas of teaching and the medical profession. The MRC's work is concerned with the 'nuts and bolts' issues of registering RCOs with the Charity Commission, helping with filling in funding applications, developing a written constitution and networking with statutory authorities, the voluntary sector and NGOs. Through its team of community development workers the MRC directly supports the principal Kurdish organisation, the Afghan association, the Sudanese Midland association and the Somali community development association. Other organisations are supported indirectly through advice and support.

The Birmingham Refugee Network, consisting of representatives from the principal RCOs and nationalities in the city, held its first meetings in the summer of 2003. At the time of the fieldwork, the network was only tentatively taking shape. From the perspective of one of its participants, the network had a series of definite advantages, both in raising their level of representation with NGOs and statutory authorities and internally in relation to the needs of individual refugee groups:

"When the RCOs had the meeting [April 2003] from that conference the RCOs realised it is important to work together and identify issues.... Birmingham City Council (BCC) agreed with the RCOs that OK it is important to sit and plan together.... Now we are planning together with BCC ... formal meetings.... We talk through their worker ['Ahmed'] ... he's working with newly arrived refugees .... We all meet together as RCOs with this 'Ahmed' and discuss how we want the programmes to run and what programmes we want to make.... We only started this very, very recently. We have only had two meetings. And the third meeting is going to be Friday the 12th.... This meeting will be the planning session of what we want to do. What our communities, our individual communities want ... the Somalis, the Kurds, the Ethiopians. The Somalis are in different groups ... also bigger organisations like MRC, RC [Refugee Council]. It's important not only for sharing information of what is going around, it's important in identifying problems together. Also it's important to share resources. For example, when we had our trips and we didn't have enough volunteers.... We could easily ring the other RCOs if they could help us on such a day. And then they would easily say, 'Yes'.... The present group in Birmingham is a good focus point.... RCOs can identify their problems, discuss their problems, also move forward. Because without the network I feel that people are spinning in the same place. But with the network you can easily know what stages someone has gone through so that you don't go through the same stage again. You can learn from that experience and jump the hurdle…." (Sudanese organisation)

Again, the benefits of networking across groups are spelt out: information sharing, identification of problems, resource and personnel sharing, and avoidance of duplication of effort are the main positive outcomes resulting from the networking process. However, perhaps the most salient point to note concerns the close connection between networking across the various refugee groups and the developing links with statutory agencies and NGOs. What has been the character of this relationship in Birmingham and how might the benefits to refugee groups in the city be assessed?

Linking up: the RCO–NGO nexus

It is vital to note that the principal NGOs, in conjunction with Birmingham City Council, have been instrumental in fostering new refugee community groups and in providing support for developing infrastructure and responding to the training needs of refugees. Given the deficiency in service provision for refugees that was apparent across a range of statutory bodies, voluntary organisations and RCOs in the city (interview, Birmingham City Council housing department, January 2003; Zetter et al, 2003b) the asylum team in conjunction with the MRC and Refugee Action campaigned to open a dedicated resource centre for asylum seekers and refugees in the city. The Wardlow Road Resource Centre is led by the leader of the asylum team and includes NHS Health Outreach, the Careers Service, the MRC, Refugee Action and the Neighbourhood Advice Team. It provides housing advice, neighbourhood advice, welfare support, NHS surgery and signposting to other agencies, including Refugee Council information and data collection. Connexions, which runs training programmes relating to employment and education, is also based at the centre.

Refugee community involvement in the centre is actively encouraged through the provision of office space. This can be used for training purposes for RCOs in relation to capacity development and project management. As Birmingham City Council's 2001 Report to the Director of Housing indicates:

> Where new asylum seekers and refugees do not have
> established and resourced community organisations the
> centre can offer a venue for new groups to meet while
> they establish themselves and secure funding. The
> development of Refugee Community Organisations is an
> essential element in an integration strategy.

The aims of the centre in relation to the capacity building of RCOs
are explained in more detail in related documents ('Project description
for the Refugee Resource Centre – Appendix One'). The MRC
similarly supports a variety of RCOs through paying for community
development posts in different organisations. Refugee Action was
particularly active at the time of the fieldwork in examining the ways
in which refugee communities relate to existing organisational
structures in the city. The importance of networking was high on the
agenda, specifically concerning non-duplication of effort, information
sharing and securing legitimacy and 'clout' for refugee organisations
in the city.

It is important to note that the role of NGOs and the voluntary
sector in supporting refugee settlement predates the dispersal
arrangements that came into effect in 2000. As indicated in the literature
review in Chapter Three, they are a central feature of the reception
and settlement arrangements that have been set in place for various
programme refugees in the past. Under the NASS arrangements, as
discussed in Chapter Three, both the Refugee Council and Refugee
Action have taken on the responsibility in designated consortia areas
of running the One-Stop Service (OSS) of asylum seeker support.
From discussion with representatives of the main NGOs in the city, it
was clear that dispersal had impacted on their work in various ways,
not least by increasing workloads and shifting the emphasis from long-
term community development to day-to-day crisis management (Zetter
et al, 2003b). The Refugee Council in particular had been inadequately
resourced to run the OSS in the city from the outset of its contract.
This has had the unfortunate result of alienating a large number of
refugees and asylum seekers from the organisation. By contrast, the
locally based Refugee Action and MRC appear to be perceived in
more positive terms. There are nevertheless more general questions
that might be raised around the role of the principal NGOs in
facilitating and supporting the formation of RCOs.

In general, the community development work practised by these
organisations is seen by them as a series of active interventions that
increase self-sufficiency and empower refugee communities (Craig

and Mayo, 1995). For newly emerging RCOs, the support given by the NGOs was seen as necessary and beneficial. They learnt how the system worked, how to apply for funds and work towards achieving charitable status. In many respects, the relation of support was one of tutelage and instruction. In more general terms, however, the relationship between refugees and NGOs can be seen as both normative and regulatory in character. In effect, refugees are obliged to learn the set of rules that apply in the new society, in order to organise and secure legitimacy. Opportunity structures or institutional frameworks, as noted in Chapter Two of this book, define what is normal, acceptable and feasible and "define logics of appropriate behaviour" (Hay, 2002, p 105). Again, as one representative of the Refugee Council in Birmingham, who was quoted earlier, remarked, "We force an idea of something that they don't really understand" on refugees. Perceived largely in positive terms by the recipients there was nevertheless a compulsory element to the acquisition of the norms of 'appropriate behaviour'.

In this respect, it was interesting to note that internal, community-based alternatives to the official sponsoring of RCOs had been actively considered in the past by one of the organisations interviewed. As the former chair of the Kurdish association remarked:

> "I've been involved with this organisation in November 1999. We were about 15 members. Later on we were separated....After that a new management committee, we tried to go back to the statutory.... *But there were some other voices inside the Kurdish community who were saying we can do this for ourselves. There are some rich Kurdish people in Birmingham who can do something. There was a different idea of how to start. And still like that for quite a long time until 2001.* When in 2001 we had a new election. I've been a chairman of the Kurdish community. I said this is the time to work in partnership with some organisation because we don't have the skill to set up an organisation. And at that time we've been involved with the MRC and they agreed to help us. *At that time, people wanted to do something for themselves, not anybody to give them to do it. It was going like that for quite a long time....* We tried to go to the MRC and say look we are here, we are doing this for quite a long time, what can you do for us. At that time the MRC agreed to get the proposal together for Community Fund. And we got a start fund to get some support for the Kurdish community

through the RCO as an umbrella. Until 2001. From 2001 we started to be not just involved with those agents and organisations but to have a contribution to the decision makers ... give them advice and access essential services." (emphasis added)

Playing outside the rules of the game is difficult, not to say impossible, for RCOs seeking to establish themselves in Birmingham. Partnership working and reliance upon NGOs skilled in the workings of the system are essential prerequisites for establishing viable RCOs. This is not to say that RCOs do not in significant respects rely heavily upon their own internal resources. Many, as is the case in London, actively seek to become income generating in order to gain a degree of independence from funding bodies and the vagaries of local politics. In practice, even organisations with funding rely upon a pool of volunteers and donations to survive. In Birmingham, entering into networks with official bodies, NGOs and the local authority, was clearly perceived as beneficial to the RCOs interviewed. Securing greater representation with Birmingham City Council, for example, was regarded as one of the main potential benefits of the evolving refugee network. Nevertheless, there was also, on occasion, an undercurrent among several of the RCOs interviewed that suggested that tokenism and political concerns predominated in the local authority's relations with the refugee sector:

"I don't like this. I attend meetings. I don't learn very much ... it's mostly politics. It's mostly you know the highest level, employees like managers or other people.... They might talk to each other but they forget that all these communities have so many problems, for example. Some of them, or the majority of them, don't know a thing about these problems. Even if you explain to them they might say, 'Oh, forget it', or 'Oh, we are not able', because the state has its own way.... If I discuss what can they do – nothing!" (Ethnic Albanian group)

Another volunteer in a Sudanese organisation simply remarked of the local authority that, "They send us information, they invite us to their meetings but they don't take RCOs very seriously".

These impressions, although difficult to verify and only rarely explicitly expressed during the course of discussions, are significant. 'Linking up' with the relevant authorities, as appears to be assumed in

Putnam, for example, is no guarantee of being taken seriously or consulted by them on a regular basis. It is significant, for example, that the integration proposals in the West Midlands Consortium for Asylum Seeker and Refugee Support (WMCARS) Business Plan (WMCARS, 2003) were not developed in consultation with NGOs or RCOs in the West Midlands. This has been a matter of concern for many of the parties involved (interviews with Refugee Council, Refugee Action in Birmingham, July 2003). One representative from the Refugee Council roundly condemned the Business Plan as having "nothing to do with an integration strategy". On the other side, newly emerging RCOs in Birmingham appear to face a continual demand to legitimate their position as trustworthy representatives of their communities. The professional codes operating within local authorities (Clarke and Newman, 1997), including professional demarcations and areas of responsibility, may also mean that representatives of RCOs are 'not taken seriously', as the Sudanese individual quoted earlier suggested. The development of linking social capital therefore, although a necessary condition of establishing viable RCOs, is not in itself sufficient to secure equal treatment for refugees. The broader institutional context, in this as in other cases, is the decisive variable.

RCOs in the North West: fragmentation and unity in refugee communities

Reporting on the development of RCOs in Manchester and Liverpool, Gameledin-Ashami et al (2002, p 25) have noted that:

> There was an overwhelming sense of fragility about the RCOs found in each locality [Manchester and Liverpool]. They faced a wide range of demands with very limited resources. They commonly had weak structures, little money, sometimes no meeting place, limited knowledge of the British system, and dependency on a small number of enthusiastic individuals whose dedication led them to work very hard, bringing them, in some cases, close to burn out.

Refugee community organisations, according to Gameledin-Ashami et al's survey, were small and too few to meet the scale of demand in the region. In Liverpool, for example, there were only nine RCOs in 2001. On the other hand, as our own fieldwork indicates, asylum seekers arriving under the dispersal arrangements have in many cases brought a new lease of life to the established refugee organisations, often challenging them to the organisational limits. The same process of dispersal to the regions has stimulated among the newcomers themselves the need to form their own organisations, especially after they have received refugee status and begun to feel more settled in their new environment. Alternately, asylum seekers lead many of the newer organisations; this has a significant impact upon their way of working and life expectancy.

It is important to note that the number of refugee organisations in Liverpool and Manchester has risen significantly since the advent of the NASS dispersal arrangements. Due to the range of forms and structures they take, it is hard to provide an exact estimate for the number of RCOs in the region. Several local initiatives aiming at reviewing their number, scope, nationality, status and composition are ongoing. According to respondents, the number of RCOs operating in Liverpool is currently between 40 and 60. A similar figure was estimated in Greater Manchester. Nevertheless, it was a consistent theme in interviews that not all RCOs are actively involved in the support of their communities. On the contrary, in many cases it appears that organisations have been formed primarily as an expedient to acquire funding for a few individuals and their relatives and friends. This is a theme that is developed more fully below. In addition, no RCO appears to be operating outside the city level. Despite some efforts to 'extend their reach to the North West' (RWP, 2001) that took place after the introduction of the dispersal policy, few local branches of London-based refugee organisations have been established in Liverpool and Manchester. The relationship between London-based RCOs and those in the regions is addressed in Chapter Seven.

One of the fieldwork aims was to examine the emergence of RCOs and the possible causes of their development and underlying organisational rationale. The common assumption of a direct link between the number of asylum seekers and the growth in RCOs was investigated by focusing, in particular, on the interplay between internal and external factors. Among the internal factors, it was suggested in the interviews that homeland ties and history as well as settled community and newcomer relationships are the most relevant. For example, a respondent from Refugee Action noted:

> "Pakistani refugees have an uneasy relationship with settled Pakistani migrants. The latter tend to have a strong mythical link with Pakistan that, in most cases, is not shared by refugees who fled recently from the country."

Two other factors were also often cited, specifically the fragmentation along clan and family lines of the Somali community and the division of Kurds according to political factions (see Griffiths, 2002).

Among the external factors, the way the funding system is organised and the lack of cultural understanding of refugee communities, both in relation to the donors and statutory authorities, were mentioned as key points. Three more factors are of central importance:

- the role of NGOs and support networks that provide training and instruction in the development of constitutions and access to funding;
- the increasing number of asylum seekers who receive status and decide to stay in the North West;
- the difficulty that skilled and qualified refugees have in gaining employment that reflects their qualifications and experience.

"All these factors," a Kensington regeneration officer stated, "create the scope for launching an RCO".

A total of eight organisations in the North West were interviewed as part of this research (see Appendix). As in the case of the fieldwork more generally, the specific selection of RCOs was based upon predetermined criteria such as principal countries of origin but also depended upon the prevalence of particular groups in specific localities. Accessing the groups was often extremely difficult in practice. Some groups, for example, appear not to rely on public funding and mainstream support agencies and are able to support community members using internal skills and resources (for example, wealthy communities have in place a system of self-taxation for social and cultural events and initiatives). For this reason alone, certain RCOs have a high level of invisibility to the outside researcher and may be bypassed as a result. This necessarily skews the fieldwork results towards those refugee organisations that have, either through choice or compulsion, entered the sphere of public accountability and representation.

Resource base and organisational issues

Table 6.2 gives a general indication of the date of establishment, legal and financial status of RCOs interviewed and provides an approximate indication of the size of the refugee community.

Table 6.2: Summary of RCOs interviewed in the North West

Nationality/group represented	Date established	Charity	Paid worker	Funding	Approximate size of community
Congolese (Liverpool)	1998	N	N	N	500
Iranian (Salford)	2003	N	N	Y	1,000: "it is just a guess"
Kurdish (Salford)	2003	N	N	N	500 – mainly dispersed asylum seekers
Refugees' organisation (Liverpool)	2000	No profit company limited by guarantees	Y	NA	NA
Sierra Leone women's group (Manchester)	1997	N	N	Y	1,500-1,600
Somali (Manchester)	2003	N	N	Y	16,000-18,000 including settled community, asylum seekers and refugees
Somali (Liverpool)	2001	N	Y	Y	5,000-8,000 including settled community, asylum seekers and refugees
Tamil (Liverpool)	1997	N	N	Y	300 families scattered in Merseyside

Nationalities

Information supplied by a variety of sources in Liverpool and Greater Manchester – for example, Multi-Agency for Refugee Integration in Manchester (MARIM), Merseyside Refugee Support Network (MRSN) and Refugee Action – indicated around 100 RCOs in the two areas, although not all of them are active or even functioning. The ethnic community with the largest number of organisations is the Somali. The two oldest groups have been registered as charities since the 1970s. Central Africans and Congolese have well-established RCOs in the region. The Kurdish community has some long-running RCOs and a few new ones that have emerged in the dispersal areas. Iranians, Iraqis and Afghans have also recently established organisations.

Date of establishment

Five out of eight organisations interviewed have been recently or only very recently established. Some older groups have changed their aims and activities in the last few years, reshaping themselves to respond to the needs of the new arrivals. For some new organisations, the lack of pre-existing groups in dispersal areas was the main reason for initiating a new organisation.

Legal status

Of the eight organisations interviewed, none is registered as a charity. Stringent requirements for obtaining charity status was the main reason supplied. In one case, the decision not to register as a charity had been taken deliberately:

> "We chose not to register. We will go in that direction only if people will. We need people committed first. We are not ready yet. The trouble is, when you have a charity status, people try to apply for huge amount of money without preparation and commitment to the community. By not applying for the status yet, it is a way of making sure that we work with people that are knowledgeable and reliable." (Congolese organisation, Liverpool)

In two cases, the registration process was ongoing. The quotation below offers a perspective on the way that recently constituted groups perceive registration:

> "We start to support people before of establishing our organisation. At some point we realised: why not to make an arrangement for an organisation? We thought it would facilitate our work and it could take part of the burden out from us. Now we are in the process of registration as a charity, but we can't stop in the meantime. People continue to need us." (North Manchester Somali Community, Manchester)

The burden mentioned in this quotation is better defined in another section of the interview. Talking of the relationship with social services, the coordinator of the North Manchester Somali Organisation (NMSO) saw the receipt of official recognition primarily as a means of establishing an effective communication conduit with statutory services. It was also an effective tool for accessing the resources that the group needed in order to address the increasing number of requests from their community.

> "We just get in touch with social services for specific cases: when we escort a person who needs language support. We do this work voluntary. We don't want somebody else to pay for us doing it. The reason we made this organisation is we were no more able to continue to support the increase number of people that were coming to us. In order to bypass this situation we really need to be official and be able to redirect the burden on the real people who are in charge." (NMSO, Manchester)

Membership

Most RCOs interviewed did not have a formal membership system in operation. In most cases, organisations only kept a record of their clients because this is requested by donors as evidence of accountability and the efficient monitoring of service provision to clients.

Funding

Funding was raised as a key issue throughout the interviews conducted. New organisations as well as old ones continuously face the problem of guaranteeing adequate funding for their activities. Bureaucratisation in bidding procedures, accountancy requirements, short-term grants, and a lack of understanding of refugee communities and their cultures were mentioned as the main problems by most interviewees. For some organisations, financial support from within their own community was also an important factor.

> "Our time is very tight, we move like turtles and funding applications are very time-consuming, they require a lot of office work. It is normal, we know. But the time we have is so short and we have very little capacity to do these things." (NMSO, Manchester)

> "There are many small organisations from Black Africa in this area. They are small but they are so important for refugees' life. They support their people as a natural thing. They don't even know that they can ask for funding for doing these things. Thus, the few times they prepare a bid for funding they fail. They don't have the skills for doing it." (Sierra Leone Women's Group, Manchester)

Another concern was the negative impact of purely funding–driven initiatives on organisational development. As a Congolese refugee stated:

> "Since the beginning we chose not to rely on public funding, at least as long as there will be more people in the community willing to be committed to our vision. Besides, this allowed us to be independent and act as watchdog." (Congolese organisation, Liverpool)

A further point raised by Liverpool Asylum Seekers and Refugees Development Project (LASAR) concerns the side effects of the funding system, which appears to promote duplication of projects, fragmentation among refugee groups and the proliferation of short-term organisations, rather than enabling the consolidation of existing RCOs and supporting good practice and networking. In addition, a Refugee Action officer pointed out the lack of adequate monitoring measures to assess the outcomes of projects. "Till now," she argued, "there have been neither resources nor will to really monitor and evaluate the way grants are spent and the success of initiatives". Finally, it was suggested that most resources go to individuals who want to set up an organisation and that insufficient support is directed towards the actual communities and their long-term development.

Staff

Two of the organisations had paid workers on their staff. The other organisations relied exclusively upon volunteers to provide services. One consequence of this is the lack in most cases of resources for adequately training temporary staff.

> "Training is very important. Some of us are entering a different field and need a specific training. Sometimes what we do is to assume that what is good for us is good for our people too. But to work properly you need also to have specific knowledge." (NMSO, Manchester)

Reported cases of high staff turnover were also commonplace, with individuals leaving organisations once they had secured employment in other or related areas.

Services provided

Almost all RCOs are involved in on-site interpreting, advice, and signposting. The vast bulk of this work is done on a voluntary basis. In addition, most RCOs provide some form of cultural activity to strengthen ethnic solidarity and to alleviate the experience of boredom and isolation. In reality, however, the vast majority of work performed by RCOs tends to go unrecognised. Further up the institutional hierarchy, statutory services rely heavily on the work performed by RCOs to cope with the demands and needs of asylum seekers and refugees in their area.

> "You are not just translating the language. Doing this job, you are translating a culture, explaining to newcomers how this system, full of formalities, works." (Kurdish community, Salford)

Organisational aims and rationale

One of the themes discussed in the interviews concerned what RCOs can and cannot do, or what constitutes the principal rationale for refugee organisations. "From the host society perspective, in a place like Liverpool," as a Refugee Action manager argued, "where there have been a lot of problems of understanding communities and mistrust, a well-established refugee network could help to overcome some of these problems. It could build a refugee voice to challenge misinformation, for example. What Liverpool really needs is a celebration of diversity". The following passages show how individual history and motivation are fundamental driving forces behind the creation of organisations.

> "I arrived in Liverpool in December 1998. A year later I participated to a conference in London that was supposed to launch the National Asylum Support Service. There, I find out more people were coming to North West and I realised the absence of any sort of support service would have caused even more troubles for us and for the newcomers. This is why I started my commitment as a one-man-run organisation." (Congolese organisation, Liverpool)

The gaps left in service provision by the statutory authorities were the main reason, according to those interviewed, for setting up organisations.

> "The Congolese community started to arrive to Liverpool in late 1990s. We were few people at the time scattered in different areas. I was one of them; at the time there were no language provision or translation services or interpreting, it was very difficult for us to access information and guidance on any kind of services. It was very difficult as a stranger, coming from another country. The language was really a major barrier." (Congolese organisation, Liverpool)

Having gone through the experience of migration and the asylum process enables RCOs, according to some respondents, to better understand and address the needs and problems faced by new arrivals.

> "Having underwent the asylum process myself, having absorbed this experience, being lonely, unable to trust anyone, that has helped me a lot to realise what a refugee need. I know what they suffer. What we are trying to do is to make for other people the process less painful." (NMSO, Manchester)

> "For many of them it's a cultural shock [to come here]. We know what that means. It's alright for them to be crazy, to

be mad. Each of us went through this; each of us has been affected by these problems. But we coped with them by helping and supporting each other." (Sierra Leone Women's Group, Manchester)

Acting as a bridge to the receiving society, providing newcomers with the necessary tools for understanding the new system and articulating the needs and demands of the community to statutory agencies were also primary stated aims of most organisations. The following extract further explores this point and introduces another important element: the experience of isolation that may result from policies such as dispersal but that also appears to be part of a more general response to differences in lifestyle and culture:

"The Iraqi society is a simpler society. The life is easier. People can help each other. There are stronger family and neighbourhood ties and support. There are always people around you to get help. In the UK, although everything is available, if you are ill and you need to go to hospital, you need to ring the ambulance and it'll arrive in five minutes, but if you don't ring, there is no one to help you. You have to do everything by yourself. The only way to get support, if you don't know how the system works here, it's your community. If you have a proper community [organisation], with a small management, some paid workers able to translate and support you and a venue to gather together, life could be much easier. It would be like an alternative to family. Because, you know, there is no family here. We are all single men." (Iraqi Kurdish refugee, Salford, Greater Manchester)

Defining RCOs

As indicated in the previous part of this chapter on the West Midlands, rather than offering to those interviewed a received definition of 'RCO', they were invited to provide their own. The following quotations indicate a wide variety of responses that reflect both the conceptual and the policy ambiguities surrounding the term RCO:

"We give a broad definition of the term 'RCO'. For us, it is any organisation run predominantly by refugees. Some are single community organisations, other are grouped by common language [for example, French speakers, Latin-Americans]." (MRSN, Liverpool)

"Refugee community organisations can be placed in a spectrum that goes from formal organisation with bank accounts, constitution statutes, employees to loosely and informally connected people. The large majority is more on the side of informality, although recently they are getting more formal. Our aim is to support the development of refugee-led groups with a specific aim rather than developed according to what they are asked to do." (Refugee Action, Manchester)

An interesting view was expressed by Remisus, an organisation founded in 2000 and comprised of refugees from various ethnic backgrounds:

"Since we started, we tried not to be labelled as RCO. The problem with labels is they are too narrow. What we try to do is to apply equal opportunities regardless of ethnic background; we work with and for individuals." (Remisus, Liverpool)

Another significant point was raised by the coordinator of the Sierra Leone community organisation in Moss Side (Manchester):

"Support groups want to apply to all refugee organisations the same templates but they don't really know how to relate with the communities individually. They look at them as a whole but they never go to talk with them." (Sierra Leone Women's Group, Manchester)

As in the case of the West Midlands, what these comments clearly highlight is that there is no clear definition of what RCOs are, even among those working in the field. Refugee organisations can be portrayed along a "spectrum of different organisational forms", as one individual from Refugee Action suggested. The key point remains the degree to which government policy acknowledges and addresses this variety of forms. It is evident among refugees that there are ambivalent attitudes towards RCOs, which are alternately perceived as a useful instrument for accessing resources, or as a means of creating a political/ social space for action. In other instances, they are seen as a necessary instrument and interface for communicating with local and national government and NGOs. Finally, they may be perceived as an imposed package that does not allow those willing to participate and intervene in the public arena to do so, unless within this given, predetermined framework.

Defining and representing communities

Defining a community and representing it through community organisations, as indicated in the earlier part of this chapter concerning the West Midlands, is a complex and at times conflictual process. Far from being straightforward, it appears to be a circular process whereby organisations determine the boundaries of their client group. This tends, in turn, to be identified with the community as a whole. In reality, communities develop a contrasting set of attitudes towards the existing organisations, reacting to the boundary-marking process by instigating new organisations and competing boundary definitions.

A further element highlighted by respondents was the complexity of the relationships between community leaders, community members and organisations. The executive committee or board of members was often made up of skilled and well-educated individuals whose relation to the wider community is often tangential. The relation between the leadership of organisations and the communities they aimed to represent, therefore, was often ambiguous. Replicating the results of interviews in the case of the West Midlands, it appeared that the main reasons for the gap between RCOs and their respective refugee communities stemmed from a lack of understanding of the way formally constituted organisations work and manage funding; cultural issues, such as the different meanings attached to the role of organisations; and, on occasion a lack of communication between members, leadership and the organisations themselves.

An example that was mentioned several times concerned the Somali community and its internal conflicts and divisions along clan and family lines.

> "In our community there is a very strong social networking; it is a very sophisticated network of social security based on clans, sub-clans and families. Wherever you go, you will be soon signposted to the right place." (Somali refugee, Liverpool)

From interviews and observation in Manchester and Liverpool, it appears that the clan structure has a stronger appeal for the older generation, whereas younger people tend to be less impressed by clanship and identify with a broader range of identity options, including pan-Somali ideals. Due to clan factionalism and in particular the marginalisation of minority groups in Somalia (Griffiths, 2003), RCOs "tend to represent the majority of Somali community, the dominant families and clans. Therefore, minority groups are reluctant to work with them because of the fear of being marginalized". Among the Somali community organisations, men's groups tended to represent mainly the older generation of Somalis. Women's groups were more mixed. The youth on the other hand appear to be less involved with community groups. In part this is because 'they feel the community is pulling them down', but also because the elders are quite reluctant to accept young people into the fold, according to several of the young Somalis interviewed.

Nevertheless new groups in the Somali community are emerging. A recently established Somali RCO in Manchester observed:

> "Our group is totally different. Whoever comes to us, we don't ask: where are you from? We represent the whole Somalia. Our members have never met before; they are not from the same clan. Our main idea is that we Somalis are Somalis. When other people saw us, regardless all our differences, we are Somalis for them. We all suffered the consequences of the situation in our country. For that now we are here, for that we have to be united now." (NMSO, Manchester)

In Liverpool, divisions within the Somali community, along with its relative isolation (some respondents talk of 'insularity') led the bishop of the city to chair a Commission of Inquiry into the Somali Community in Liverpool. The inquiry found that the Liverpool local authority had failed to recognise the distinctive needs of Somalis in the city. As a consequence, the city council decided to fund the establishment of a Somali Umbrella Group (SUG). The outcomes of this attempt will be explored later in this chapter.

> "They don't trust each other. That is way many people find more comfortable to work with me rather than with a Somali. They want to see Somalis involved in the running of the group but there is a general consensus to have a

non-Somali person as a manager. Sometimes I felt myself as a sort of colonial presence. It's very embarrassing." ('White' manager of the SUG, Liverpool)

In relation to the role that RCOs can play in helping newcomers to settle into their established ethnic communities, the Merseyside Tamil School coordinator argued:

> "There are tensions between Tamil migrants, refugees and recently arrived asylum seekers. My objective is to create bridges between these groups. NASS people [dispersed asylum seekers] are quite economically weak and they depends on the established refugee and ethnic community for finding a job. They don't have language skills. Therefore, there has been a tendency by the established community to exploit their work. And even if they get the leave to remain they don't find a job easily in Liverpool. We try to overcome these barriers by organising public events, free of charge [the school, for example, is free for children]. But you can still see a kind of constraints on the two groups to interact when they met in public events, a kind of class structure." (Merseyside Tamil School, Liverpool)

Building networks

Building well-functioning networks was generally acknowledged as an essential tool for improving RCO capacity to cope with the increasing demands on their services. There was less agreement, however, on exactly how to build and manage a well-functioning refugee network. The diverse forms of refugee support networks or fora highlight the complexity of the issue. As a Refugee Action officer suggested:

> "Most RCOs are very pressed from the basic needs of their community. As a result, they have no time for strategic thinking. A network may help to overcome this limitation." (Refugee Action, Manchester)

A LASAR officer also supported this view and argued, "How can you have time for strategic thinking when your challenge is how do I pay for office space?". The importance of improving networks, although differently accented in this quotation, is more clearly expressed in the following comment by Remisus:

> "The lack of coordination among RCOs leave a lot of room for established generic organisations to take over and to work on behalf of refugees. A good change would be not to encourage a divide-and-rule strategy among RCOs but rather encourage a local forum of various RCOs: a place where coming up together and sharing resources and expertise; a common structure that would simplify the working process and allow a better use of resources. This means that the door would be always open. Whenever and whoever knocks to the door, he/she would be signposted in the right place and find the advice needed. But unfortunately, what I see at the moment, it's a deep-rooted pigeonhole mentality." (Refugees and Ethnic Minorities Support Service, Liverpool)

Refugee Action is the main voluntary sector organisation that is directly involved in the dispersal process in the North West. It has national contractual agreements with the Home Office to provide emergency accommodation for those claiming asylum within the region and also to provide advice and information services for asylum seekers. The direct involvement of voluntary sector organisations in the process has been highly controversial and fraught with problems. The main problem has been the large number of asylum seekers being sent to, and arriving in, the region. This was unanticipated at the beginning of the process and Refugee Action has simply been unable to cope with the numbers of people requiring emergency accommodation and advice and information. Given the ongoing process of settlement of former dispersed asylum seekers, integration initiatives are gaining more attention. Refugee Action has two personnel in the North West devoted to community development and supporting refugee integration. The organisation also plays a major role in promoting networking between agencies and RCOs.

Several networks are currently in operation. Their relationships are not always constructive. Competition for the allocation of limited resources appears a key reason for this. A brief outline of the different networks in operation follows.

Multi-Agency for Refugee Integration in Manchester (MARIM)

The Multi-Agency for Refugee Integration in Manchester (MARIM) arose in recognition of the need to develop a coordinated response to the dispersal of asylum seekers into Manchester following the IAA99. It works as a forum where different council departments share information. The work of the multi-agency is structured on seven theme-based task groups: Advice and Information Task Group; Education Task Group; Post-16 Education, Employment and Training Task Group; Health Task Group; Housing Task Group; Mental Health Task Group and the Supporting Communities Task Group. Additionally, there are two area-based groups situated in the regeneration areas of East Manchester and North Manchester.

The overarching objectives of each of the task groups are:

- the coordination, planning and delivery of services to refugees and asylum seekers in Manchester;
- the development of strategies and working practices necessary to improve service delivery;
- to maximise resources used to support asylum seekers and refugees by reducing the duplication of work across agencies.

The forum seeks to ensure that the membership of each of the task groups is drawn from the appropriate statutory, non-statutory and voluntary sector organisations working in each of the themed areas. Refugee organisations are not greatly involved in MARIM, with the exception of the Supporting Communities Task Group. The task groups have therefore created action plans based on specific, agreed objectives and are further divided into sub-groups or working groups to implement the identified actions necessary to meet these objectives.

Liverpool Asylum Seekers and Refugees Development Project (LASAR)

The LASAR Partnership is funded through the EQUAL Programme. It assists asylum seekers and refugees in Liverpool by offering new projects and assistance in the following areas:

- information networks and sharing;
- family learning and education support through schools;
- orientation ESOL;

- health link/support;
- capacity-building support activities with RCOs.

The project operated between May 2002 and July 2004.

Merseyside Refugee Support Network (MRSN)

Merseyside Refugee Support Network (MRSN, administered since November 2001 by Liverpool Network for Change [LNC]) exists to support those organisations whose objective is the relief of refugees and asylum seekers in Merseyside and the surrounding area by bringing together all those voluntary organisations concerned with their welfare and assisting those organisations in their effective networking, and communications with local and central government and other agencies of the state.

The network was initially established by Refugee Action and partner agencies. Since 2001, the new management has developed a database of members, registered MRSN as a charity and thereby gained access to funds for refugee and asylum seeker events, held regular meetings and acted as a networking conduit. It has also assisted many RCOs, through LNC, to establish themselves as formally organised groups.

As a respondent noted, MRSN is very much an agency-led network rather than a refugee community-based network. That was often given as one of the main reasons why very few refugee participants actually attended their meetings.

> "MRSN is not a refugee-led organisation, as it was expected to be at the beginning, when the idea came out. What happened is that some people, right or wrong, took control of this organisation, no refugees are involved at management level. I personally don't see refugees taken adequately into account when it comes to take decisions that really matter for us. They behave quite paternalistically. For me they should change name." (Congolese organisation, Liverpool)

Manchester Refugee Support Network (MARSN)

This network emerged in the early 1990s with the aim of better serving the needs of the various refugee communities in Manchester. Working with local authorities, voluntary agencies and refugee community groups, its main aim was to build a multi-agency approach to meeting these needs. It has some paid staff and a voluntary committee of representatives from refugee communities manages it. It brings together a number of communities including Afghanis, Africans, Bosnians, Chileans, Kosovar/Albanians, Kurds, Iraqis, Somalis, Sudanese, Tamils, Vietnamese and Zimbabweans. Its main objectives are:

- to facilitate access to support and information to newly emerging refugee communities;
- to promote RCOs' access to multi-agency forums where they can influence policy and service development;
- to support RCOs in consolidating their activities and benefiting from their development in size and capacity;
- improving RCOs' ability to manage money, staff and volunteers and to deliver successful projects;
- to provide an ad-hoc programme of integration for RCOs;
- to allow RCOs free access to meeting spaces and resources.

With the increasing complexity of refugee communities that has resulted from dispersal, MARSN has had to partially review its membership rules. In terms of its constitution it is allowed only one group per refugee community. Although there have been a few amendments to this rule, as several interviewees noted, the rule nevertheless tends to exclude many of the more recent RCOs.

As regards the churches and faith groups, overall, their main activity has been to provide assistance, often in the form of food parcels and related support, to asylum seekers and local authority asylum teams for distribution. There is a widespread perception that the churches have stepped in and provided a service precisely where the statutory process has 'broken down'. Other activities that churches have generally been involved in are such things as providing social and cultural events for asylum seekers and refugees, but also allowing refugee communities to use church premises for holding meetings and develop their own community initiatives.

Dealing with local authorities

Dealing with local authorities, according to most interviewees, is often quite problematic. The range of issues raised by respondents varied greatly but included:

- a lack of support in implementing projects they themselves funded;
- poor understanding of community needs;
- the overriding assumption of homogeneity within refugee communities despite the existence of fragmentation.

Pervasive differences in cultural orientations between service providers and refugee communities reinforced a sense that statutory provision often failed to adequately address the character and extent of refugee community needs. For example:

> "The lack of support of Liverpool City Council is one of the major problems I have faced. They have put their money in the project but not their mouth. They are not open to listen and to discuss the umbrella group proposals. 'No, this is not our policy', is their answer." (SUG, Liverpool)

> "There is a huge problem of representativeness. Local authorities want to have one RCO speaking for community and this often is not possible due to social, cultural and historical reasons." (Refugee Action, Manchester)

> "The city council decides this is how we are going to tackle the problem and we are forced to fit a square peg into the round hole." (SUG, Liverpool)

The assumption of homogeneity within the refugee community drives the policy agenda. Yet the communities encountered in Manchester and Liverpool were characterised by their diversity. Indeed, differentiation appears to be growing rather than declining in significance:

> "I saw the work Manchester City Council undertook with the Somali community. They attempted to pigeonhole and box a lot of different and conflicting interests in just one community organisation: the Somali Cultural Association. It banged. Not just banged, it went bang and left a shambles all around…." (MARIM development officer, Manchester)

This view of Manchester City Council's attempts to harmonise the Somali community provides a warning shot for Liverpool, where the city council is pursuing a similar approach through the SUG. After more than a year in post, the SUG development officer acknowledges:

"Whether or not this approach is a success, I don't know. Is this the best way to move forward? If the community does not feel enough ownership of the project, then it is a problem. Sometimes I wonder whether it would be best to continue as it was happening before, to fund each individual group as an individual group, ignoring the fact they are Somalis and deal with them as any other voluntary organisations working with a client group, funding them on the same basis as any other." (SUG development officer, Liverpool)

The impacts of dispersal and legislative change

In relation to Birmingham, it is important to reiterate the main impacts of dispersal on the size of the city's refugee and asylum seeker population. According to representatives of the WMCARS and NGOs in the city, there was a tripling in the number of asylum seekers arriving in the West Midlands region throughout 2001. Most of these individuals came to Birmingham. In-region arrivals rather than individuals dispersed from the NASS offices in Croydon have been a large proportion of new arrivals in the city from 2001 onwards. Secondary migration to Birmingham from the NASS system has also been an important factor in raising the number of asylum seekers and refugees in Birmingham (Robinson, 2002). At one point, it was estimated that up to 10 Somalis a day were arriving in Birmingham from other EU countries. As a result, there has been a corresponding growth in the number of RCOs in Birmingham, from only a few in 2001 – largely Sudanese, Bosnian, Somali, Afghan and Kurdish – to over 30 in 2003. But what of the impacts of dispersal on RCOs, refugees and asylum seekers in the city?

For the better-established RCOs in Birmingham, the beginnings of the NASS dispersal in 2001 raised a series of new issues and problems that they had to address. In addition to their role of aiding the settlement of refugees the increasing numbers of asylum seekers in the city generated a whole new set of problems. The quality of accommodation was a particular issue affecting asylum seekers (Carter and El-Hassan, 2003; Zetter et al, 2003b). One Somali organisation noted the problem of unsupported mothers on housing estates in run-down areas with no support networks in place. In general there was a lack of support infrastructure for asylum seekers arriving in dispersal areas. Again, several organisations have had to deal with telephone calls from individuals dispersed throughout the West Midlands. "Terrible things happened outside Birmingham. Birmingham is easy," as one Somali community development worker noted. The more general issues raised by several RCOs concerned the lack of accountability and transparency of the principal organisations charged with coordinating dispersal in the West Midlands, the NASS and the Refugee Council:

> "They [NASS] send some people to the Refugee Council for dispersal. That people they never get support. And they come to us. We support them. So I said, OK, if you bring them why you don't ... I want to meet those people [from NASS] and discuss about these issues. So I said, 'OK, I only need one thing. I need a direct line. If somebody comes to me ... some Somali who is in danger so I can phone direct to that person'. I've waited for that direct line for a year now!" (Somali organisation)

The majority of RCOs interviewed commonly expressed high levels of dissatisfaction with both the NASS and the Refugee Council. One Sudanese organisation that was established in 1990, argued that dispersal has had a big impact on their performance and the demands made upon them. One consequence has been that they have recently appointed a part-time worker to deal with the increased workload. According to the chief executive of the association, "It is us dealing with the problems" raised by the dispersal process. Formal advisory services are very often unable to deal with the volume and character of the work needed. Refugee community organisations, on the other hand, are ideally placed to do this. In relation to this, there was also a generalised perception that organisations like the Refugee Council and Refugee Action are adjuncts to the Home Office and are not able to act independently in fulfilling their customary role of intervention and advocacy on behalf of asylum seekers and refugees. The executive committee believed that there should be more recognition and direct funding of RCOs to deal with the increased workload caused by dispersal. From their perspective, the RCOs are key: "they are refugees serving their own people".

Other groups had begun to respond to the ad-hoc dispersal of asylum seekers from London before the IAA99 and had used this as the basis for forming their own community organisations:

> "Talk about the dispersal scheme: when there were a lot of people coming from London, some of them they don't know the system, especially the health care system. We help

them to accept the primary health care, to help them get into the system. And then what we did when we called a meeting … the community in 1997, one of the proposals was for the African community to help Africans to come together. For to reach everybody we had to form a community-based organisation, based on countries in Africa." (African organisation)

The specific health needs of individuals and the impact of vouchers and poorly organised support for asylum seekers were priorities for this particular organisation:

"I was one of community in London called African Refugee Network. I was on one of the sub-committees. Because of that dispersal scheme and the policy of vouchers and dispersal it was not well thought and people did not prepare the regions. So that when they come here there will be good reception for them. They are not prepared … it was very difficult. Vouchers, it was very difficult especially for people with HIV and AIDS. People for example who are taking some drugs and some medicines and special food.… Then also to go to different appointments, they don't have money even for tickets to attend the meeting.… That one I used to coordinate. It was very difficult.…"

In addition, there are a number of common issues that both established and more recently formed RCOs have to address. These include, at the time of the fieldwork, the introduction of section 55 of the 2002 Nationality, Immigration and Asylum Act and the withdrawal of the right to seek permission to work. Referring to the effects of both legislative changes several individuals interviewed referred to their negative impacts upon asylum seekers and the relentless downward pressure into illegality and the black market:

"The problem with NASS, for example, is that people are left in a limbo. Nothing at all. They cannot feed themselves. The next thing they will hanging on the streets. How do they feed themselves? Encouraging crimes 'cos that's the only way they can get something to eat. You're encouraging crimes… People are becoming overstayers, doing illegal work and things like that.… I don't get out of my homeland so I can do crime in England, definitely not." (Central African organisation)

Other organisations had attempted to respond positively to the changes by networking with other agencies, but again the consequences for illegal overstaying and entry into the black market were emphasised:

"About Section 55, when Home Office decide on this ... we find there is someone dealing with that from the Red Cross.... Refugee and asylum seeker project. Whenever something happens like this they come to us ... or make a phone call. We have contacts with other service providers including MRC and sometimes NASS comes for our meetings.... If the Home Office do not go to think about those people, those people will very easily disappear. And they will stay illegally. And they will go to the black market to work. And I know that's happened to the Albanians and Kosovans and I'm sure that is going to happen to the Kurdish too.... They have some relatives but they are going to fake some documents, get some work...." (Kurdish association)

Taken as a whole, these remarks indicate a high degree of negative response to the management of the dispersal process and the effects of recent legislative change. The resources available to RCOs to challenge or accommodate these changes are, however, extremely limited.

A similar range of themes was evident in the case of the North West. In this instance, support groups and networks had helped, to some degree, to alleviate the impact of successive policy change and the intensified administrative burdens placed on RCOs. The most complex of these requirements relates to the financial accountancy of projects. In addition, according to Remisus, networks are doing a good job in selecting and disseminating information – "They work as a filter". This helps RCOs to cope, on the whole, with the effects of policy change. Their role, however, is primarily defensive (Gameledin-Ashami et al, 2002), as their limited resources make them unable to counter the negative effects of legislative change. These include, as indicated earlier, the adverse effects of section 55 of the 2002 legislation and the withdrawal of the right to seek permission to work for asylum seekers. As was noted in the case of the West Midlands, these changes have resulted, according to several of those interviewed, in an increase in the pool of unregulated, casual labour in both Manchester and Liverpool.

Conclusions

This chapter has concentrated on RCOs in Birmingham, Liverpool and Manchester. Birmingham was selected as it has the largest number of asylum seekers in the West Midlands and also hosts a sizeable refugee population, estimated at some 10,000-15,000. The period since 2001 has seen a rapid increase in the number of asylum seekers in Birmingham and also in the rate of recognised refugees settling in the city. Birmingham had a limited number of RCOs throughout the 1990s, consisting of a few key nationalities: Somalis, Sudanese, Bosnians and Kurds. The period since 1999 has seen a rapid expansion in the number of RCOs in the city, from four or five principal RCOs to over 30, although these are of varying size, status and composition. Of the 12 RCOs interviewed, 10 have been established since 1999. Over half of the 12 have some form of funding, although in most cases this is small scale (below £50,000 per year) and dependent upon combining a number of small, short-term funds from a variety of sources. Funding tends to be associated with charity status and allows RCOs to employ paid staff. Despite this, organisations remain heavily dependent upon voluntary work. The RCOs provide a number of services, principal of which are advice and signposting to statutory agencies. Cultural and social activities, provision of ESOL and training were also common across those RCOs with access to funding. One of the organisations that has been more successful in obtaining funds has also managed to establish a particular niche, supplying specialist services in the area of refugee health issues.

Although the majority of RCOs interviewed shared common objectives – to help their communities and build up a form of collective social capital that would aid community development – there were specific obstacles that all of the RCOs encountered. Foremost of these was the difficulty in obtaining funding. Developing a track record with funders and securing legitimacy were particular problems for newly emerging RCOs. Competition for funds was another problem that RCOs were aware of and attempted to combat in their organisational practice and aims. Newly emerging organisations in particular were in the process of defining and building their communities, although this was in the early stages in Birmingham. Some of the more established RCOs had encountered difficulties in encouraging participation in organisational activities. A variety of factors including educational background and prior negative experiences of state-controlled organisations in the home country may have been partially responsible for this. The pressure from funding agencies and statutory authorities to form unified communities was tangible for many RCOs. The reality of community formation in particular nationalities was, for a variety of reasons, far from this ideal.

Drawing critically upon Putnam's distinction between bridging and linking social capital, the chapter noted the development, largely in response to dispersal, of networks across refugee groups in Birmingham and the formation of an RCO–NGO nexus in the city. The advantages of building bridges between refugee groups were clearly acknowledged by those RCOs interviewed: information, resource and personnel sharing; identification of problems; and avoidance of duplication of effort were the primary benefits noted. Building bridges of this sort was limited by organisational constraints, particularly for newly emerging RCOs. These were principally concerned to define their organisational aims, acquire funding and secure representation in the local policy arena. In relation to the role of NGOs it was noted that their traditional support function had a number of implications for RCOs. In particular, NGOs are often the primary route for RCOs to learn the 'rules of the game' in relation to setting up community organisations, obtaining funding and receiving some form of legal status. Non-governmental organisations and other agencies supporting refugees help to define the institutional 'opportunity structures', the parameters within which organisational activity may legitimately take place. There was some evidence of a tension between taking the route of institutionalised support or a more exclusive reliance on the community's own resources. In practice, emerging RCOs were constrained to follow a process of induction that was on the whole perceived in positive terms. The formation of links with NGOs and the statutory authorities was regarded as necessary and desirable by the RCOs interviewed. This was in fact perceived to be one of the main benefits and rationales of the new refugee network in Birmingham. In some cases, however, there was a pronounced awareness of the imbalances in decision-making capacity between RCOs and the statutory services. Partnership and participation were seen in this sense as largely tokenist in character and more concerned with the logistics of political presentation than with assisting refugee communities. A similar pessimism marked the response to the management of dispersal and recent legislative changes affecting refugees and asylum seekers in the city.

In relation to the North West, the period since 2000 has seen a rapid growth in the number of asylum seekers in Liverpool and Greater Manchester and also in the rate of recognised refugees settling in the city, although there are no reliable statistics available. The last few years have also seen a considerable increase in the number of RCOs, which are currently estimated at around 90-100 across the region. Most of them, according to interviewees, are not very active and are often just 'one-person' organisations or, at best, family-run groups. Of the eight RCOs interviewed, five have been established since 2000. A majority of them have some form of funding, although in most cases this is small scale and from a diverse range of sources. The RCOs provide a number of services, principal of which are interpreting and translation, advice and signposting to statutory agencies. Organising cultural and social activities is another key feature of their activities, which thereby enables asylum seekers and refugees to set up networks of mutual support.

Formally constituted refugee organisations act as the interface to deal with the 'host society' and its bureaucracy. In several cases the relationship between newcomers and the settled community of co-ethnics has been far from harmonious. The newcomers, arriving as asylum seekers rather than economic migrants, often represent different histories and political affiliations and are unable to find what they need in the established community organisations. This is one important reason for the proliferation of RCOs that has occurred since the beginning of dispersal. In addition, considering the difficulties faced by skilled refugees in accessing the labour market in the North West, especially in Liverpool, RCOs appear as one of the few options available for these individuals to gain some form of social recognition and employment. In turn, as the interview narratives suggest, they are often compelled to base their organisational rationale on the principle of 'ethnicity' (in effect 'capitalising' on their ethnicity) and to play on a stage that has been set up by other actors and interests. The space for refugee participation in the public arena is, to adopt Tarrow's perspective (1994), based upon the resources available in the political environment. The variety of nationalities and cultures brought about by dispersal in the North West, where these groups have no longstanding tradition of settlement and mobilisation, has meant an even stronger dependency upon organisational models and know-how developed elsewhere in the country. Nevertheless, the appearance of so many RCOs in a short space of time is a clear indication that newcomers have learnt the lesson. The fragility and rapid turnover of many these organisations, their almost total dependency upon public funding and consequently their difficulty in absorbing working practices required by the funders indicate that RCOs are not yet a consolidated reality in the regions. More importantly, perhaps, they may not always be best adapted to meet the growing needs of refugee communities.

As emphasised in the case of the West Midlands, networking is widely perceived as a key tool for building the capacity of RCOs. Networks may also allow RCOs to gain more power in the decision-making process, in relation to which they tend to participate only as implementing partners. As one interviewee said, "They are forced to fit the square peg in the round hole". The different networks currently in operation in the region highlight another key element: the power relations between statutory services, NGOs, voluntary organisations and RCOs. The conflict over the allocation and control of limited resources in the local political and policy environment clearly affects the structure that several of the networks in the region take. For example, in the Merseyside area, the lack of a formal contract between Liverpool City Council and the Home Office that, as mentioned earlier in this chapter, can be seen as the result of the general political competition in the area, has meant poor coordination of initiatives, frequent lack of resources and patchy outcomes. Moreover, it has moved the governance of the dispersal process outside the control of the council and made dispersal an explicitly partisan issue. Those groups that have been able to establish, for whatever reason, a direct connection with central government and key funders, have also managed to play a key role in decision making and agenda setting at the local level.

Concerning the role of RCOs in integrating refugees, until recently very little 'structural' consideration has been given to the process of 'move on' in the region. The situation is characterised by a lack of 'joined-up' thinking concerning the role of RCOs and their relationships with their communities. In many areas of support, including housing, social security and employment, the asylum seeker is potentially abandoned.

Although integration is one of the primary concerns of the local policy agenda in both the West Midlands and the North West, the future role that RCOs will be asked to play in regional and local integration strategies is as yet unclear. The emergence of new organisations in both regions is a dominant feature in the fieldwork. As is clearly demonstrated in this chapter, the assumption of homogeneity and unity within the refugee community drives the local policy agenda in both regions. According to some respondents, despite being one of the causes behind the failure of many projects, this assumption is rarely questioned. There is, rather, a tendency for local authorities to 'blame the victims' and their internal conflicts.

Note

[1] The Iranian community was set up as a response to the tragic death of Israfil Shiri. "Mr Shiri, 30, had been thrown out of his Salford council flat and been denied benefits, under the government's tough new rules. He told friends that he would do something to prove that 'this government cares more about animals than people fleeing torture and persecution'. On 4 September 2003, he went to the offices of Refugee Action in Manchester, went into a toilet to douse himself in petrol and then returned to the front desk and set himself alight with a lighter" (reported on 4 September 2003 by IRR).

SEVEN

Dispersal, RCOs and refugee communities

This book has examined the changing pressures faced by refugee community organisations (RCOs) in the UK in a period of rapid legislative change. Our objectives were broadly focused. Based upon fieldwork with RCOs in London, the West Midlands and the North West, they related in the first case to the impact of dispersal policies upon refugee organisations and their capacity to respond to these changes. In addition, our objectives were to explore the barriers and resource constraints affecting refugee organisations and any resulting conflict between the traditional settlement role of RCOs and their involvement in the dispersal arrangements. Further issues were raised in relation to the problem of accountability and representation in refugee communities and the need to specify the internal differentiation within the RCO sector as a whole. This chapter draws together the different strands of the argument and summarises the fieldwork evidence from London and the regions. In particular, the comparative issues raised by the fieldwork are discussed and the research objectives outlined in the Introduction addressed in further detail.

The chapter first reviews the contrasting institutional frameworks in the two dispersal regions outside London. Then the comparative development of refugee communities and RCOs in London and the regions is discussed. The principal themes examined are the organisational and social issues affecting RCOs, including their resource base; the contested process of defining and building refugee communities; the significance of networks; and finally, the impacts of dispersal upon RCOs in London and the regions.

The institutional framework

In this section, we review the comparative issues raised by the fieldwork in relation to the operation of the consortia structure in the regions and finally the formal position of RCOs in relation to the broader institutional arrangements for reception and settlement.

In the West Midlands, the National Asylum Support Service (NASS) began dispersing asylum seekers to the region from April 2000 and worked with the West Midlands Consortium for Asylum Seeker and Refugee Support (WMCARS) from December 2000 to manage the dispersal process. According to sources in Birmingham City Council, the consortium, the Refugee Council and NASS itself, the early stages of dispersal were largely ineffective in the West Midlands. Particularly relevant are a number of related problems around non-compliance and organisational deficiencies: for example, asylum seekers often failed to get on designated coaches to the West Midlands, while different criteria were applied to the booking process for accommodation by NASS and the local housing providers. A combination of administrative problems and non-compliance were therefore key issues around the turn of 2001. It was also suggested by those interviewed that the large number of dispersal points from London affected the coordination of dispersal to Birmingham. The inability of NASS to produce 'clean lists', with accurate names and details for asylum seekers, was also a recurrent problem in the administration of dispersal. After a slow take-up of places, NASS agreed to a system of in-region dispersal for those arriving from the main motorway routes to the region. This has generally proven to be effective in managing the process, although the popularity of Birmingham as a destination point has placed a continuing strain on emergency accommodation. Problems over internal and external coordination have been central to the operation of NASS in the region although, according to interviews with the NASS regional manager, these had been addressed by an increase in staff and the greater regionalisation of NASS operations throughout 2002 and 2003.

The performance of NASS in the North West has been heavily conditioned by the bifurcation of the region into Western and Eastern sub-regions. The Western sub-region is characterised by the absence of a consortium contractual relationship with NASS. In the absence of centralised coordination, Refugee Action has assumed a steering role in this part of the region. The remaining coordinating agency is the regional NASS office that covers the whole of the North West. With limited personnel and resources NASS has been severely stretched to fulfil a fully directive role in the region. By way of contrast, Manchester, as the lead authority in the Eastern sub-region, has a contract with NASS to provide accommodation to approximately one third of asylum seekers arriving in the Eastern sub-region. Here a more integrated approach to dispersal has taken place, with effective liaison between partner agencies providing a more coherent managerial approach to supporting asylum seekers in the region. As in the case of the West Midlands, the transparency and accuracy of information flows between NASS and the consortium are considered to be one of the main impediments to the successful operation of the dispersal arrangements.

Concerning the role of the consortia, it is clear that, even accounting for regional differences, there are significant variations in their approach, structure, and their degree of engagement with dispersal. There are also substantial variations in the autonomy of consortia within and between the two regions examined here. According to Zetter et al's (2003b) typology of the consortia, the West Midlands can be characterised as 'integrated', with a coherent, strategic managerial structure and clear relations between the different partner agencies. By contrast, the North West is 'multi-centred', albeit with integrated sub-regions. This distinction is clearly brought out in the contrast between Birmingham, which occupies a central position in the West Midlands, and the bifurcated model in the North West where Manchester and Liverpool effectively divide the region. In both cases, however, the regional consortia are defined by a series of conflicting relationships and often poor coordination between the actors and agencies involved in the dispersal arrangements. The distinction between 'integrated' and 'multi-centred' consortia structures necessarily obscures important detailed variations in the cases examined in this book. Nevertheless, in general, it is clear that the consortia lack cohesion, either as region-wide agencies or as regionally integrated partnership arrangements. The broad distinction between the consortia is heavily influenced by a range of factors that, in many cases, pre-date dispersal. These factors include:

- *Historical allegiances/enmities:* this is evident in examining the relative development profiles of different consortia. The North West Regional Consortium bifurcated into two very distinct operational hubs, Manchester and Liverpool, in May 2001, that operate as two separate organisations with little or no reference to each other. This is in sharp contrast to Birmingham, where the consortium officers are tasked with a much more strategic role for the whole consortium area.
- *Variations in political control:* there are indications, linked closely to the first point here, that political differences between local authorities forming part of the same consortium may militate against effective collaboration in programme development and service delivery.
- *The existence (or otherwise) of effective mechanisms for joint working:* in localities where joint working between local authorities was already well developed, the development of dispersal appears to have been

implemented in a more collaborative manner, for example in Greater Manchester and the West Midlands.

- *The state of local community relations:* this has been an important influence on the success or otherwise of local dispersal initiatives. Although there is no evidence of a widespread groundswell of racist activity throughout the cluster areas, there are some exceptions to this.

- *The reputation for autonomy and an independent 'municipalist' stance by local authorities:* Liverpool, for example, has arguably constrained its willingness to operate in local partnerships.

- The *insularity* of some statutory agencies that operate within a very narrow or isolationist focus (often sectoral, departmental or organisational) that inhibits the joint working, partnership and coordination necessary to develop and implement public policies, processes and projects.

The variations between regions in terms of NASS operational activity and consortia structure are highly significant factors. In particular, they influence the modes in which refugee communities and RCOs have been incorporated into the formal, institutional arrangements for dispersal and integration.

The relationship between RCOs and the main players in the dispersal arrangements remains ambiguous, at best, in both the West Midlands and the North West. Birmingham City Council, as the lead authority in the West Midlands, has a strong commitment to refugee settlement and integration. This has been translated into a number of initiatives that involve the city council, the main non-governmental organisations (NGOs) and the principal refugee groups in the city. The Birmingham Refugee Network is a prime example of coordinated activity between the council, NGOs in the city and the larger RCOs. From the fieldwork in Birmingham, there are several issues around the impact of dispersal on the settlement of refugees that can be raised. The centralised character of decision making was also perceived as a problem in Birmingham, with the hierarchical model of the National Refugee Integration Forum (NRIF) and subgroups failing to effectively filter down to the regional level. Consultation and strategic coordination across statutory agencies, NGOs, the voluntary sector and RCOs remained in need of improvement according to many sources in Birmingham. For many RCOs, there were also clear issues raised concerning the impact of growing numbers of asylum seekers and the neglect of integration and community development due to increased workloads.

At consortium level, the progress in developing a coherent integration strategy for refugees has been more modest. Although the consortium provides a potential framework for integration work, there are continuing tensions with NASS concerning the aims of the dispersal programme. One of the key aims of dispersal is to deter 'unwanted economic migration', an approach that although differentiating between 'unfounded' and 'genuine' asylum claims, in practice tends to tar all asylum seekers with the same brush. Most significantly, the principle of deterrence promotes a negative framework in which to enact public policies geared to the long-term integration of recognised refugees. One representative of the Midland Refugee Council (MRC) in Birmingham argued that the Home Office "played the business card for internal purposes"; that is, in order to gain legitimacy for the economic goals of its integration strategy within government circles but not in relation to the treatment of public opinion, where a hard-line stance on immigration and asylum was seen as the only electorally viable solution.

These essentially negative conclusions can be balanced by several factors. There is, for example, a growing research base on asylum seekers and refugees in the West Midlands, some of that is focused on labour market integration and the skills base of asylum seekers and refugees in the region (Phillimore and Goodson, 2001). There are also a number of initiatives by Birmingham City Council, the MRC and Refugee Action that aim to promote the integration of refugees in employment and housing in the region. Housing Association Charitable Trust (HACT) is similarly active in the region, promoting integrated approaches to refugee housing (Carter and El-Hassan, 2003). The growth in the number of RCOs in the region and the establishment of the Refugee Resource Centre in Birmingham and comparable initiatives in Coventry, Wolverhampton and smaller areas in the consortium such as Stoke-on-Trent and Walsall also provide solid grounds for future development.

As yet, however, there is little evidence to suggest that the integration policy framework in the West Midlands has begun, in its own terms, to work. If integration occurs (and there is no local research to show how and in what way and over what period of time this happens), it would appear that this takes place through the work of local agencies, including RCOs and through diverse networking practices that depend very much upon the will and energy of the individuals involved. The informal character of these networks in relation to the formally constituted dispersal and settlement arrangements needs to be emphasised. The relative importance of the different kinds of networks in operation, relating in particular to the integration of refugees, is addressed in Chapter Eight of this book. In this context, what is clear is that the development of a coherent regional strategy in the West Midlands would facilitate the process of networking and the pooling of information that is vital to effective refugee settlement. The degree to which this is happening at present is open to question.

The situation in relation to Manchester and Liverpool is considerably more mixed. Differences between asylum teams in local authorities and a lack of clear central direction have impeded the development of integration and settlement strategies for refugees in both cities. The situation here is characterised by a series of ad-hoc initiatives from a variety of voluntary organisations and fora. Liverpool City Council, for example, chairs the Liverpool City Council Refugee Strategic Planning Committee. In interviews, concerns were consistently raised about its effectiveness and the degree to which it includes refugees and RCOs in the decision-making process. In Manchester, by contrast, some significant improvements have been made in preparing the ground for capacity building in refugee communities. The contrasting ethnic composition of the two cities is significant here, with Manchester having a strongly multi-ethnic composition in contrast to the more mono-cultural character of Liverpool. The difficulties encountered in Liverpool in part reflect this different ethnic heritage and the composition of the city's population. Specific examples of local initiatives were noted in the fieldwork that aimed to promote the integration agenda for refugees. In Manchester, for example, Multi-Agency for Refugee Integration in Manchester (MARIM) is currently lobbying the city council to prioritise the issue of refugee integration. Overall, however, the absence of a central coordinating body for these initiatives would appear to be a fundamental problem in the North West. The proliferation of networks and fora in the regions suggest that networking processes are taking place but within an overall environment that lacks centralised strategic control.

In relation to RCOs in both regions, while they are formally part of the consortium arrangements, there was little evidence of them occupying fully integrated roles within the existing structures. Lack of consultation and tokenism in partnership were the negative characteristics noted in both regions. The next part of this chapter elaborates on the position of RCOs in more detail.

The development of RCOs

In the principal cities examined, Manchester and Liverpool have an estimated 40 to 60 RCOs each, while Birmingham has over 30 refugee organisations and a growing number in the neighbouring cities of Coventry and Wolverhampton (Coventry City Council, 2003; Phillimore and Goodson, 2001). In both regions, there has been a rapid growth in the number of RCOs since the introduction of dispersal. The majority of RCOs interviewed in the regions had been established within the last three to four years. In London, by contrast, the sample reflected the settlement of refugees particularly from the 1980s onwards. The majority of RCOs interviewed in London had been established for more than 10 years.

Summarising the main factors affecting refugee settlement in London and the dispersal areas in the regions, the principal points of contrast are:

- *Infrastructure and services*
  Many of the support services needed for effective refugee settlement are located in London and the South East. These include a dense network of statutory, NGO and voluntary groups as well as the bulk of RCOs in the country. These necessarily act as a pull factor for refugees and asylum seekers, for example in the case of requiring legal aid (Harvey, 2001) or specialist health services (Johnson, 2001) that are relatively undeveloped in the regions.
- *Existing community settlement and size of refugee communities*
  The basic contrast between locations in terms of the history of refugee settlement and the size of refugee communities has been drawn out in the fieldwork. It is well established in the literature that pre-existing networks and communities act as significant pull factors for migrants (Breton, 1964). Refugees appear to be no exception to this rule. The broad distinction in the spatial concentration of refugee communities in London and the regions nevertheless conceals significant local variations and diversity in settlement patterns that require further explanation.
- *Policy and administrative centralisation*
  The centralisation of policy formation and administration relating to asylum seekers and refugees is an important contrast between London and the regions. Although dispersal and settlement is effected through the regional consortia these remain restricted in terms of their decision-making capacity. The regional consortia have no independent policy-making function but operate through a system of decentralised control, consultation and 'partnership' with Home Office institutions. The room for manoeuvre of the regional consortia is therefore limited in terms of policy innovation, in

particular as this affects refugee settlement and the provision of services to refugees.

These general points of contrast between London and the regions are subject to a number of qualifications. In particular, dispersal has effected significant developments in the new areas of settlement, in relation to processes of community formation, the formation of networks comprising NGOs, RCOs and statutory authorities and in the emergence of an infrastructure of refugee support mechanisms and institutions in the regions. These issues are further developed in later sections of this chapter. The establishment of increasing numbers of RCOs in the regions and throughout London is one of the most significant changes to have occurred and relates both to the introduction of dispersal and to the more general growth in asylum applications that had taken place throughout the 1990s.

The resource base and organisational issues affecting RCOs

Reviewing the fieldwork results, a limited number of RCOs were selected for interview in each locality, totalling 40 across the three cases. While in no sense representative in a statistical sense, the sample obtained can be regarded as illustrative and indicative of certain general trends and characteristics affecting RCOs. The resource base of RCOs was one of the central issues addressed in the fieldwork and reflects in large part the questions raised by the research objectives. What are the resources available to RCOs and how far do these meet the demands of a rapidly changing policy environment and increasing numbers of asylum seekers? The organisations in the regions were 'small', with funding in most cases well below £50,000 for the current year. Typically they were in the range of £10,000 to £20,000. In some cases in the North West, information was not given concerning the amount of funding that organisations had acquired. In London, by contrast, the sample of RCOs was mainly 'medium'-sized with a funding base between £50,000 and £250,000. The majority were in the region of £100,000, with a few large organisations with budgets in excess of £400,000.

This degree of variation, both between the regions and London and within London itself, suggests that the RCO sector is clearly not homogenous but marked by significant internal differentiation. There are significant inequalities between different-sized RCOs on the one hand, but also between RCOs and other voluntary agencies in addition to the principal NGOs in the field (Zetter and Pearl, 2000). The RCO sector therefore appears to be marked by a high degree of structural instability, with a solid core of established organisations surrounded by an indeterminate periphery of semi-secure and insecure organisations. High turnover of organisations and general volatility appear to be important defining characteristics.

Funding was a fundamental organisational issue. Some of the key themes raised in interviews were:

- the impacts of short-term funding on sustainability;
- increased competition for funding with a shrinking overall amount of money available;
- increased bureaucratisation of funding requirements;
- competition between small RCOs and other, larger agencies and difficulties in providing match funding; for example, under the terms of the European Refugee Fund.

All of the organisations, with the exception of the refugee women's organisations in London that had substantial budgets in excess of £400,000, were affected by these factors to varying degrees. The smaller and more recently established RCOs in the regions were on the whole the most vulnerable to one, or several of these factors in combination.

Staffing levels and the availability of training and the degree of professionalism in organisations were also dependent upon the overall resources available. Some London-based RCOs had significant staffing levels, in excess of eight personnel, while between two and four individuals was more typical. In the regions, with their significantly smaller resource base, a smaller number of staff tended to perform a broad variety of functions. A high turnover of staff also appeared to be endemic to the RCOs sector as a whole. This was either due to volunteers gaining employment or trained staff leaving organisations in order to benefit from the higher salary levels outside the RCO and voluntary sector.

In terms of the services provided by RCOs, these again reflected fundamental differences in the resource base of organisations. On the whole, there was considerably more diversity in the services provided in London than in the regions. The basic activity of most of the organisations was in providing advice and signposting to the statutory authorities. Only a minority of organisations in the different areas were able to offer more specialised services such as health advice in the case of one Department of Health-funded organisation in Birmingham or assistance with education, training and employment, as in the case of several London-based RCOs. On the whole, these facilities were provided by the larger, better-funded organisations that had built up expertise after running projects for several years.

Organisational aims and rationales were also considered in the different locations. In all cases, meeting the needs of refugee communities and filling the gaps in service provision were the main reasons given for the development of organisations. There were, however, some important differences in the interviews between the newer organisations in the regions and the established organisations in London. For the newly emerging organisations in the regions, consolidating a name and organisational procedures, defining their community base and solidifying social capital were overriding concerns. The better-established organisations in London encountered a different set of organisational problems relating to the change from 'grassroots' mobilisation, largely of an informal character in the early days of organisation, to the benefits and penalties of increased bureaucratisation. In some cases, accountability to funders had taken precedence over maintaining contact with the needs of the refugee clients or 'users'. Increased organisational diversification had been one result of an ageing population and the development of the long-term settlement needs of refugee families in London.

Defining RCOs and refugee communities

How RCOs saw their own role and function was one of the central issues explored in the interviews with representatives of refugee organisations. Given the ambiguity surrounding the definition of RCO and the partial incorporation of formally constituted refugee organisations in the dispersal and settlement arrangements, it is important to clarify the understanding and perceptions of refugee organisations themselves. A wide variety of conceptions of refugee organisations emerged in interviews, with some RCOs refusing the category of 'refugee organisation', preferring a more general ethnic conception of membership, or of affiliation to a particular country or region of origin. Linguistic, cultural and religious markers were also routinely used to provide the basis for the establishment of an RCO. In practice, inclusiveness of definition and plurality of organisational forms was the norm, with the provision of services on the basis of ethnicity to refugees and asylum seekers as the defining feature of an 'RCO'. Organisational forms were fluid in nature and varied from 'one-person' shows to complex and sophisticated bureaucratic structures. The term 'RCO', therefore, embraced a variety of informal networks and more formalised, bureaucratic arrangements.

The defining of RCOs was in turn related to the active constitution of source or founding communities: RCOs were substantially responsible for the delineation of community boundaries and characteristics – based as above on a range of ethnic, cultural, geographic and linguistic markers – rather than merely reflecting pre-given social entities. Illustrations were given of this process in both of the regions, notably in relation to Central African and Somali organisations. In both cases, there was significant competition between different factions in the community, based in part upon country of origin factors but also the need to demarcate separate identities and organisational 'missions' in the local policy context. In Birmingham in particular, there was strong evidence from the Central African organisations emerging in the city of incipient competition between the groups as they sought to define themselves alternately in geographical, cultural, or linguistic terms. Competition over the material and symbolic resources offered by RCOs, their facilitating role in relation to the formation of social capital, was suggested as one of the prime factors, alongside meeting the unmet welfare needs of refugee and asylum seekers behind the formation of refugee community organisations. In part the product of weak networking and poor information flows between groups, the local policy and funding environment also generated a tangible need for organisations to compete against one another in order to represent their respective 'communities'. The active role of organisations in constructing the 'public face' of community (Cohen, 1985) was evident throughout the fieldwork and is an important consideration in relation to the broader context of migrant incorporation operating in the UK, a point that we develop further in the conclusions to this book.

While the effort to establish coherent refugee communities and organisations was particularly evident in the regions, by contrast, other aspects of the fracturing and dissolution of nationality-based community organisations were apparent in the case of some of the RCOs interviewed in London. In particular, better-established organisations were often prone to the divisive effects of politicisation in the community. In the case of one Sudanese organisation, political affiliations and authority relations within the organisation neatly replicated those in place in the country of origin. The organisation was effectively treated as a conduit for the appropriation of funds that were channelled according to the political and organisational 'weight' of the individual concerned. That this process was heavily gendered in this particular instance adds an important dimension to the analysis and one that is often overlooked in the literature on RCOs.

Although nationality and ethnicity appear to form the primary organising principles of RCOs, there are important exceptions. In this respect, the relationship of gendered identities to the communal basis of nationality-based organisations can be particularly problematic. The construction of the national imagined identity by diasporic groups often occurs in terms that reinforce or create a 'traditional' version of gender relationships and a specific role for women as the bearers of the nation's honour (Yuval-Davis, 1997). As the keepers of the biological and cultural purity of the nation, women may be assigned a role that sits uneasily alongside the more 'liberal' sexual codes that they encounter in the country of reception. For this reason, the process of defining communities that appears to be central to the process of organisational consolidation, a significant part in this sense of the constitution of social capital in refugee communities, may exhibit a characteristically 'dark side' in relation to the position of women (Portes, 1998). Women – that is, according to whether they conform to the designated ideal of female behaviour – may be either included or excluded from the dominant national paradigm of community organisation and representation. The formation of women-only organisations is a significant development in this context, as it departs from the nationality-based model of refugee organisation in order to proclaim a wider basis of affiliation and allegiance. Multinational, age-based and specialist employment, training or health-related refugee organisations were evident across the three locations. These also provide an important alternative to the nationality-based model of refugee organisation that tends to predominate in the refugee sector (Evelyn Oldfield Unit, 2003a).

Building networks: the broader structural context

The concepts of bridging and linking social capital derived from Putnam were explored in connection with the capacity of refugee groups to forge links across communities and in relation to NGOs and statutory authorities. The importance of networks in terms of information sharing and pooling resources was emphasised time and again in all of the fieldwork locations. This was particularly the case in relation to the newly emerging refugee communities in the regions. Here, there were pronounced difficulties in organising these networks, largely due to resource and time constraints. The peculiar character of these relationships was emphasised in the case of the West Midlands where a discernible RCO–NGO nexus had been established. As in the other fieldwork locations, NGOs had a constitutive role in the formation of RCOs, providing training and assistance and the back-up and know-how involved in setting up organisations. The regulatory and normative character of NGO interventions in assisting and promoting the formation of RCOs is illustrative of the opportunity structures and the forms of migrant incorporation that refugee groups encountered, as we argue further in the conclusions to this book. In some cases, as in the North West, RCOs had opted to build their networks outside the existing channels. Dependence upon own-community resources was, however, necessarily problematic and limited in scope.

The newly emerging organisations interviewed in the regions typically looked to partnerships in order to gain a foothold in the local policy environment. The better-established organisations interviewed in London, on the other hand, reported a variety of experiences in relation to networking practices with both the key NGOs and statutory authorities. Several examples were given of this in the London fieldwork. The case of the RCO development project stands out as particularly illustrative of the power imbalances that affect even the established RCOs in their relations with their strategically more powerful partners. From a refugee community-based initiative that involved the development of important networks between RCOs based in London and the regions, the RCO development project appears to have been absorbed into the organisational agendas of the principal NGOs involved in dispersal. The dependency of RCOs upon Home Office funding, channelled in this case through the NGOs, had set definite limits to their room for manoeuvre and control.

Concerning the broader structural conditions affecting RCOs, our fieldwork in London had suggested that for the practitioners themselves there is a lack of a coherent 'integration framework' to inform their daily practice. Integration activities, conceived in terms of improving refugees' access to services and employment, do not appear to be closely related to policy formulation but occur independently through formal and informal networks of refugees, RCOs, statutory agencies and NGOs. In this respect, there are a number of key issues affecting refugee settlement in London that are raised by the fieldwork and substantiated by a review of the literature:

• the lack of strategic coordination of the different agencies – RCOs, statutory, NGO and voluntary – on a borough basis and across London;
• a failure to record and disseminate good practice across London boroughs;

- the need for improvements in the networking capacity, funding, training, and coordination of RCOs and their 'interface' with statutory authorities;
- the need for adequate, precise information on the numbers of refugees and asylum seekers in particular boroughs to allow advance planning and the provision of services.

These issues have been pinpointed in a number of other contexts (Robinson, 1998a; Zetter and Pearl, 1999) but warrant repetition in the light of current policy interventions. There are of course exceptions, notably in the case of Renewal West London (see www.renewalsrb.org.uk) and the efforts at cross-borough collaboration, but in general the picture in London remains fragmentary and undeveloped.

If the lack of a coherent policy framework acts to impede refugee integration, the broader socioeconomic position of refugees and asylum seekers is also undoubtedly of great importance. The research evidence has consistently suggested that refugees in London and the regions continue to face problems in accessing employment, education, health services and housing (Bloch, 1996, 1999, 2000; Africa Educational Trust, 1998; Audit Commission, 2000a; Sargeant and Forma, 2001; DWP, 2002). The most common obstacles facing refugees and asylum seekers include:

- language barriers;
- waiting lists for ESOL classes;
- lack of recognition for overseas qualifications;
- lack of familiarity with labour markets;
- absence of specialised training routes for professionally qualified refugees;
- lack of interpreters for accessing services;
- specific health needs including mental health needs and gender issues;
- racism and discrimination.

That these obstacles are particularly acute in the case of refugees in comparison with other minority ethnic communities is also borne out by research (Bloch, 2002; Bloch and Atfield, 2002). This is despite the fact that research has clearly established that refugees are often highly educated and qualified in their countries of origin (Bloch, 2002; Carey-Wood et al, 1995).

In terms of the progress of the Home Office national integration strategy for refugees, the NRIF and employment sub-group have worked cross-departmentally with the Department of Work and Pensions (DWP, 2002), for example, in developing an employment strategy for refugees. However, as we noted in Chapter Three of this book, the NRIF occupies an ambiguous position in terms of its own accountability and remit. As we have seen, the regional consortia, including the London Asylum Seekers' Consortium (LASC), provide a potential framework for action in relation to integration. To date, however, the focus appears to have been on the logistical problems of dispersal and the immediate needs of asylum seekers rather than the long-term issues posed by refugee settlement. In particular, lack of data on refugees, their demographic characteristics, location, qualifications and professional skills (Robinson, 1998a; Home Office, 2001) is a significant obstacle to the long-term planning that is vital to an effective integration strategy.

The impacts of dispersal

As we noted in Chapter Three of this book, the existing literature on RCOs and dispersal falls into four broad categories:

- London-based studies have pointed to increased workloads that have occurred as a result of dispersal (Audit Commission, 2000b; Esa Feka, 2001). A general weakness in networking practices and in the ability to access basic infrastructure, funding and services by RCOs, are the dominant themes in the literature.
- Research based in the regions (Stansfield, 2001; Fletcher, 2002) has replicated many of these themes, pinpointing the importance of regional and local features and the recent date of arrival of asylum seekers and refugees. In effect, dispersal has created new refugee communities, often in areas without prior experience of minority ethnic settlement or appropriate services for asylum seekers and refugees.
- The limited comparative research between London and the regions (Gameledin-Ashami et al, 2002) has contrasted the more developed administrative structures of RCOs in London to those that have been newly formed in the regions. The difficulty in forming viable networks in the new dispersal areas is emphasised in comparison to London. Despite these contrasts, RCOs in both London and the regions are believed to exhibit similar structural deficiencies in terms of funding base and organisational sustainability.
- The general commentary on RCOs and dispersal (Zetter and Pearl, 2000) has situated the analysis of RCOs in the context of welfare

restructuring and restrictive asylum policy. According to this perspective, the continued marginalisation of RCOs and the divorce of refugees from established means of community support are two of the most immediate outcomes of dispersal. In relation to asylum seekers, reduced levels of state provision and exacerbated processes of non-integration are the dominant features.

The fieldwork conducted as part of this research has confirmed and reinforced many of these conclusions. Summarising the fieldwork evidence and based upon a critical reading of the literature, it is possible to identify four main clusters, or constellation of factors, that impact upon RCOs in the context of dispersal:

- *The local political and policy context*
  The most significant factors here include the character of the NASS management and the composition of the consortia, in addition to the specific institutional and political history of the region. The outcomes of dispersal for RCOs are heavily dependent upon the political, social, economic and geographical characteristics of the region or locality in question. In this research, the bifurcated political and geographical model in the North West, with control divided between Liverpool and Manchester, contrasts strongly with the more centralised consortium arrangements in the West Midlands with the dominant position of Birmingham in the region. Distinctive political factors are also involved here relating to the degree of coherence of strategic approaches to dispersal. What in particular are the different stances of the consortia towards refugees and the issue of refugee integration? Geographical factors are another vital consideration. For example, the degree to which the regional consortium is spread over a large geographical area that obstructs networking processes and communication between refugees and RCOs, is highly significant (Fletcher, 2002). The distinction between London and the regions in terms of differences in infrastructure, community settlement and policy centralisation has also been noted.

- *The date of establishment of RCOs*
  A fundamental distinction between RCOs in the sample related to their date of establishment. As Zetter and Pearl (2000) have argued, the twin processes of the consolidation of established RCOs and the emergence of newer organisations, often originating in refugee groups with no prior experience of settlement in the UK, are highly characteristic developments. While consolidation was more

commonly noted in the RCOs interviewed in London, due in part to the earlier settlement of refugees there, both processes were evident across the three locations. On the other hand, the emergence of new RCOs was more evident in the regions, given the generally negligible basis of RCO development prior to dispersal. In relation to the established RCOs, it was noted that their organisational rationale had changed over time, from grassroots mobilisation to sustaining a bureaucratic organisation and meeting the requirements of funding and monitoring bodies. The processes of consolidation and emergence also relate to the date of arrival of the refugee group and a range of other factors, including the organisational capacity of the group and its internal coherence, as we argue later in this chapter.

- *The size and funding base of organisations*
  Newer and less-developed RCOs may on the whole be more vulnerable to the changes brought about by dispersal, as they will often lack the resources to adapt to situations of rapid change. Questions of organisational capacity are of fundamental importance. In this respect, it is important to emphasise that the RCO sector is not homogenous but appears to be highly differentiated. The internal differentiation of the RCO sector is important to register, as organisational capacity and funding base affect the ability of an organisation to adopt to changing circumstances and to diversify the services it provides according to changes in its client base. It was evident, for example, that some of the established organisations in London were able to adapt to dispersal by committing themselves to outreach work in the regions. Declining asylum applications and the growth in the asylum seeker and refugee population outside London had prompted a change of approach by these organisations that was in part prompted by ethnic solidarity, in part by a need to diversify activities in order to maintain organisational operations.

- *The character of the refugee community*
  The internal organisation of the community itself is of central importance. What are the processes of fragmentation and competition within a particular refugee group and how are the different bases of identification and belonging – nationality, ethnicity, gender and religious belief – negotiated within the group (McDowell, 1996; Griffiths, 2000, 2002; Kelly, 2003)? Issues of community solidarity and coherence, of fragmentation and competition have been consistently recorded in the fieldwork. In

this context, it is important to note the ways in which factors stemming from the country of origin – existing social and political divisions, for example – are often overlaid and reinforced by the political economy of the local funding environment and the dominant forms of multicultural 'community representation'. Within this cluster of variables affecting the community, we should also consider demographic characteristics, language and educational qualifications, prior experience of organisational activity and the existence of a community of settled co-ethnics, including the establishment of an 'ethnic economy', as important variables impacting on the organisational capacity of a particular group. In practice, the ways in which dispersal has affected refugee communities and RCOs is context specific and will depend upon the complex configuration of these and related variables.

A final consideration, relating to one of our initial research objectives, is the potential conflict between the traditional role of RCOs in assisting the settlement of refugees and the new demands placed upon them as a result of dispersal. In this context, it was evident that the RCOs interviewed in the regions did not have the capacity or resources to respond in other than an ad-hoc and uncoordinated way to the exigencies brought about by dispersal. Increasing numbers of asylum seekers had resulted in increased workloads and strain on organisational capacity. In many cases RCOs reported that they were unable to respond effectively to the needs of asylum seekers in the dispersal areas. Yet, more positively, new organisations had clearly also arisen in response to the changes.

London-based organisations had responded to dispersal in a number of ways. Several of the RCOs interviewed had been involved in the RCO development project that had aimed to provide assistance to RCOs in the regions. Individual initiatives had also been developed, between Tamils in South London and Tamil groups in Liverpool, for example. An Iraqi Kurdish organisation in London had similarly sponsored support and assistance programmes for Kurds in the regions. In a similar vein, the response to other legislative changes – the introduction of section 55 of the 2002 Nationality, Immigration and Asylum Act and the withdrawal of the right to seek permission to work – was marked by disquiet in those organisations interviewed but also a general sense of impotence concerning their ability to respond effectively to the changes. Individuals prohibited from receiving benefits under section 55 cannot be effectively helped by RCOs as this would automatically disentitle them from assistance. In other cases, asylum seekers returning from the regions, in particular when their appeals' procedures had been exhausted, were often supported by community members. Over a period of time, this necessarily placed additional strains on the coping capacity of relatives and friends providing support. Destitution and the inexorable push down into the black market were recorded by RCOs in London and the regions as one of the principal effects of these legislative changes.

The degree to which the support functions traditionally ascribed to RCOs have been affected by dispersal is at present unclear. Many organisations, for example, although working under severely constrained conditions, appear to have an institutional commitment to running particular programmes that aid integration – promoting access to services and limited language, educational and training provision – or in developing new ones. Given the limits upon RCO capacity and the inability in many cases to directly improve the position of asylum seekers and refugees, it is difficult to argue that dispersal in itself, or the restrictive policy environment affecting asylum seekers and refugees, have resulted in the increased marginalisation of RCOs. Marginality for RCOs has rather been a continuous feature, related both to the race relations framework that underpins refugee settlement and to the more general under-resourcing of the voluntary and black and minority ethnic (BME) sectors (McLeod et al, 2001). Moreover, the marginality experienced by RCOs is also subject to significant processes of renegotiation under the dispersal arrangements. While the removal of asylum seekers to areas without community support has been one of the more damaging effects of dispersal, the long-term implications for refugee community formation would appear to be more ambiguous in nature. What is most striking about cities such as Birmingham is the rapidity with that refugee communities are in the process of developing from fragmentary and often diffuse social networks. Weakly developed at present, these emergent networks nevertheless provide the basis for future refugee community formation in the regions.

Conclusions

This chapter has reviewed the comparative fieldwork evidence from our examination of RCOs in London and the regions. Our research objectives were to describe how policy changes are impacting upon RCOs in established areas and the new dispersal regions. In particular, we have been concerned to outline the institutional, organisational and resource constraints affecting RCOs in the context of dispersal.

As we have argued, the outcomes for specific RCOs are dependent upon a number of factors, including their date of establishment, the regional and local context (including the composition and characteristics of the consortium arrangements and their levels of institutional support), the size and diversity of the organisation in question and the internal composition of the refugee community. The fieldwork pointed to some significant divergences between RCOs in London and the regions in relation to funding base, organisational rationale, capacity and size. There were, however, notable common features: in terms of funding restrictions, competition between groups, issues of community representation in the local policy and political context and evidence of asymmetrical relationships in networking with NGOs and the statutory authorities.

While there has been a tendency in the literature to highlight the negative impacts of dispersal upon RCOs, setting this within the context of an erosion of entitlements for asylum seekers and what Gibney (2003) has termed a general 'teleology of restrictionism', our research suggests that this is far from a complete picture. As Gibney (2003) remarks, the converse of the general climate of restrictionism and the assault launched on asylum and refugee rights by nation states has been an enlarged role for due process and the courts in constraining the executive. In parallel terms, there is a marked tension between the policy discourse on the social inclusion of refugees, with its emphasis upon integration and citizenship and the politics of exclusion and restriction underpinning these same policies. It would, therefore, be difficult to argue for an undifferentiated process of social exclusion for refugee communities and RCOs as a result of dispersal, however fraught the process has been for particular groups and individuals. In particular, organisational proliferation in refugee communities and the development of new refugee networks are two of the major by-products of dispersal, which we address at greater length in Chapter Eight.

EIGHT

Conclusions

"If you look at the institutions in Britain, you don't have to look at refugees – look at any sector – how many black people, or how many ethnic people are in positions of power? It's not about the RCOs, it's not about refugees, it's about our society. We do not have the opportunity to manage, it doesn't matter how good you are. If you don't have the right colour, if your accent isn't the one they want.... It's all about that: the discrimination, the racism. It's all about that." (Somali coordinator, London)

Chapter Seven summarised the results of the fieldwork and provided an assessment of the institutional context in the regions; the background to refugee settlement and the development of refugee community organisations (RCOs); and finally, an initial evaluation of the impacts of dispersal upon refugee communities and RCOs. The main factors identified were the variability of the local political and policy context; the date of establishment of RCOs; the size and funding base of organisations; and the character of the refugee community concerned. In this concluding chapter, we approach the fieldwork results from a more theoretical perspective. Our concerns here are with the integrative role of RCOs; the institutional constraints and opportunities for mobilisation affecting refugee communities; and finally, the role of networks, resources and social capital in the formation of refugee organisations. In the concluding part, we address the implications of the analysis for the issues of social cohesion and the broader refugee settlement context in the UK.

The integrative role of RCOs

One of the central concerns in this book has been to raise a series of questions about the role of RCOs in the integration process. The positive role of RCOs for the integration of refugees is a dominant assumption in the literature, but one that is more often asserted than fully demonstrated. On one level, there is indeed strong evidence in the literature to suggest that RCOs make a vital contribution in meeting the welfare needs of their communities. They can also, in some cases, provide training and routes into paid employment. By assisting asylum seekers and refugees to understand the welfare system they are also acting, in a sense, to integrate them into the patterned relationships of the receiving society. These arguments have a general validity. What is problematic in many of these accounts is the lack of precision over the term 'integration', that is very often used to describe the process of settlement; that is, 'getting used to' the new environment, or forms of individual adaptation among refugees. Integration, conceived as a long-term, two-way process between refugees and the receiving society (Castles et al, 2003) that occurs in a number of different social, economic and political arenas, is not on the whole a central factor in these accounts.

While an intensive spate of research at the European and national levels has begun to address the question of refugee integration in some detail (ECRE, 1998, 1999, 2000; Robinson, 1998a; Penninx, 1999, 2000), there is both continuing terminological confusion and a protracted policy debate around the best ways to measure integration (Valtonen, 1999). The understanding of integration as a long-term, complex, and two-way process between the refugee and the receiving society, is nevertheless now generally accepted by academics, non-governmental organisations (NGOs) and refugee organisations working in the field. At the policy level, however, 'hard', quantifiable measures in terms of employment and training tend to be favoured over more qualitative 'soft' indicators such as the sense of well-being and inclusion experienced by refugees. As documented in previous chapters of this book, a largely instrumental approach to refugee integration predominates in the policy field, with the result that refugee perceptions and evaluations of integration tend to be under-valued. The Home Office draft document, *Integration matters* (Home Office, 2004), deploys an essentially pragmatic understanding of integration as the fulfilment of the potential of refugees, the promotion of access to services and the ability to participate fully in society. The emphasis is moreover very much upon 'swift' integration and the acquisition of citizenship, rather than any lengthy process of negotiation and dialogue between refugees and the 'host society'.

As we have indicated, the literature appears to be strong on assertion but often weak in terms of providing demonstrable evidence on the long-term, integrative role of RCOs. In this respect, Gameledin-Ashami et al (2002, p 42) have distinguished between the settlement functions of RCOs, including the satisfaction of basic needs and the opportunity to associate with co-ethnics, in contrast to the potential role of RCOs in promoting the integration of refugees into mainstream social relations. In particular, the authors have convincingly noted that RCOs at present simply do not have the resources that would enable them to contribute to the long-term integration of refugees. Their current role is essentially 'defensive' – filling gaps in services, providing a basis for association and meeting essential needs – rather than being actively engaged in the development of individual and community resources. As in the sample used in this research, only a minority of RCOs interviewed by Gameledin-Ashami et al had the resources to run the education, training and employment programmes that would promote long-term integration into the labour market, for example. In this respect, it is worth pointing out that Gameledin-Ashami et al's sample of 22 London-based RCOs is small and necessarily limited in scope. It is certainly difficult to generalise conclusively from this sample in the way that the authors are perhaps inclined to do. As in relation to the present study, it can be argued that more large-scale, quantitative research is required in order to draw firmer conclusions in relation to the organisational capacity and characteristics of RCOs. Despite these drawbacks, what their argument does suggest is that a more critical interpretation of the role of RCOs is necessary and in particular that there is a need to take into account the broader structural framework affecting the mobilisation and organisation of refugee communities.

There are additional reasons that cast further doubt on the privileged role that RCOs have come to assume in the literature. The fieldwork had suggested that there was an important distinction between formal and informal networking in refugee communities. There was, for example, a notable resistance on the part of specific refugee groups to formalising networks. Not wishing to be part of formal channels or to participate in the funding-driven political economy of refugee organisation were the primary reasons given. As Rex (1987) had long ago pointed out, formal organisations are only one part of a larger picture that includes a vast network of informal, transient, unnamed and unofficial forms of social organisation. One Sudanese community activist who had worked with RCOs in London in capacity building for several years remarked of a community organisation in London, that there were several groups who held meetings at the centre who were not affiliated to the organisation. As he argued:

> "For example, me and a friend we started doing these public talks.... I think that's a Sudanese community organisation ...

> but we didn't want an address for it….I do it, or a friend does it….We said, 'Don't even give it a name'."

In this particular case, giving a name to an activity would have had immediate political connotations by labelling the activity in a certain way, which the individual concerned wanted to avoid. By maintaining activities at an informal level, politicisation and factionalism in the community could be avoided. Rather than one organisation 'speaking for' the community, a multiplicity of 'communal options' was opened up through the operation of informal networks. In this context, the degree to which formally constituted RCOs are at the centre of refugee networks or peripheral to the main sources of community activity is a vital empirical question. Korac (2001), contrasting the cases of Italy and the Netherlands, has argued that informal networks and the ability to participate freely in the social life of the receiving society – freedom of movement, access to employment and the ability to mix with members of the receiving society – may be more effective in promoting integration than state-directed programmes, or other formal community-based organisational means. Critics of dispersal, for example, point to the ways in which it has had the effect of by-passing networks and the processes of ethnic community formation that appear to be vital to effective refugee settlement (Robinson et al, 2003). It is precisely the elements of freedom of choice in relation to settlement location and the right to work that have been withdrawn under the dispersal programmes initiated by a spectrum of European Union (EU) member states (Pfohman and Amrute, 2004). The move towards an accommodation centre model of reception in the EU, where facilities are provided in situ to asylum seekers while their claims are processed, may have the effect of attenuating the social contact with the receiving society that is essential to long-term integration.

In the current context, what we cannot assume is that RCOs are automatically the hub of refugee community activity and the prime movers in fostering integration in community members. As several respondents indicated in the fieldwork, RCOs may be said to work at the periphery of their communities rather than at the centre. In addition, RCOs may perpetuate marginality through a needs-based approach to service provision, including the mutual adaptation between RCOs and the statutory authorities (and here we should include the key NGOs) in reproducing this system. Far from being central to the integration of refugees, RCOs may on the contrary perpetuate marginality from within their designated roles as service providers on the edges of their communities.

It can be further questioned whether the designation of RCO itself militates against acceptance within the so-called 'mainstream'. Tomlinson and Egan (2002, p 1038), for example, have argued that the discourse of community seems most often used for those "groups and categories located on the 'margin' or 'outside'." There may, therefore, be a core conflict between participation in RCOs and acceptance within official networks and social relations. On the other hand, as the fieldwork evidence suggests, while several of the newly developing organisations in the regions chose to organise outside recognised channels, the possibilities for doing so were limited and heavily dependent on the viability of own-community resources.

There is, on the other hand, anecdotal evidence from several of the fieldwork locations that informal economic networks among Somalis have been instrumental in promoting business activity in specific areas of Birmingham and London. This is based around a proliferating number of internet cafes, the *hawilad* system of transfer of remittances to Somalia, and a variety of small shops and restaurants. The *hawilad* system and its role in economic reconstruction in Somalia have been investigated by de Monclos (2000). Individuals come together in cities in the UK to pool resources and typically set up businesses on a joint basis. The part of the Stratford Road in Birmingham that is nearest to the city centre has been transformed from a run-down area, once Irish and then Asian-dominated, to a bustling centre of Somali business activity. Currently small scale and subject to rapid turnover in ownership, the potential of this business activity for the economic integration of refugees may be equal if not greater to that offered by service provision through RCOs, or by using RCOs themselves as a form of self-employment. While self-employment may not be a viable alternative to the need to mainstream economic opportunities for refugees, the development of training programmes for refugee self-employment is now widely practised (Refugee Council, 2004). The structural obstacles to refugee employment noted in the previous chapter (Bloch, 2002) suggest that self-employment and the development of small businesses may be important, alternative ways to promote the economic integration of refugees.

We can conclude that the integrative benefits of participation in RCOs and the services provided by them in comparison to other forms of networking, such as the economic activity outlined earlier, is in need of further examination. While it is clear that RCOs provide vital welfare services it is not clear how far they act to promote the long-term integration of refugees. RCOs may play a part in the integration of refugees but this is quite likely not as central as is commonly assumed in the literature.

Opportunity structures and modes of migrant incorporation

The discussion has already anticipated the role of opportunity structures and forms of migrant incorporation that was another of the theoretical themes raised at the outset of the research. Opportunity structures had been defined as institutional settings that define the parameters for effective political mobilisation. They have a normative and regulatory character in setting the boundaries of what is permissible and possible. The term 'incorporation' was borrowed from Soysal (1994) to describe the ways in which the membership model of a receiving state influences how migrants are enabled to participate in the new social setting. For Soysal, 'incorporation' goes beyond the question of the integration of the individual, to investigate the modes in which the state 'handles' its outsiders. What are the terms on which they are allowed to participate in the social, economic and political spheres of the receiving state? The basic assumption is that the 'terms' set the limits to migrant activity and mobilisation, with direct results for the specific organisational forms they adopt. Soysal's use of incorporation is also to be distinguished from Portes and Rumbaut's (1990) notion of 'modes of incorporation', which refers to the complex formed by the policies of the host government, the values and prejudices of the receiving society, and the characteristics of the co-ethnic community. Portes and Rumbaut use this to develop a typology of different 'assimilation' outcomes for ethnic groups depending on the specific configuration of these variables. This concept is closely linked to that of 'segmented assimilation' that has come to dominate migration discourse in the North American context.

A large part of the discussion has been concerned with describing how the dominant form of migrant incorporation, predicated upon the race relations framework, impacts upon the organisational activities of refugee groups. Depending on the degree of organisational coherence and the motivations of the different actors involved in the regional consortia, it was suggested that the statutory authorities and NGOs involved in the dispersal process actively foster the development of RCOs as the legitimate channel for refugee organisation and representation. In practice, however, there is considerable variation in terms of outcomes across the different regions. As in the context of the race relations framework more generally, there is a wide gulf between policy prescription, based upon community representation, integration and equal opportunities and the actual outcomes for specific ethnic groups. In this respect, we have argued that the integrative role of RCOs is more often assumed than carefully examined in the ethnic relations and policy literature. There are, on the contrary, clear indications that the impediments affecting RCOs are rooted in the broader structural inequalities that continue to hamper minority ethnic communities in Britain (McLeod et al, 2001).

Rather than treat RCOs as a naturally occurring part of the policy landscape, as is typically the case in the literature, it is necessary to contextualise the role and function of RCOs by using a comparative framework. Gold (1992), for example, has suggested that the centralised refugee resettlement model in the US actively inhibits the development of RCOs and refugee communities. As indicated in Chapter Two of this book, Wahlbeck's (1997) comparative study of Kurds in Finland and the UK had contrasted the negative impact of a largely assimilationist model in Finland upon refugee community formation and the development of RCOs, in comparison to the process of organisational proliferation in refugee communities that had appeared to result from the multicultural model prevalent in the UK.

Organisational proliferation in refugee communities in the UK may be less a case of 'vibrancy' in civil society (as suggested in Putnam's analysis) than of the efficacy of state-sponsored forms of migrant incorporation and the limited options open to refugees to participate on an equal footing in other social spheres. In this case, is organisational proliferation a positive or negative development? The ethnic relations literature is again instructive here. Werbner (1991), drawing on the theory of urban movements, and referring to the post-war migrants from the Caribbean and South Asia, points to a three-stage process of mobilisation in migrant communities, from associational empowerment, to ideological convergence and finally mobilisation. The first stage is marked by associational proliferation and the competition for state-allocated resources. Local-level processes of segmentation, and the accentuation of class and ideological differences within ethnic communities are the defining feature of this first stage. Are refugee communities similarly at a 'first stage' in their organisational development or do differences in size, demographic composition, legal status and the character of forced migration, draw a firm dividing line between the broader category of migrants and refugees? Future trends in asylum applications and refugee settlement patterns in Britain will allow a clearer picture to emerge. For Werbner, the stage of organisational proliferation and competition for state-allocated resources is by no means entirely negative, as it opens up new channels for ethnic mobilisation and advancement. Similarly, the partial incorporation of refugee organisations in the dispersal arrangements (however asymmetric these relations may be) also increases the potential of refugee groups to develop networks and organisational forms that more accurately reflect their emerging needs and interests.

Networks, resources and social capital

Turning to the question of networks, it would appear that the effectiveness of any emerging organisational forms in refugee communities depends upon the character of the networks and the relations between the actors involved in those networks. As the fieldwork component of the research indicated, the networks formed by RCOs in relation to statutory authorities and NGOs were often characterised by imbalances in the decision-making capacity of agents and by the more general agenda setting inherent in the institutional arrangements. In addition to linking people, therefore, it is clear that the operation of networks also involves the circulation of resources and power (Vertovec, 2001, p 9). The notion of resources has indeed been central to this research. Often used in a descriptive sense to refer to the financial assets of organisations, the meaning of the term embraces a variety of factors including the material and symbolic rewards derived from participation in networks (Lin, 2001, p 29), most notably in this context, refugee community organisations. Drawing upon resource mobilisation theory (Drury, 1994, pp 19-20), it has been noted that the skills and capacities of particular groups, including their degree of internal coherence, can also be considered as significant resources that may affect the groups' capacity to develop effective community organisations. Al-Ali et al (2001) similarly underline the importance of community resources in relation to the comparative transnational organisation of Bosnian and Eritrean refugees. In the fieldwork chapters of this book, the case of the Somalis was used to illustrate the organisational proliferation and competition that appeared to stem from the politics of an internally divided community. The issue of resources is also inherent in the possession, direction and allocation of funding streams and the superior organisational capacity, expertise and technical knowledge of the large NGOs and Home Office institutions in their relationship with the (on the whole) weaker RCO sector (Zetter and Pearl, 2000). Conflict over resource allocation would appear to be endemic to the operation of RCOs and also to their relations with the other agencies involved in the refugee field.

The term 'social capital' has also been used in a critical vein to describe the material and symbolic benefits deriving from participation in networks and RCOs in particular. One of the questions raised in Chapter Two concerned the relative strengths and weaknesses of Putnam's conception of social capital, in contrast to Bourdieu's, for example. The concepts of bridging and linking social capital derived from Putnam (the latter aiming to account for the question of power) were utilised in an instrumental fashion in this book. Arguably, however, Putnam's perspective as a whole suffers from a weak understanding of institutional constraints and the corrosive effects of structured inequalities. While this is by no means to advocate an analysis based solely upon Bourdieu, it is important to acknowledge, as we have emphasised throughout this book, the conflictual fields and differential power relations affecting refugee organisations. The broader geopolitical context is relevant here. As Harriss (2002) has noted at length, the current vogue for the concept of social capital, in the variants derived from Putnam in particular, lies in its very flexibility and in its suggestive, metaphoric character. It chimes in comfortably with neoliberal concerns to constrain welfare provision and to increase processes of self-reliance and 'participation' in civil society.

As Molyneux (2001) has further argued, social capital is in the process of emerging as the new development paradigm, building on and in some cases replacing the earlier participatory model of development. Notions of participation and partnership, as we underlined in Chapter Three, are at the heart of the community development models commonly utilised by the state and para-state institutions involved in the dispersal process. In this context, participatory development had aimed to increase the control of marginalised groups and individuals over the decision-making process that affected their lives (Cooke and Kothari, 2001, p 5). Posited upon a 'grassroots' approach to development, the participatory paradigm has been subject to an increasingly widespread critique. The re-evaluation of participatory development models points to several interconnected shortcomings, relating in particular to a dependence upon simplistic notions of 'community' and the erasure of internal differentiation and power relations within social groupings. From this perspective, the incorporation of participatory models within a generally managerial approach to development has had negative, long-term implications. In effect, for many commentators, the rhetoric of participation now "masks continued centralisation in the name of decentralisation" (Cooke and

Kothari, 2001, p 7). Similarly, Cleaver (2001) has cogently argued that erstwhile radical notions of empowerment rooted in Freirian politics have been gradually de-politicised and individualised as a result of their absorption within the policy sphere. More generally, interlocked concepts such as social inclusion, citizenship, community and democracy have been incorporated within the broader discourses of participation and partnership that are now dominant within the public policy domain.

It is particularly significant in this context that discourses of participation are closely related to an emphasis on institutional analysis. As Cleaver argues, referring here to the concept of social capital (2001, p 40):

> Associations, committees and contracts channel partici-
> pation in predictable and recognisable ways.... Ideas about
> social capital and civil society are also strongly
> institutionalist, although often vague. Visible, often formal,
> manifestations of association are attributed normative value,
> denoting initiative ... as well as allegedly facilitating vibrant
> economic activity.

Recalling here our earlier observations on the significance of informal networks in refugee communities, the deficiencies of the participatory approach and more significantly that of social capital include the following factors:

- *An over-emphasis on formal organisations to the expense of informal networks.* Formal organisation is assumed to be more accountable and transparent than informal networks, although the latter may be more significant for the maintenance of support mechanisms in a community.
- As Cleaver argues (2001, p 45), *participation in committees or organisations is no guarantee of broader participation by the community.* In this respect, socially embedded institutions carry on despite of, or in addition to, more formal arrangements.
- There is *an over-reliance on 'solidarity models' of community* rather than recognising the overlapping and diverse forms of social networking based upon family, religion, locality and other factors.
- *A tendency to play down the role of structural constraints.* As Cleaver has noted (2001, p 46), although there is a strong assumption that communities only require sufficient mobilisation to achieve their aims, "Even where a community appears well motivated, dynamic

and well organised, severe limitations are presented by an inadequacy of material resources, by the very structural constraints that impede the functioning of community-based initiatives".

• *The assumption of cultural foundationalism*, with communities rooted in and expressing their own unique 'cultural identities', or what Gerd Bauman (1997) has called the 'dominant discourse of culture'. Communities on the contrary are diverse and contain conflicting interpretations of identity and belonging, many of which cross both territorial and cultural boundaries.

A reassessment of the discourse of participation is therefore necessary according to Cooke and Kothari (2001). Henkel and Stirrat (2001), for example, argue that participatory approaches share the same goal as more top-down development approaches, to 'change hearts and minds', to 'make people modern'. For development agencies, the advantage of participatory models is to make 'participating individuals' responsible for their own fates, thereby avoiding development workers' responsibility for the outcomes of projects. Many of these critical points apply with equal force to the current usage of social capital as an explanatory catch-all and panacea for community development in socially marginalised groups, including refugees (Johnston and Percy-Smith, 2003). As we have seen, the emphasis on formal organisation in refugee communities, simplistic notions of community and the neglect of structurally embedded inequalities, are dominant features in the literature on RCOs and are also key determinants of the policy and practice of refugee settlement in the UK.

To summarise the argument, first, we have argued that the state context of migrant incorporation provides the framework within which refugees are allowed and encouraged to organise. The state level is therefore one of the preconditions of the 'efflorescence' of associational activity that produces social capital, rather than simply its outcome as appears to be assumed in Putnam (Serra, 1999). The operation of state power (exercised through a variety of agencies) is in this sense both productive and directive. The parallel with Foucauldian notions of power, as inscribed in discursive and institutional practices, is important. The state, through the operation of NGOs and the considerable history of devolution to partner agencies in the reception and settlement of refugees, sets the parameters within which refugee groups may legitimately organise to represent their interests.

This general framework recalls the earlier discussion of welfare state restructuring in Chapter Three, where we had referred to the development of a new type of governmentality in relation to public policy. As we had noted concerning the new institutional arrangements for the reception and settlement of asylum seekers and refugees, 'partnership' and 'participation' aim towards the transformation of 'hard-to-reach' groups such as refugees, into "compliant collaborators in creating a more inclusive society" (Ling, 2000, p 90). In practice, however, there is no tight fit between policy prescription and outcome. Many refugee communities appear to operate outside the parameters set by the dominant forms of migrant representation, while the organisational proliferation brought about by dispersal may itself result in new or emerging organisational forms that more closely mirror the changing needs and interests that are developing within refugee communities. While dispersal has partially disrupted the networks that would be formed by allowing asylum seekers freedom of movement – the dispersal of asylum seekers to areas where there are no existing refugee communities is a particularly damaging illustration of this process – it has also created new opportunities for the development of refugee communities in the regions. Many of these, as we have noted, have been set up from scratch, or with only fragmentary networks in operation in particular localities. The secondary movement of refugees, who currently enjoy freedom of movement, adds to the counter-pressures that refugees are able to exercise in relation to centrally formulated dispersal policies. Rather than being simply repressive and prohibitive, the introduction of dispersal has set in train a series of events and processes, which to some degree evade attempts at centralised managerial control.

In the second case, we have noted that the encounter with blocked opportunities in the labour market and the deficiencies of public service provision are two of the primary spurs to the formation of RCOs in refugee communities. Counter to the romanticism of Putnam's perspective, the formation of social capital in refugee communities is a product of crisis and social breakdown. As Molyneux (2001) has suggested, recourse to social networks occurs typically as a 'coping strategy' in situations of social collapse. The analysis of social capital in refugee communities should not therefore seek to celebrate and reinforce what arises, in large part, from desperation. Again, the broader institutional and structural level needs to be brought back into focus. As Molyneux (2001, p 34) has argued:

> Social capital in the form of networks and associational activity can be an important resource in tackling poverty and social disintegration and in assisting in the effective delivery of social welfare. But it is no substitute for policies

designed to achieve a more socially integrated society through redistributive measures and sound economic policies....

Concerning this broader policy framework, the themes of social cohesion and integration have come to occupy centre stage in debates on immigration and asylum in the UK. This is evident in the 2002 White Paper, *Secure borders, safe haven: Integration with diversity in modern Britain* (Home Office, 2002a), in the development of the Home Office national refugee integration strategy and in a number of related policy documents. In general, there has been an increased emphasis upon the significance of citizenship in government discourse. A single theme in particular – that of social cohesion – has now come to dominate the policy field. In the concluding section of this chapter, we address the relevance of social cohesion to the current issues affecting RCOs and refugee communities and set this within the context of the broader immigration debate in the UK.

Social cohesion, immigration and refugee integration

Social cohesion is a relatively novel addition to the constellation of policy terms. But what precisely is social cohesion and why has it assumed such heightened political saliency? Turning first to the question of definitions, it is useful to return here to the initial discussion on the integrative role of migrant associations, as this was outlined in Chapter Two. A pressing concern with the sources of social cohesion is common among those writing within the classic sociological tradition. Durkheim's (1933) distinction between mechanical and organic solidarity contrasted social cohesion resulting from shared values – mechanical solidarity in the case of small-scale and structurally simple societies – to the 'organic' cohesion stemming from the interdependence and individualism that characterises complex societies. Tonnies (1955) distinguished between the different types of social cohesion based upon *Gemeinschaft* and *Gesellschaft*: commonality of social bonds based upon family and peers in contrast to cohesion based upon impersonal associations. Finally, Parsons (1971), writing from the standpoint of mid-20th century functionalist sociology, accounted for social cohesion in terms of normative integration: the internalisation and institutionalisation of norms and values are here the basis of social cohesion. As Vertovec (1997) has noted, two contrasting conceptions of social cohesion are in operation, particularly in Durkheim and Tonnies, where romantic communitarianism is positioned against 'hetorogeneous' cohesion based upon difference. In relation to the latter, complexity, specialisation, differentiation, reciprocity and interdependence are the key terms. Policy debates seldom reflect these more nuanced understandings of social cohesion. Indeed, there is a strong tendency to refer to an imagined state of monocultural social cohesion, rather than the more complex notion of reciprocity and structural interdependence that characterises modern societies (Pahl, 1991).

Further clarifying the concept of social cohesion, Woolley (1998) has noted that different and co-existing conceptions of the term are commonly in operation. In the first place, social cohesion can be defined both in terms of process (building shared values) and outcome (reducing inequalities). Added to this basic distinction, the concept of social cohesion can be further subdivided:

(1) *Cohesion as inclusion:* not being excluded from the dominant types of social and economic activity.
(2) *Cohesion as interaction:* Elster (1989) in common with Putnam, argues that there is an important connection between interaction and social cohesion. Voluntary activities and engagement in associations in particular create and cement relations of trust.
(3) *Cohesion as shared values:* social solidarity resulting from shared values, cultural norms and so on.
(4) *Associationalism* is another way of conceptualising social cohesion. In this context, social cohesion is regarded as resulting from membership in a number of unrelated 'clubs' – ethnic, religious, leisure pursuits and so on – that constitute the diverse range of activities in civil society.

If social cohesion appears to suffer from a terminological confusion similar to that of social capital (and with a similar principle of selectivity in relation to the notion of social cohesion we choose to adopt), then the question remains concerning its current popularity and political significance. In this context, it is important to differentiate between the general and the more immediate factors underlying the high profile of social cohesion in the policy arena. In general terms, as Vertovec (1997) has noted, the current significance of social cohesion stems from real or perceived threats resulting from economic and political restructuring and the erosion of the nation state, from either supranational or sub-national factors. Berris (1995) further elaborates on the concept of social cohesion and its application in different economic, social and political contexts. In her view, there are multiple social crises or threats in operation, ranging from the nation-state level and the undermining of welfare provision, to the growth in global poverty and social exclusion. In this broader geo-political context, immigration and the transnational movement of peoples more generally, are often singled out as the most important obstacles to social cohesion. In particular, international migration is believed to endanger the assumed bases of social solidarity in likeness and commonly accepted norms. It is also thought to weaken the integrity of the nation state in cultural and economic terms, by promoting cultural plurality and by placing burdens upon welfare spending and domestic labour markets.

In UK policy discourse, in contrast to Canada and some of the Scandinavian countries, an explicit concern with the issue of social cohesion has been late in developing. A general preoccupation with 'community', on the other hand, has been a mainstay of the communitarianism of the Third Way (Giddens, 1998) and the moralisation of political discourse that is characteristic of the New Labour policy agenda. As Maile and Braddon argue (2003, p 128), it is necessary to differentiate between the critical strand of communitarianism commonly associated with MacIntyre (1990), for example, and the 'emotive' form of communitarianism advocated by the sociologist Anthony Giddens. While in the former perspective, individuals are socially embedded within historically constituted communities, in the latter case communities merely form the backdrop to "abstracted notions of individual choice in the pursuit of free-floating and therefore quite arbitrary 'lifestyle practices' " (Maile and Braddon, 2003, p 127). In the context of the social fragmentation brought about by globalisation and economic restructuring, the overriding goal of social policy now appears to lie in promoting individual choice in a variety of markets, while laying the foundations for the *re-creation* of viable, cohesive communities.

The immediate backdrop to the increased saliency of social cohesion in the UK policy agenda is the heritage of post-war immigration and the dramatic rise in asylum applications that had occurred throughout the 1990s. The evidence on the post-war settlement of migrants has consistently suggested both the limitations of formal, legal equality and of the race relations framework more generally. In particular, there are continuing tensions between the equality enshrined in race relations legislation and the evidence of discrimination and inequality that pervades most aspects of public life, for at least significant sections of the minority ethnic population in Britain. The increasingly restrictive policy environment and the marginality experienced by the growing numbers of asylum seekers arriving during the 1990s have only added to this general picture of exclusion and discrimination. The emergence of what are perceived as forms of ethnic separatism, particularly among the South Asian community, and sporadic rioting in the major areas of urban settlement in Northern England, have led to official concerns about a growing 'parallel society'. In particular, it is the failure of 'Muslim youth' to fully integrate into British society that appears to have created the highest levels of official concern.

A series of policy documents has addressed the question of social cohesion directly. The 2002 White Paper *Secure borders, safe haven* (Home Office, 2002a, p 10) notes that "last summer's disturbances in Bradford, Oldham and Burnley painted a vivid picture of fractured and divided communities, lacking a sense of common values or shared civic identity to unite around". It is in this context that the need to "rebuild a sense of common citizenship" is affirmed as a key political and policy priority. This includes the cultivation of a sense of 'active citizenship' in both 'working-class communities' and those entering the country as immigrants. The White Paper reinforces recognition of multiculturalism and diversity, while arguing for the need for language training and education for citizenship. Although addressed in general terms in the White Paper, changes in citizenship are central to the 2002 Nationality, Immigration and Asylum Act. A citizenship 'test' (in English language and citizenship) is to be reinforced by a ceremony celebrating the acquisition of citizenship. The overall aim of the test is to promote "individuals' economic and social integration" (Home Office, 2002a, p 11). The assumption of an underlying 'Britishness' to which newcomers will have to adapt, clearly informs policy making in relation to citizenship norms. At the same time, however, there is also a formal commitment to promoting cultural diversity and multiculturalism (Favell, 1999). As Castles (1995) has noted, in key respects, the British mode of migrant incorporation appears to be an uneasy halfway house between assimilationism and multiculturalism.

In common with the 2002 White Paper and the Nationality, Immigration and Asylum Act, the Cantle Report (Cantle, 2001), commissioned by the Home Secretary in the aftermath of the riots in Oldham and Burnley in 2001, takes as its starting point the question of ethnic separatism in British cities. The conception of social cohesion used in this report refers, in particular, to the importance of cross-cultural communication and respect for cultural diversity. In terms of practical recommendations, it suggests that local community cohesion plans should be set in operation, involving community leaders at a variety of levels. Cantle advocates the use of regeneration programmes and cohesion activities throughout the education system and most especially in relation to promoting cross-cultural understanding in young people. Lynch (2001), in an appendix to the Cantle Report, bases her evaluation of the concept of social cohesion on the North American literature, especially from the Canadian Social Cohesion Network (Government of Canada, 1996). In line with the general tenor of the report, she proposes a limited conception of social cohesion in terms of shared values, trust and equality of opportunity for all members of society.

Another related policy document, *Building cohesive communities: A report of the ministerial group on public order and community cohesion* (Denham, 2001), or the Denham Report, repeats many of the themes developed in Cantle. In particular, there are the consistently raised issues of separatism and the growth of parallel worlds, the need for inclusive citizenship and the promotion of dialogue and understanding between communities. Above all, 'segregation, along racial lines', is identified as a growing problem. Finally, the Crick Report (Home Office, 2003b), entitled *The new and the old: The report of the 'Life in the United Kingdom' Advisory Group*, has as among its main goals the widening of citizenship, the encouragement of community cohesion and the valuing of cultural diversity. The aims of the citizenship test and ceremony are further outlined and described in this report. Their aim, according to Crick, is to promote a core set of British values while acknowledging the importance of cultural diversity. Crick further proposes a programme of studies relating to citizenship and underlines the importance of English language acquisition to full citizenship. With the Crick Report, the current debate on social cohesion returns full circle to the 1960s and Roy Jenkins' original pronouncements on the nature of integration, "not as a flattening process of assimilation, but as an equal opportunity, accompanied by cultural diversity in an atmosphere of mutual tolerance" (quoted in Home Office, 2003b, p 12).

Surveying the policy literature, there is therefore a general consensus across a range of reports that a lack of shared values and the 'fragmentation and polarisation of communities' are the main impediments to social cohesion. As the Denham Report (Denham, 2001, p 13) concludes, "we cannot claim to be a truly multi-cultural society if the various communities within it live, as Cantle puts it, a series of parallel lives that do not touch at any point".

How, in practice, is social cohesion to be achieved? In common with the literature on social capital, a dominant theme in the policy documents on social cohesion concerns the importance of participation in voluntary associations. According to Lynch (2001), for example, volunteering can be seen as a means of increasing social cohesion by encouraging communication across community boundaries. Volunteering is a part of social capital, which in turn promotes social cohesion. As we have seen, Woolley (1998), in common with Putnam, argues that associationalism, or voluntary interaction across social boundaries, is one of the principle indicators of social cohesion. In Woolley's (1998, p 8) terms, "voluntary activity promotes social cohesion by making society work better through provision of personal and public goods, and by providing charity to the marginalised, thereby preventing social exclusion". The key question that she raises is whether the prevalence of volunteering, instead of directly indicating the presence of social cohesion and solidarity, rather reflects a deficiency in the level of support provided through the state. In this context it may be useful to recall Molyneux's (2001) suggestion that the recourse to voluntary networks and associations is an effect of social breakdown and crisis, rather than to automatically idealise the 'coping strategies' of the poor.

Despite these ambiguities concerning the role of participation in voluntary networks, there is an important economic basis to the role assigned to the voluntary sector in government policy. As HM Treasury (2002, p 5) notes, voluntary and community organisations (VCOs) "are often uniquely placed to reach marginalised groups and enable individuals to participate actively in their local communities". There is, moreover, a high degree of untapped 'added value' in the sector, involving the provision of specialised services, cost effectiveness, flexibility and innovation, advocacy and citizen participation. In sum, VCOs provide specialist knowledge, sensitive working practices, independence from the state, and flexible working conditions, all at a fraction of the cost of more professional, mainstream service provision.

Turning to the case of RCOs, can the prevalence of voluntary organisations in refugee communities be said to reflect or indeed promote a high degree of social cohesion? In this respect our research has indicated a number of significant tensions and contradictions. We have argued that the mode of migrant incorporation and the experience of discrimination in service provision and in the labour market are the primary determinants explaining organisational proliferation in refugee communities. We have suggested that participation in RCOs, although often assumed to be highly integrative in the literature, may on the contrary reinforce a condition of institutionalised marginality: it is difficult for refugees to evade or circumvent it. As Tomlinson and Egan (2002, p 1027) have argued, refugees are subject to competing discourses in government policy, as either "helpless and incompetent" (referring on the whole to asylum seekers) or "active and empowered" (that is, generally applied to recognised refugees). While the change in policy towards a participatory model of community development and empowerment in refugee communities may appear to be positive, it carries with it the continued likelihood of marginalisation for refugees, who continue to belong 'outside the mainstream'. The discourse of 'community', as Tomlinson and Egan (2002, p 1038) note, "seems most often used to characterise groups and categories located on the 'margin' or 'outside'". The main issue is the degree to which the retention of a distinctive 'refugee identity' is advantageous, or helps to perpetuate marginality (Zetter, 1991). For the authors, a more nuanced approach is necessary, whereby RCOs adopt a "genuinely intermediary rather than marginal" position, strengthening the identity of refugee communities while challenging the resistance of "groups and institutions within the so-called 'mainstream'" (Tomlinson and Egan, 2002, p 1041).

In relation to refugee communities, there is evidently a balance to be struck between promoting independent organisation without, at the same time, reinforcing the marginality of refugee-specific initiatives. One possibility increasingly advocated by NGOs and the Home Office is the mainstreaming of provision for refugees (Evelyn Oldfield Unit, 2003a, 2003b; Home Office, 2004; Refugee Council, 2004). Within this perspective, there is a renewed role for the state in mainstreaming provision for refugees, in particular through the Home Office institutions and the regional consortia. Ideally, cultural sensitivity in the provision of services and the opportunity for independent organisation in refugee communities should be encouraged, but not driven (as at present) by the political economy of funding regimes, the politics of 'community' representation or the perpetuation of institutionalised marginality. Despite the degree of consensus around the need for mainstreaming provision for refugees, there are some important divergences between the principal NGOs and the Home Office. A particular sticking point for NGOs and RCOs is the inclusion of asylum seekers in the integration process. Integration "must begin at the point of arrival" (Refugee Council, 2004, p 5) rather than being deferred, as under current Home Office policy, until formal recognition has occurred. A positive commitment to the 1951 Geneva Convention on Refugees and to the right to seek asylum should also be clearly evident in government policy. In the absence of an effective political leadership that fully endorses the right to seek asylum, the subsequent integration of refugees will be hampered and the possibilities for social cohesion impaired. As Robinson et al (2003) have convincingly argued, in relation to asylum seekers and refugees there is a general need for public education concerning their reasons for flight and why they are arriving and settling in the UK. There is furthermore, a need to re-legitimise asylum seeking (Robinson et al, 2003, p 172) as one among several possible migration routes to the UK. Misinformation and moral panics around the issue of asylum have meant that the different routes have become blurred in public discourse, with the consequence that the terms illegal immigrant, asylum seeker and refugee often appear to be identical in meaning.

Situating refugee communities and RCOs within the broader debate on social cohesion and integration, there is, first, a need to promote the political and social integration of refugees through the increased participation, consultation and mobilisation of local organisations across group lines. Integration, as is now generally recognised, is a two-way process between refugees and the receiving society. Hence, there is a clear need for a more inclusive approach that engages the principal components of the community, rather than merely segments of it. Second, there is a need to foster cross-national and inter-ethnic activity among refugee groups themselves, rather than the nationality-based model that tends to dominate in the refugee sector. Other bases of allegiance should be developed that run counter to a restrictive interpretation of 'refugee identity': gender, human rights, migrant rights and development issues offer the most ready alternatives. Indeed, there is evidence from the fieldwork conducted in London and the regions that such multi-ethnic and gender-based forms of organisation are already well established (Evelyn Oldfield Unit, 2003a, p 7).

The goal of a socially cohesive society is to overcome fracturing along class, ethnic and residential lines (Forrest and Kearns, 2001). While there is no shortcut to achieving this goal, and even in the long term it may be impossible to realise without radical social change, there is clearly a need to promote the political and social integration of minority ethnic communities, including refugees. In this respect, the integration of minorities is one of the basic preconditions of effective social cohesion. For Vertovec (1997), the main question is how the issue of social cohesion might most usefully be addressed without recourse to a nostalgic version of mono-cultural Britain. The implication is to reconsider the notion of social cohesion, not as marked by a "homogenous fabric of common values and close reciprocal relationships" but as the acknowledgement of heterogeneity and "cooperative activity surrounding common causes" (Vertovec, 1997, p 8). A shared political culture rather than an ethnically based nationalism would properly form the basis of social cohesion in diverse, multicultural societies (Habermas, 1992). This ideal situation has to be counter-posed to the strong movement towards an ethnic conception of citizenship that has taken place in the UK since the 1980s. According to Cohen (1994, p 19), for example, the changes introduced in the 1981 British Nationality Act, including the departure from *ius soli* (citizenship based upon place of birth), were "designed to buttress a racially-based British identity". The 2002 Nationality, Immigration and Asylum Act further enhances this process and actively promotes what might be termed a neo-assimilationist approach in immigration and refugee policy.

Asylum, as we suggested in Chapter One of this book, manages to condense a number of anxieties and perceived threats: to national and cultural identity; to enlarged welfare spending; and to security issues. Governmental response on the whole has tended to restrictionism, prompted in part by media-generated moral panics and by the political manipulation of the asylum issue. There has, however, been a discernible move towards instigating a system of managed migration in which the opening of formal migration channels would ease the flow of asylum seekers. The development of rational debate around the asylum issue is to be welcomed. Yet profound ambiguities in the policy framework remain. To take the case of asylum, pre-entry controls and reception policies are explicitly formulated to act as deterrents and measures of control. The overriding assumption is one of abuse of the asylum system by unfounded applications. The high level of initial rejections of asylum claims is used as evidence that the vast majority of claims are unfounded. However doubtful the merits of this case – poor initial decision making and the general culture of disbelief operating in the Home Office are significant factors – it sets up a framework in which both the 'unfounded' and 'genuine' asylum seeker will be deterred, first, from entering the state and, second, from enjoying freedom of movement and a range of other entitlements once inside it. The non-integration of asylum seekers is now official policy in a spectrum of EU member states. By contrast, once accepted into the UK as recognised refugees, many of these same individuals are invited to integrate as 'full and equal citizens'.

The shadow of the race relations and multicultural framework falls heavily upon the whole enterprise. Restrictive and racialised immigration control is complemented by the emphasis on promoting harmonious race relations through equal opportunities legislation and other forms of community involvement and representation. The often-repeated need to forestall the rise of the Far Right that underpins restrictive asylum policies echoes a long line of proselytisers for 'harmonious race relations' in the post-war period. Only by 'acting tough on asylum', so it is argued, will race relations be maintained. The effect, on the contrary, is to more deeply entrench negative public perceptions of migrants and asylum seekers. This broader framework, therefore, properly contextualises the analysis of RCOs and the role of social capital in their formation. Public debate and policy interventions relating to refugee communities need to begin from this starting point if they are to be effective in promoting long-term solutions to the pressing questions of integration and social cohesion.

References

Africa Educational Trust (1998) *Refugee education, training and employment in Inner London*, London: Africa Educational Trust.

Al-Ali, N., Black, R. and Koser, K. (2001) 'The limits to "transnationalism": Bosnian and Eritrean refugees in Europe as emerging transnational communities', *Ethnic and Racial Studies*, vol 24, no 4, pp 578-600.

Al-Rasheed, M. (1992) 'Political migration and downward socio-economic mobility: the Iraqi community in London', *New Community*, vol 18, no 4, pp 537-50.

Al-Rasheed, M. (1994) 'The myth of return: Iraqi Arab and Assyrian refugees in London', *Journal of Refugee Studies*, vol 7, no 2/3, pp 199-219.

Albrow, M., Eade, J., Durrschmidt, J. and Washbourne, N. (1997) 'The impact of globalisation on sociological concepts: community, culture, milieu', in J. Eade (ed) *Living the global city*, London: Routledge, pp 20-36.

Anderson, B. (1983) *Imagined communities: Reflections on the origins and spread of nationalism*, London: Verso.

Arango, J. (2000) 'Explaining migration: a critical view', *International Social Science Journal*, vol 165, pp 283-96.

Ashami, M. and Dumper, H. (2003) *Sudanese community and information centre*, Research Report, London: HACT.

Audit Commission (2000a) *Another country: Implementing dispersal under the Immigration and Asylum Act 1999*, London: Audit Commission.

Audit Commission (2000b) *A new city: Supporting asylum seekers and refugees in London*, London: Audit Commission.

AWM (Advantage West Midlands) (2001) *Regional economic strategy: Creating advantage*, Birmingham: AWM.

Balibar, E. (1991) '*Es Gibt Keinen Statt in Europa*: racism and politics in Europe today', *New Left Review*, vol 186, pp 5-19.

Bang Niesen, K. (2004) *Next stop Britain: The influence of transnational networks on the secondary movement of Danish Somalis*, Sussex Migration Working Paper 22, University of Sussex, Falmer.

Baron, S., Field, J. and Schuller, T. (eds) (2000) *Social capital: Critical perspectives*, Oxford: Oxford University Press.

Bauman, G. (1997) 'Dominant and demotic discourses of culture: their relevance to multi-ethnic alliances', in P. Werbner and T. Modood (eds) *Debating cultural hybridity: Multi cultural identities and the politics of anti-racism*, London: Zed Books.

Bauman, Z. (1997) *Postmodernity and its discontents*, Oxford: Blackwell.

Bell, C. and Newby, H. (1971) *Community studies*, London: George Allen and Unwin.

Berris, S. (1995) *From social exclusion to social cohesion: Towards a policy agenda*, Management of Social Transformations (MOST) UNESCO, Policy Paper 2, presented at the Roskilde Symposium, University of Roskilde, Denmark, 2-4 March.

Bhabha, H.K. (1990) 'Introduction: narrating the nation', in H. Bhabha, (ed) *Narrating the nation*, London: Routledge, pp 1-7.

Black, R. (2001) 'Fifty years of refugee studies: from theory to policy', *International Migration Review*, vol 35, no 1, pp 57-78.

Bloch, A. (1996) *Beating the barriers: the employment and training needs of refugees*, London: London Borough of Newham.

Bloch, A. (1999) 'Refugees in the job market: a case of unused skills in the British economy', in A. Bloch and C. Levy (eds) *Refugees, citizenship and social policy in Europe*, London, Macmillan, pp 187-210.

Bloch, A. (2000) 'Refugee settlement in Britain: the impact of policy on participation', *Journal of Ethnic and Migration Studies*, vol 26, no 1, pp 75-88.

Bloch, A. (2002) *Refugees' opportunities and barriers in employment and training*, Research Report 179, London: DWP.

Bloch, A. and Atfield, G. (2002) *The professional capacity of nationals from the Somali regions in Britain: Report to Refugee Action and IOM*, London: Goldsmiths College and Refugee Action.

Boswell, C. (2001) *Spreading the costs of asylum seekers: A critical assessment of dispersal policies in Germany and the UK*, London: Anglo-German Foundation for the Study of Industrial Society.

Boswell, C. (2003) *European migration policies in flux: Changing patterns of inclusion and exclusion*, Royal Institute of International Affairs, London: Blackwell.

Bourdieu, P. (1967) *Reproduction*, London: Routledge.

Bourdieu, P. (1986) 'The forms of capital', in J. Richardson (ed) *Handbook of theory and research for the sociology of education*, New York, NY: Greenwood Press, pp 241-58.

Bousquet, G. (1991) *Behind the bamboo hedge: The impact of homeland politics in the Parisian Vietnamese Community*, Ann Arbor, MI: University of Michigan Press.

Breton, R. (1964) 'Institutional completeness of ethnic communities and the personal relations of immigrants', *American Journal of Sociology*, vol 70, pp 193-205.

Buijs, G. (ed) (1993) *Migrant women: Crossing boundaries and changing identities*, Oxford: Berg Publishers.

Bulle, A. (1995) *Profile of the Somali community in Liverpool*, Community Development and Equality Unit, Liverpool: Liverpool City Council.

CAB (Citizens Advice Bureau) (2001) *Welcome advice: Business plan' of a project to deliver advice to refugees and asylum seekers in Stoke on Trent*, Stoke on Trent: CAB.

Cabinet Office (1999) *Modernising government*, Cm 4310, London: The Stationery Office.

Camino, L.A. and Krulfeld, R.M. (eds) (1994) *Reconstructing lives, recapturing meaning: Refugee identity, gender and culture change*, New York, NY: Gordon and Breach Science Publishers.

Campbell, C. (2001) 'Putting social capital in perspective: a case of unrealistic expectations?', in G. Morrow (ed) *An appropriate capitalisation? Questioning social capital*, (www.lse.ac.uk/Depts/GENDER/an_appropriate_capital.htm).

Cantle, T. (2001) *Community cohesion: A report of the independent review team*, London: Home Office.

Carey-Wood, J. (1997) *Meeting refugees' needs in Britain: The role of refugee-specific initiatives*, London: Home Office.

Carey-Wood, J., Duke, K., Karn, V. and Marshall, T. (1995) *The settlement of refugees in Britain*, Home Office Research Study 141, London: HMSO.

Carter, M. and El-Hassan, A. (2003) *Between NASS and a hard place*, London: HACT.

Castles, S. (1995) 'How nation-states respond to immigration and ethnic diversity', *New Community*, vol 21, no 3, pp 293-308.

Castles, S. (2003) 'Towards a sociology of forced migration and social transformation', *Sociology*, vol 37, no 1, pp 13-34.

Castles, S., Korac, M., Vasta, E. and Vertovec, S. (2003) *Integration: Mapping the field*, London: Home Office.

CCCS (Centre for Contemporary Cultural Studies) (1982) *The Empire strikes back: Race and racism in 70's Britain*, London: Routledge.

Census (2001) *National statistics online*, (www.statistics.gov.uk/census2001).

Cheetham, J. (1985) *Ethnic associations in Britain*, Research Study Project for Refugee Studies Programme (RSP), Oxford: RSP.

Clarke, J. and Newman, J. (1997) *The managerial state*, London: Sage Publications.

Clarke, J., Gewirtz, S. and Mclaughlin, E. (eds) (2000) *New managerialism, new welfare?*, London: Sage Publications.

Cleaver, F. (2001) 'Institutions, agency and the limitations of participatory approaches to development', in B. Cooke and U. Kothari (eds) *Participation: The new tyranny?*, London: Zed Books, pp 36-55.

Cohen, A.P. (1985) *The symbolic construction of community*, London: Routledge.

Cohen, R. (1994) *Frontiers of identity: The British and the others*, London: Longmans.

Cohen, R. (1997) *Global diasporas: An introduction*, London: UCL Press.

Coleman, J.S. (1988) 'Social capital and the creation of human capital', *American Journal of Sociology*, vol 94, pp 95-121.

Cooke, B. and Kothari, U. (2001) 'The case for participation as tyranny', in B. Cooke and U. Kothari (eds) *Participation: The new tyranny?*, London: Zed Books, pp 1-35.

Coventry City Council (2003) *Strategy for asylum seekers and refugees in Coventry*, Coventry: Asylum Team, Coventry City Council.

Craig, G. and Mayo, M. (1995) *Community empowerment*, London: Zed Books.

Crawley, H. (1997) *Women as asylum seekers: a legal handbook*, London: ILPA (Immigration Law Practitioners' Association).

Crawley, H. (2001) *Refugees and gender: Law and process*, Bristol: Jordan Publishing.

de Monclos, M. (2000) 'Reseaux financiers et hawilad: le role de la diaspora somalienne dans la reconstruction de son pays', in L. Cambrezy and V. Lassailly-Jacobs (eds) *Migration forcées de populations: Refugiés deplacés, migrants*, Paris: IRD, pp 136-56.

Deakin, N. and Cohen, B. (1975) 'Dispersal and choice: towards a strategy for ethnic minorities in Britain', Reprinted in E. Jones (ed) (1975) *Readings in social geography*, London: Oxford University Press, pp 307-16.

Denham, J. (2001) *Building cohesive communities: A report of the ministerial group on public order and community cohesion*, London: Home Office.

Dick, M. (2002) 'Celebrating sanctuary: Birmingham and the refugee experience 1750-2002', *Refugee Week 2002*, Birmingham: Refugee Week.

Dorais, L.J. (1991) 'Refugee adaptation and community structure: the Indochinese in Quebec City', *Canada, International Migration Review*, vol 25, no 3, pp 551-73.

Drury, B. (1994) 'Ethnic mobilisation: some theoretical consideration', in J. Rex (ed) *Ethnic mobilisation*, London: Routledge, pp 13-22.

Duke, K. (1996) 'Refugee community groups in the UK: the role of the community group in the resettlement process', Paper presented to the British Sociological Association Annual Conference, 'World of the Future: Ethnicity, Nationalism and Globalisation', University of Reading, 1-4 April.

Dumper, H. (2002) *Missed opportunities: A skills audit of refugee women in London from the teaching, nursing and medical professions*, Report for the Mayor of London, London: Refugee Women's Association.

Durkheim, E. (1933) *The division of labour in society* (2nd edn), New York, NY: Free Press.

DWP (Department of Work and Pensions) (2002) *Working to rebuild lives: A preliminary report towards a refugee employment strategy*, London: DWP.

Eade, J. (1991) 'The political construction of class and community: Bangladeshi political leadership in Tower Hamlets, East London', in P. Werbner and M. Anwar (eds) *Black and ethnic leaderships: The cultural dimensions of political action*, London: Routledge and Kegan Paul.

Eastmond, M. (1993) 'Reconstructing life: Chilean refugee women and the dilemmas of exile', in G. Buijs (ed) *Migrant women: Crossing boundaries and changing identities*, Oxford: Berg Publishers, pp 35-53.

Eastmond, M. (1998) 'Nationalist discourses and the construction of difference: Bosnian Muslim refugees in Sweden', *Journal of Refugee Studies*, vol 11, no 2, pp 161-81.

ECRE (European Council on Refugees and Exile) (1998) *The state of refugee integration in the European Union*, Background paper for the Conference on the Integration of Refugees in Europe, Antwerp, Belgium, 12-14 November.

ECRE (1999) *Position on the integration of refugees in Europe*, London: ECRE.

ECRE (2000) *Good practice on refugee integration in Europe*, London: ECRE.

El-Solh, C. (1991) 'Somalis in London's East End: a community striving for recognition', *New Community*, vol 17, no 4, pp 539-52.

ELCHA (East London and City Health Authority) (1999) *Refugee health in London: Key issues for public health*, London: ELCHA.

Elster, J. (1989) *The cement of society: A study of social order*, Cambridge: Cambridge University Press.

Esa-Feka, R. (2001) *Community based initiatives with the capacity to assist integration of refugees and asylum seekers in London*, London: Home Office.

Evelyn Oldfield Unit (2003a) *The changing role of refugee women: Conference report from the West London Refugee Women's Forum*, London: Evelyn Oldfield Unit.

Evelyn Oldfield Unit (2003b) *Refugee integration: Opportunities and challenges*, Report of a conference organised by the Co-ordinators Training and Support Scheme (COTASS) and the Evelyn Oldfield Unit, July, London: Evelyn Oldfield Unit.

Evelyn Oldfield Unit (2003c) *Refugee settlement: Can communities cope?*, Report of a Conference held in February, London: Evelyn Oldfield Unit.

Faist, T. (2000) *The volume and dynamics of international migration and transnational social spaces*, Oxford: Oxford University Press.

Favell, A. (1999) *Immigration and the idea of citizenship in France and Britain*, London: Macmillan.

Field, S. (1985) *Resettling refugees: The lessons of research*, Home Office Research Study 87, London: HMSO.

Fine, B. (1999) 'The developmental state is dead – long live social capital?', *Development and Change*, vol 30, pp 1-19.

Fletcher, G. (2002) *Investigating community groups in the North East of England dispersal area and community-based integrative initiatives*, Foundation Study for the NASS Dispersal Programme, London: Home Office.

Forrest, R. and Kearns, A. (2001) 'Social cohesion, social capital and the neighbourhood', *Urban Studies*, vol 38, no 12, pp 2125-43.

Foucault, M. (1980) *Power/knowledge: selected interviews and other writings 1972-1977*, C. Gordon (ed), London: Harvester.

Gameledin-Ashami, M., Cooper, L. and Knight, B. (2002) *Refugee settlement: Can communities cope?*, London: Evelyn Oldfield Unit.

Geddes, A. (2000) *Immigration and Fortress Europe: Towards Fortress Europe?*, European Policy Research Unit Series, Manchester: Manchester University Press.

Gibney, M. (2003) 'The state of asylum: democratisation, judicialisation and evolution of refugee policy', in S. Kneebone (ed) *The refugee convention fifty years on: Globalisation and international law*, Ashgate: Aldershot, pp 19-45.

Giddens, A. (1998) *The Third Way: The renewal of social democracy*, Cambridge: Polity Press.

Gilroy, P. (1987) *There ain't no black in the Union Jack: The cultural politics of race and nation*, London: Hutchinson.

Gold, S.J. (1992) *Refugee communities: A comparative field study*, London: Sage Publications.

Goldberg, D.T. (1993) *Racist culture*, London: Blackwell.

Goulbourne, H. (1991) 'The offence of the West Indian political leadership and the communal option', in P. Werbner and M. Anwar (eds) *Black and ethnic leaderships in Britain*, London: Routledge, pp 296-322.

Goverde, H., Cerny, P.G., Haugaard, M. and Lentner, H.H. (2000) *Power in contemporary politics: Theories, practices, globalisations*, London: Sage Publications.

Government of Canada (1996) *Social cohesion network, policy research initiative*, Government of Canada.

Granovetter, M.S. (1973) 'The strength of weak ties', *American Journal of Sociology*, vol 78, pp 1360-80.

Griffiths, D. (2000) 'Fragmentation and consolidation: the contrasting cases of Somali and Kurdish refugees in London', *Journal of Refugee Studies*, vol 13, no 3, pp 281-302.

Griffiths, D. (2002) *Somali and Kurdish refugees in London: New identities in the diaspora*, Aldershot: Ashgate.

Griffiths, D. (2003) *Somalia*, Country Guide, University of Oxford, Forced Migration Online (www.forcedmigration.org).

Gurak, D.G. and Caces, F.E. (1992) 'Migration networks and the shaping of migration systems', in M. Kritz, L. Lim and H. Zlotnik (eds) *International migration systems: A global approach*, Oxford: Clarendon Press, pp 150-76.

Habermas, J. (1992) 'Citizenship and national identity: some reflections on the future of Europe', *Praxis International*, vol 12, no 1, pp 1-19.

Hall, S. (1991) 'Old and new identities: old and new ethnicities', in A.D. King (ed) *Culture, globalisation and the world system*, London: Macmillan Education, pp 41-68.

Hall, S. (1992) 'New ethnicities', in J. Donald and A. Rattansi (eds) *'Race', culture and difference*, London: Open University/Sage Publications, pp 252-9.

Haringey Council (1997) *Refugees and asylum seekers in Haringey*, Research Project Report, London: Haringey Council.

Harris, H. (2004) *The Somali community in the UK: What we know and how we know it*, Commissioned and published by The Information Centre about Asylum and Refugees in the UK (ICAR), King's College, London: ICAR.

Harriss, J. (2002) *Depoliticizing development: The World Bank and social capital*, London: Anthem Press.

Harvey, C. (2001) *Provision of legal services in the dispersal areas*, NASS Foundation Reports, London: Home Office.

Hassan, L. (2000) 'Deterrence measures and the preservation of asylum in the United Kingdom and United States', *Journal of Refugee Studies*, vol 13, no 2, pp 184-204.

Hay, C. (2002) *Political analysis: A critical introduction*, Hampshire: Palgrave.

Henkel, H. and Stirrat, R. (2001) 'Participation as spiritual duty: empowerment as secular subjection', in B. Cooke and U. Kothari (eds) *Participation: The new tyranny?*, London: Zed Books, pp 155-80.

Henry, N., McEwan, C. and Pollard, J. (2000) *Globalisation from below: Birmingham – Post-colonial workshop of the world*, Transnational Communities Working Paper, WPTC-2K-08, Oxford: University of Oxford.

HM Treasury (2002) *The role of the voluntary and community sector in service delivery: A cross cutting review*, London: HM Treasury.

Home Office (1998) *Fairer, faster, firmer: A modern approach to immigration and asylum*, White Paper, Cm 4018, London: The Stationery Office.

Home Office (1999a) *Asylum seeker support*, London: Home Office.

Home Office (1999b) *Process manual*, London: Home Office.

Home Office (1999c) *Accommodation specification document*, London: Home Office.

Home Office (1999d) *A consultation paper on the integration of recognised refugees in the UK*, Immigration and Nationality Directorate, Asylum Support Project Team, London: Home Office.

Home Office (1999e) *Full and equal citizens: A policy and implementation model for the integration of refugees into UK society*, London: Refugee Section, Home Office.

Home Office (2000a) *Asylum statistics in the United Kingdom*, London: Home Office.

Home Office (2000b) *Full and equal citizens: A strategy for the integration of refugees into the United Kingdom*, London: Refugee Integration Section, NASS, and Home Office.

Home Office (2001) *Migration: An economic and social analysis*, RDS Occasional Paper 67, London: Home Office.

Home Office (2002a) *Secure borders, safe haven: Integration with diversity in modern Britain*, White Paper, Cm 5387, London: Home Office.

Home Office (2002b) *Asylum statistics in the United Kingdom*, London: Home Office.

Home Office (2003a) *Asylum statistics in the United Kingdom*, London: Home Office.

Home Office (2003b) *The new and the old: Report of the 'Life in the United Kingdom' Advisory Group chaired by Bernard Crick*, London: Home Office.

Home Office (2004) *Integration matters: A national refugee integration strategy*, Draft document, London: Home Office.

ICAR (Information Centre about Asylum and Refugees in the UK) (2003) *Refugee community development resources list*, (www.icar.org.uk).

IPPR (Institute of Public Policy Research) (2003) *States of conflict: Causes and patterns of forced migration to the EU and policy responses*, London: IPPR.

Jenkins, S. (1988) *Ethnic associations and the welfare state*, New York, NY: Columbia University Press.

Johnson, M.R.D. (2001) *Synthesis and overview of dispersal, A report for the National Asylum Support Service Foundation Study for the NASS Dispersal Programme (IRSS)*, London: Home Office.

Johnston, G. and Percy-Smith, J. (2003) 'In search of social capital', *Policy & Politics*, vol 31, no 3, pp 321-34.

Joly, D. (1996) *Haven or hell: Asylum policies and refugees in Europe*, London: Macmillan.

Joly, D. (1999) 'A new asylum regime in Europe', in F. Nichols and P. Twomey (eds) *Refugee rights and realities: Evolving international concepts and regimes*, Cambridge: Cambridge University Press, pp 336-56.

Jones, P.R. (1982) *Vietnamese refugees: A study of their reception and resettlement in the UK*, Research and Planning Unit Paper 13, London: Home Office.

Kay, D. (1987) *Chileans in exile: Private struggles, public lives*, London: Macmillan.

Kaye, R. (1992) 'British refugee policy and 1992: the breakdown of a policy community', *Journal of Refugee Studies*, vol 5, no 1, pp 47-67.

Kelly, L. (2003) 'Bosnian refugees in Britain: questioning community', *Sociology*, vol 37, no 1, pp 35-49.

Kelly, L. and Joly, D. (1999) 'UNHCR workshop', referenced in *Refugees' reception and settlement in Britain: A report for the Joseph Rowntree Foundation*, York: JRF.

Khan, V.S. (1979) 'Work and networks: South Asian women in south London', in S. Wallman (ed) *Ethnicity at work*, London: Macmillan, pp 84-112.

Koopmans, R. and Stratham, P. (2000) 'Migration and ethnic relations as a field of political contention: an opportunity structure approach', in R. Koopmans and P. Statham (eds) *Challenging immigration and ethnic relations politics: Comparative European perspectives*, Oxford: Oxford University Press, pp 13-56.

Korac, M. (2001) 'Dilemmas of integration: two policy contexts and refugee strategies for integration', (www.rsc.ox.ac.uk/dilemmasofintegrationrep.htm).

Koser, K. (2001) 'New approaches to asylum', *International Migration*, vol 39, no 6, pp 85-103.

Koser, K. (2002) 'From refugees to transnationals', in N. Al-Ali and K. Koser (eds) *New approaches to migration*, London: Routledge, pp 138-52.

Koser, K. and Pinkerton, C. (2002) *The social networks of asylum seekers and the dissemination of information about countries of asylum*, London: Development and Statistics Directorate, Home Office.

Kuhn, T. (1962) *The structure of scientific revolutions*, Chicago, IL: University of Chicago Press.

Kunz, E.F. (1973) 'The refugee in flight: kinetic models and forms of displacement', *International Migration Review*, vol 7, no 2, pp 125-46.

Kunz, E.F. (1981) 'Exile and resettlement: refugee theory', *International Migration Review*, vol 15, no 1, pp 42-51.

Kushner, T. and Knox, K. (1999) *Refugees in an age of genocide: Global, national and local perspectives during the twentieth century*, London: Frank Cass.

LGA (Local Government Association) (2000) *Asylum seekers: Briefing for LGA talks group meeting of 17/5/2000*, London: LGA.

Lin, N. (2001) *Social capital: A theory of social structure and action*, Cambridge: Cambridge University Press.

Ling, T. (2000) 'Unpacking partnership: the case of health care', in J. Clarke, S. Gewirtz and E. McLaughlin (eds) *New managerialism, new welfare?*, London: Sage Publications, pp 82-101.

Loescher, G. (1992) *Refugee movements and international security*, Adelphi Papers 268, London: IISS.

Loftman, P. and Nevin, B. (1996) 'Going for growth: prestige projects – three British cities', *Urban Studies*, vol 33, pp 991-1019.

Loizos, P. (2000) 'Are refugees social capitalists?', in S. Baron, J. Field and T. Schuller (eds) *Social capital: Critical perspectives*, Oxford: Oxford University Press, pp 124-41.

Lukes, S. (1974) *Power: A radical view*, London: Macmillan.

Lynch, R. (2001) 'An analysis of the concept of community cohesion', *Cantle Report on Community Cohesion*, London: Home Office, pp 110-20.

McDowell, C. (1996) *A Tamil diaspora*, Oxford: Berghahn.

MacIntyre, K. (1990) *Three versions of moral enquiry*, London: Duckworth.

McLeod, M., Owen, D. and Khamis, C. (2001) *Black and minority ethnic voluntary and community organisations: Their role and future development in England and Wales*, London: Policy Studies Institute.

Maile, S. and Braddon, D. (2003) *Stakeholding and the new international order*, Ashgate: Aldershot.

Maile, S. and Hoggett, P. (2001) 'Best value and the politics of pragmatism', *Policy & Politics*, vol 29, no 4, pp 509-19.

Majka, L. (1991) *Into the 1990s: The needs of refugee based organisations and refugees in Britain*, Oxford: Refugee Studies Programme.

Marcuse, P. (1996) 'Of walls and immigrant enclaves', in R. Baubock and A. Zolberg (eds) *The challenge of diversity: Integration and pluralism in societies of immigration*, London: Avebury.

Marx, E. (1990) 'The social world of refugees: a conceptual framework', *Journal of Refugee Studies*, vol 3, no 3, pp 189-203.

Massey, D.S., Arango, J., Hugo, G., Kouaouci, A., Pellegrino, A. and Edward Taylor, J. (1998) *Worlds in motion: Understanding international migration at the end of the millennium*, Oxford: Clarendon Press.

May, T. (1996) *Situating social theory*, Buckingham: Open University Press.

Medical Foundation (1997) *Past misery, present muddle*, London: Medical Foundation.

Michael Bell Associates (2002) *Renewing West London: Refugee communities, their hopes and needs*, Michael Bell Associates for the Evelyn Oldfield Unit, London: Evelyn Oldfield Unit.

Miles, R. (1993) *Racism after 'race' relations*, London: Routledge.

Miles, R. and Cleary, P. (1993) 'Migration to Britain: racism, state regulation and employment', in V. Robinson (ed) *The international refugee crisis: British and Canadian responses*, London: Macmillan, pp 57-75.

Miles, R. and Thranhardt, D. (1996) *Migration and European integration: Dynamics of inclusion and exclusion*, London: Pinter.

Molyneux, M. (2001) 'Social capital: a post-transition concept? Questions of context and gender from a Latin American perspective', in G. Morrow (ed) *An appropriate capitalisation? Questioning social capital*, (www.lse.ac.uk/Depts/GENDER/an_appropriate_capital.htm).

Moran, R. (2003) *From dispersal to destitution: Dialectical methods in participatory action research with people seeking asylum*, Working Paper, Presented at the conference 'Policy and Politics in a Globalising World', University of Bristol.

MORI (2000) *Asylum seekers and refugees in Ealing: Research conducted for London borough of Ealing*, London: MORI.

MORI (2001) *Refugees in West London: Baseline mapping study*, Research conducted for Renewal SRB, London: MORI.

MRC (Midland Refugee Council) (2001) *Dispersal or disposal? Retrieving refugees' skills for our society*, Paper presented at 'Dispersal or disposal' conference, January 2001, Digbeth, Birmingham.

NASS (National Asylum Support Service) (2001) *Report of the operational reviews of the voucher and dispersal schemes of the National Asylum Support Service*, October, London: NASS.

Newman, J. (2000) 'Beyond the new public management? Modernizing public services', in J. Clarke, S. Gewirtz and E. McLaughlin (eds) *New managerialism, new welfare?*, London: Sage Publications, pp 45-61.

Overbeek, H. (1996) 'Towards a new international migration regime: globalisation, migration and the internationalisation of the state', in R. Miles and D. Thranhardt (eds) (1996) *Migration and European integration: Dynamics of inclusion and exclusion*, London: Pinter.

Page, M. (nd) *Compassionate leadership: A question of gender? The experience of women managers in refugee organisations*, London: Evelyn Oldfield Unit.

Pahl, R.E. (1991) 'The search for social cohesion: from Durkheim to the European Commission', *Archives Européennes de Sociologie*, vol 32, no 2, pp 345-60.

Park, R. (1925) 'The city: suggestions for the investigation of human behaviour', in R. Park, E.W. Burgess and R.D. McKenzie (eds) *The city*, Chicago, IL: University of Chicago Press.

Parsons, T. (1971) *Societies: Evolutionary comparative perspectives*, Englewood Cliffs, NJ: Prentice Hall.

Penninx, R. (1999) *Political participation and integration of immigrants in European cities*, (www.international.metropolis.net).

Penninx, R. (2000) *Integration of immigrants in Europe: Policies of diversity and diversity of policies*, (www.international.metropolis.net).

Pfohman, S. and Amrute, S. (2004) 'Refugee decentralisation in Europe', in J. Blaschke and S. Pfohman (eds) *The decentralisation of asylum: Refugee procedures in the European Union*, Berlin: Edition Parabolis.

Phillimore, J. and Goodson, L. (2001) *Exploring mechanisms for the integration of asylum seekers and refugees into the labour market in Wolverhampton*, Report for Wolverhampton Connects by the Centre for Urban and Regional Studies (CURS), Birmingham: University of Birmingham, CURS.

Porter, B. (1979) *The refugee question in mid-Victorian England*, Cambridge: Cambridge University Press.

Portes, A. (1995) 'Economic sociology and the sociology of immigration: a conceptual overview', in A. Portes (ed) *The economic sociology of immigration*, New York, NY: Russell Sage Foundation, pp 56-87.

Portes, A. (1998) 'Social capital: its origins and applications in modern sociology', *Annual Review of Sociology*, vol 24, pp 1-24.

Portes, A. and Rumbaut, R.G. (1990) *Immigrant America: A portrait*, Berkeley, CA: University of California Press.

Putnam, R. (1993) *Making democracy work: Civic traditions in modern Italy*, Princeton, NJ: Princeton University Press.

Putnam, R. (1996) 'The strange disappearance of civic America', *The American Prospect*, vol 7, issue 24, pp 34-48.

Refugee Council (1987) *Settling for a future: Proposals for a British policy on refugees*, London: Refugee Council.

Refugee Council (1997) *The development of a refugee settlement policy in the UK*, Working Paper 1 (Addendum), London: Refugee Council.

Refugee Council (2004) *Agenda for integration*, Consultation Draft, May, London: Refugee Council.

Reilly, R. (1991) 'Political identity, protest and power amongst Kurdish refugees in Britain', Unpublished MA thesis, Cambridge University.

Rex, J. (1987) 'Introduction: the scope of a comparative study', in J. Rex, D. Joly and C. Wilpert (eds) (1987) *Immigrant associations in Europe*, Aldershot: Gower, pp 1-10.

Rex, J. (1994) 'Ethnic mobilisation in multi-ethnic societies', in J. Rex (ed) *Ethnic mobilisation*, London: Routledge, pp 3-12.

Rex, J. and Josephides, S. (1987) 'Asian and Greek Cypriot associations and identity', in J. Rex, D. Joly and C. Wilpert (eds) (1987) *Immigrant associations in Europe*, Aldershot: Gower, pp 11-33.

Rex, J. and Moore, R. (1967) *Race, community and conflict*, Oxford: Oxford University Press.

Richmond, A. (1993) 'Reactive migration: sociological perspectives on refugee movements', *Journal of Refugee Studies*, vol 36, no 2, pp 7-25.

Ritchey, P.N. (1976) 'Explanations of migration', *Annual Review of Sociology*, vol 2, pp 336-404.

Robinson, V. (1985) 'The Vietnamese reception and resettlement programme in the UK: rhetoric and reality', *Ethnic Groups*, vol 6, pp 305-30.

Robinson, V. (1993a) 'British policy towards the settlement patterns of ethnic groups: an empirical evaluation of the Vietnamese programme 1979-89', in V. Robinson (ed) *The international refugee crisis: British and Canadian responses*, Basingstoke: Macmillan, pp 319-54.

Robinson, V. (1993b) 'Marching into the middle classes? The long-term resettlement of East African Asians in the UK', *Journal of Refugee Studies*, vol 6, no 3, pp 230-48.

Robinson, V. (1998a) 'The importance of information for the resettlement of refugees in the UK', *Journal of Refugee Studies*, vol 11, no 2, pp 146-60.

Robinson, V. (1998b) 'Defining and measuring successful refugee integration', Proceedings of ECRE International Conference on Integration of Refugees in Europe, Antwerp, November, Brussels: ECRE.

Robinson, V. (2002) *The secondary migration of dispersed asylum seekers in the UK*, Unpublished study for the Home Office.

Robinson, V. and Coleman, C. (2000) 'Lessons learned? A critical review of the UK government's programme to resettle Bosnian quota refugees', *International Migration Review*, vol 34, no 4, pp 1217-44.

Robinson, V. and Hale, S. (1989) *The geography of Vietnamese secondary migration in the UK*, Warwick: Centre for Research in Ethnic Relations, University of Warwick.

Robinson, V. and Segrott, J. (2002) *Understanding the decision-making of asylum seekers*, Research Paper 143, London: Home Office.

Robinson, V., Andersson, R. and Musterd, S. (2003) *Spreading the 'burden'? A review of policies to disperse asylum seekers and refugees*, Bristol: The Policy Press.

Rogg, E.M. (1974) 'The influence of a strong refugee community on the economic adjustment of its members', *International Migration Review*, vol 5, pp 474-81.

Rustin, M. (1991) *The good society and the inner world*, London: Verso, pp 57-84.

RWP (Refugee Working Party) (2001) *Extending our reach to the north-west: A report on refugee community organisations' visit to the North West of England 2001*, London: RWP.

Salinas, M., Pritchard, D. and Kibedi, A. (1987) *Refugee-based organisations: Their function and importance for the refugee in Britain*, Refugee Issues: Working Paper on Refugees 13.4, Oxford, London: Refugee Studies Programme, British Refugee Council.

Sargeant, G. and Forma, A. (2001) *A poor reception: Refugees and asylum seekers: Welfare or work*, London: Industrial Society.

Schuster, L. (2000) 'A comparative analysis of the asylum policy of seven European governments', *Journal of Refugee Studies*, vol 13, no 1, pp 118-32.

Schuster, L. (2003) *The use and abuse of political asylum in Britain and Germany*, London: Frank Cass.

Schuster, L. and Solomos, J. (1999) 'The politics of refugee and asylum policies in Britain: historical patterns and contemporary realities', in A. Bloch and C. Levy (eds) *Refugees, citizenship and social policy in Europe*, Basingstoke: Macmillan.

Serra, R. (1999) '"Putnam in India": is social capital a meaningful and measurable concept at Indian state level?', Institute of Development Studies (IDS) Working Paper 92, Brighton: IDS.

Siisiänen, M. (2000) *Two concepts of social capital: Bourdieu vs. Putnam*, Department of Social Science and Philosophy, University of Jyväskylä.

Simmel, G. (1971) 'The sociological significance of the stranger', in *On individuality and social forms*, (original edition 1908), Chicago, IL: Chicago University Press, pp 112-20.

Solomos, J. (1998) *'Race' and racism in Britain* (2nd edn), London: Macmillan.

Somali Conference (1998) *Somali Conference Report*, London: Evelyn Oldfield Unit.

Sorenson, J. (1990) 'Opposition, exile and identity: the Eritrean case', *Journal of Refugee Studies*, vol 3, no 4, pp 298-319.

Soysal, Y.N. (1994) *The limits of citizenship: Migrants and postnational membership in Europe*, Chicago, IL: University of Chicago Press.

Srinivasan, S. (1994) *An overview of research into refugee groups in Britain during the 1990s*, Oxford: Refugee Studies Programme.

Stansfield, R. (2001) *Another country, another city*, Nottingham: Nottingham Asylum Seekers.

Stewart, J. (1993) *Accountability to the public*, London: European Policy Forum.

Sword, K., Davies, N. and Ciechanawski, J. (1989) *The formation of the Polish community in Great Britain, 1939-1950*, London: School of Slavonic and East European Studies.

Talai, V.A. (1989) *Armenians in London: The management of social boundaries*, Manchester: Manchester University Press.

Tarrow, S. (1994) *Power in movement: Social movements, collective action, and politics*, Cambridge: Cambridge University Press.

Thomas, W.I. and Znaniecki, F. (1918) *The Polish peasant in Europe and America*, Chicago, IL: University of Chicago Press.

Tomlinson, F. and Egan, S. (2002) 'From marginalisation to (dis) empowerment: organising training and employment services for refugees', *Human Relations*, vol 55, no 8, pp 1019-43.

Tonnies, F. (1955) *Community and association*, London: Routledge.

UNHCR (2004) *Asylum levels and trends: Europe and non-European industrial countries, 2003. A comparative overview of asylum applications submitted in 44 European and 6 non-European countries in 2003 and before*, Geneva: Population Data Unit/PGDS, Division of Operational Support, UNHCR.

Valtonen, K. (1999) 'The societal participation of Vietnamese refugees: case studies in Finland and Canada', *Journal of Ethnic and Migration Studies*, vol 25, no 3, pp 469-91.

Vasquez, A. (1989) 'The process of transculturation: exiles and institutions in France', in D. Joly and R. Cohen (eds) *Reluctant hosts: Europe and its refugees*, Aldershot: Gower, pp 125-32.

Vertovec, S. (1997) *Social cohesion and tolerance*, Discussion paper prepared for the 'Second International Metropolis' Conference, Copenhagen, 25-27 September.

Vertovec, S. (1999) 'Conceiving and researching transnationalism', *Ethnic and Racial Studies*, vol 22, no 2, pp 447-61.

Vertovec, S. (2001) *Transnational social formations: Towards conceptual cross-fertilisation*, Working Paper Transnational Communities, WPTC-01-16 (www.transcomm.uk.ac.uk/working papers.htm).

Waever, O., Buzan, B., Kelstrup, M. and Lemaitre, P. (1994) *Identity, migration and the new security agenda in Europe*, London: Pinter.

Wahlbeck, Ö. (1997) 'The Kurdish diaspora and refugee associations in Finland and England', *Exclusion and inclusion of refugees in contemporary Europe*, Utrecht: ERCOMER, University of Utrecht, pp 157-86.

Wahlbeck, Ö. (1998) 'Community work and exile politics: Kurdish refugee associations in London', *Journal of Refugee Studies*, vol 11, no 3, pp 215-30.

Watson, J.L. (ed) (1977) *Between two cultures*, Oxford: Basil Blackwell.

Weber, M. (1911) 'Geschäftsbericht', in *Verhandlungen des ersten deutschen Soziologentages vom 19-22 Oktober*, Tübingen, 1991, pp 39-61, quoted in Siisiänen, 2000.

Weiner, M. (1995) *The global migration crisis: Challenges to states and human rights*, New York, NY: Harper Collins.

Werbner, P. (1991) 'The fiction of unity in ethnic politics: aspects of representation of the state among British Pakistanis', in P. Werbner and M. Anwar (eds) *Black and ethnic leaderships in Britain*, London: Routledge, pp 113-45.

Werbner, P. and Anwar, M. (eds) (1991) *Black and ethnic leaderships in Britain*, London: Routledge.

Wilson, R. (2001) *Dispersed: A study of services for asylum seekers in West Yorkshire*, York: Joseph Rowntree Foundation.

WMCARS (West Midlands Consortium for Asylum Seeker and Refugee Support) (2001) *Business Plan 2001-2002*, Birmingham: WMCARS (www.wmlga.gov.uk).

WMCARS (2002) *Purposeful activities grant 2001–2002: Progress report*, Birmingham: WMCARS.

WMCARS (2003) *Business Plan 2003-2004*, Birmingham:WMCARS (www.wmlga.gov.uk).

Wollenschläger, M. (ed) (2003) *Asylum and integration in member states of the EU: Integration of recognised refugee families as defined by the Geneva Convention considering their status with the respect to the law of residence*, Berlin: Berliner Wissenschafts-Verlag, GMBH.

Woolley, F. (1998) 'Social cohesion and voluntary activity: making connections', Paper presented at the CLSL conference, 'The State of Living Standards and the Quality of Life in Canada', 30-31 October, Ontario.

World Bank (1999) *Understanding and measuring social capital: Bonds and bridges: Social capital and poverty*, Washington DC: World Bank.

Yuval-Davis, N. (1997) *Gender and nation*, London: Sage Publications.

Zetter, R. (1991) 'Labelling refugees: Forming and transforming a bureaucratic identity', *Journal of Refugee Studies*, vol 4, no 1, pp 39-62.

Zetter, R. and Pearl, M. (1998) *Managing to survive*, Bristol: The Policy Press.

Zetter, R. and Pearl, M. (2000) 'The minority within the minority: refugee community based organisations in the UK and the impact of restrictionism', *Journal of Ethnic and Migration Studies*, vol 26, no 4, pp 675-98.

Zetter, R., Griffiths, D. and Sigona, N. (2002a) *A survey of policy and practice of refugee integration in the EU*, Final Report, Oxford: Oxford Brookes University.

Zetter, R., Griffiths, D., Ferretti, S., Romer, K. and Sigona, N. (2002b) *Asylum policy and practice in Europe: An in-depth analysis of current practices for the reception of asylum seekers, commissioned by the Home Office*, Final Home Office Report, London: Home Office.

Zetter, R., Griffiths, D., Ferretti, S. and Pearl, M. (2003a) *An evaluation of the impact of asylum policies in Europe*, London: Home Office.

Zetter, R., Pearl, M., Griffiths, D., Allender, P., Cairncross, L. and Robinson, V. (2003b) *Dispersal: Facilitating effectiveness and efficiency*, Final Report, London: Home Office.

Zolberg, A., Surhrke, A. and Aguayo, S. (1989) *Escape from violence: Conflict and the refugee crisis in the developing world*, New York, NY: Oxford University Press.

Appendix

RCOs interviewed by location

London
1. An Viet Foundation, Hackney
2. Balik Arts (Turkish and Kurdish Youth), Hackney
3. Dahidiye Somali Organisation, Kensington and Chelsea
4. Day-Mer Turkish-Kurdish Association, Hackney
5. Ethiopian Community in Britain, Finchley
6. Horn of Africa, Shepherd's Bush
7. Horn Response Project, Harrow
8. Iranian Association, Hammersmith
9. Iraqi Community Association, Hammersmith
10. Kurdish Cultural Association, Lambeth
11. Lambeth Somali Association
12. Lien Viet Housing Association, Hackney
13. Mosada Women's Organisation, Tower Hamlets
14. Refugee Women's Association, Hackney
15. South London Refugee Association, Merton
16. South London Tamil Welfare Association, Merton
17. Sudanese Community and Information Centre, Ladbroke Grove
18. Tamil Relief Centre, Edmonton
19. Tamil Welfare Association, Newham
20. The Society of Afghan Residents in the UK, Acton

West Midlands (Birmingham)
1. African Community Council for the Regions
2. Birmingham Refugee Women's Organisation: Teamwork
3. Bosnia Herzegovina UK Network
4. Central Africa Development Action (Congolese)
5. Cite Celeste French speaking community (Congolese)
6. Kurdish Community in West Midlands
7. Midlands Ethnic Albanian Foundation
8. Society of Afghan Residents in the UK
9. Somali Community Development in the West Midlands
10. Somali Immigrants Resource Development Organisation
11. Sudanese Midlands Refugee Community Association
12. Windows for Sudan

North West (Liverpool and Manchester)

1. Liverpool Congolese Organisation
2. Manchester Iranian community
3. Manchester Kurdish Organisation
4. Merseyside Tamil School, Liverpool
5. North Manchester Somali Organisation
6. Remisus, Toxteth, Liverpool
7. Sierra Leone Women's Association, Moss Side, Manchester
8. Somali Umbrella Group, Toxteth, Liverpool

Index

Page numbers in *italics* refer to tables, figures and boxes.

A

accountability, of refugee community organisations, 80-81, 137-41, 162-4
Advantage West Midlands (AWM), 106
Agenda 2010 (Manchester), 127
An Viet, 92-3
Anderson, B., 22
Another Country (Audit Commission), 110
Anwar, M., 22
Arango, J., 27, 28-9
assimilation
  asylum/immigration policy, 41-2
  definition, 12
associations
  migrant *see* migrant organisations
  refugee *see* refugee community organisations
ASD (Asylum Support Directorate), 44
Ashami, M., 87
Asylum Aid, 73
Asylum and Immigration Act, 1996, 39, 61
Asylum and Immigration Appeals Act, 1993, 22, 39
asylum seekers
  fear of, 2-3
  government policies and legislation, 1-4, 38-45
  prevalence of English language usage, 67-8
  statistics of number and applicants, 38, 66-7, 119-20, *119, 124*, 123-4, *124*
  see also dispersal; integration
Asylum Support Directorate (ASD), 44
Audit Commission, 46-7, 57-9, 110
AWM (Advantage West Midlands), 106

B

benefits, welfare
  policy regarding asylum seekers, 1-2
Berris, S., 212-13
BHUK (Bosnia Herzegovina UK) Network, 142-3
Birmingham
  accountability and community organisation representation, 137-41

asylum seeker/refugee settlement and dispersal, 120-23, 170-74, 193-7
networks of refugee organisations, 141-7, 190-93
refugee organisation-officialdom relations, 147-51, 179-80, 182-4
structure and aims of refugee organisations, 129-36, *131*, 184-8, 189
Birmingham City Council, 107, 112, 122, 147-8, 180, 184
Birmingham Refugee Forum (BRF), 144
Birmingham Refugee Network, 144-7, 182
Bosnia Herzegovina UK (BHUK) Network, 142-3
Boswell, C., 47
Bourdieu, P., 29-30, 89, 142, 207
Braddon, D., 213
BRF (Birmingham Refugee Forum), 144
British Nationality Act, 1981, 219
Building Cohesive Communities (Denham), 215

C

Campbell, C., 34
Cantle, T., 214-15
Carey-Wood, J., 19-20
Castles, S., 214
Cheetham, J., 14, 16-17
citizenship ceremonies and rules, 49
City Parochial Foundation, 74
Cleaver, F., 208-9
Cohen, B., 41
Cohen, R., 219
Coleman, J.S., 30-31
collaboration, refugee community organisations, 91-4
Commission of Inquiry into the Somali Community in Liverpool, 163
communities, ethnic
  definition and characteristics, 21-2
'community' (concept)
  gender dynamics within, 87-8
  politicisation of, 85-7
  representation by refugee community organisations, 137-41, 162-4

community organisations, migrant *see*
    migrant organisations; refugee
    community organisations
Community Relations Unit (Home
    Office), 37
competition, and politics of refugee
    community organisations, 88–91
Conservative Party/governments
    asylum and immigration legislation, 38–
    40
consortia (asylum seeker and refugee
    integration) *see* North West
    Consortium for Asylum Seekers and
    Refugees; West Midlands Consortium
    for Asylum Seeker and Refugee
    Support
Coordinators Training and Support
    Scheme (COTASS) (Evelyn Oldfield
    Unit), 95–6
cultural identities, role of refugee
    organisations, 16

D

Deakin, N., 41
Denham, J., 215
Dick. M., 50, 120–21
dispersal (asylum seekers and refugees)
    effect on refugee communities and
    organisations, 58–63
    evaluation, 46–8, *46*
    government policies, 37–45, *45*
    organisation of, 95–102, 110–11, 114–5,
    117–8, 122
    refugee community organisation
    responses, 170–74, 193–7
    see also assimilation; integration;
    National Asylum Support Service
    see also heading under Birmingham;
    Liverpool; London; Manchester
Dorais, L.J., 15
Duke, K., 19
Dumper, H., 87
Durkheim, E., 12, 211

E

East London and City Health Authority,
    72
Egan, S., 203, 216–17
Elster, J., 212
English language
    use among asylum seekers, 67–8
European Union

dispersal policies, 42–3
EC Council Directive 2003/9/EC (on
    asylum seeker reception), 43
England (North West)
    asylum seeker numbers, 119–20, *119*
    socio-economic characteristics, 106–7
    see also Liverpool; Manchester
European Convention on Human Rights,
    43, 49
Evelyn Oldfield Unit, 60, 74, 95

F

*Fairer, Faster, Firmer: a modern approach to
    immigration and asylum* (Home Office),
    40, 44
Faist, T., 29
fieldwork investigation (refugee
    community organisations)
    methodology, 66–71, 75–9, *76*
Fine, B., 142
Fletcher, G., 59
Full and Equal Citizens (Home Office), 53,
    54
funding (refugee community
    organisations)
    Birmingham, 132, 135–6, 187
    Liverpool, 156–7, 187
    London, 77–8, 82–4, 187
    Manchester, 156–7, 187

G

Gameledin-Ashami, M., 59–60, 80, 117,
    151
gender, dynamics within refugee
    community organisations, 87–8
Geneva Convention on Refugees (1951),
    217
Giddens, A., 213
Gold, S.J., 15–16, 205
Griffiths, D., 85

H

Hackney Domestic Violence Forum, 88
HACT (Housing Association Charitable
    Trust), 183
Harris, H., 50
Harriss, J., 207
Hay, C., 25
Hein, C., 43
Hoggett, P., 40
Housing Act, 1996, 39

Housing Association Charitable Trust
  (HACT), 183

I

ICAR (Information Centre about
  Asylum and Refugees), 50
identities, cultural
  role of refugee organisations, 16
immigration
  government policy and legislation, 1-4,
    38-45
  see also asylum seekers; race relations;
    refugees
Immigration and Asylum Act, 1999, 4, 11,
    41, 44-5, *45,* 52, 61, 78, 116, 171
Immigration Research and Statistics
  Service (IRSS), 53
Index of Local Deprivation, 106
Information Centre about Asylum and
  Refugees (ICAR), 50
integration (asylum seekers and refugees)
  bibliography, 50
  definition and characteristics, 12
  policy, 37-8, 50-58, *52*
  role of refugee community
    organisations, 199-203
  theories and model of partnerships,
    25-6, *54,* 204-6
  see also assimilation
Integration Matters (Home Office), 54-6
IRSS (Immigration Research and
  Statistics Service), 53

J

Joly, D., 17-18

K

Koopmans, R., 25
Korac, M., 202

L

Labour Party (New Labour)
  asylum and immigration legislation,
    40-41
LASAR (Liverpool Asylum Seekers and
  Refugees Development Project), 157,
    166-7
legal status (refugee community
  organisations)
  Birmingham, 132

Liverpool, 155-6
London, 77
Manchester, 155-6
legislation
  asylum seeker dispersal, 38-45
  impact on dispersal policies, 170-74
  see also under title eg *Asylum and
    Immigration Act, 1996*
LGA (Local Government Association), 44,
    45
Ling, T., 55-6
Liverpool
  accountability and community
    organisation representation, 162-4
  asylum seeker/refugee settlement and
    dispersal, 125-6, 193-7
  networks of refugee organisations,
    164-8, 190-93
  refugee organisation-officialdom
    relations, 168-70, 180-82, 184
  structure and aims of refugee
    organisations, 151-60, *154,* 184-8
Liverpool Asylum Seekers and Refugees
  Development Project (LASAR), 157,
    166-7
Liverpool Network for Change, 117, 127
local authorities
  relations with refugee organisations,
    147-51, 168-70
  role in dispersal, 110-11, 114-5, 118,
    122
Local Government Association (LGA), 44,
    45
Loizos, P., 34-5
London
  asylum seeker/refugee settlement and
    dispersal, 58-63, 95-102, 193-7
  limitations of refugee organisations,
    84-91
  networks of refugee organisations, 91-4,
    190-93
  refugee settlement patterns, 72-4
  structure and aims of refugee
    organisations, 75-84, *76,* 185-8, 189
London Borough Grants Unit, 74, 94
London Refugee Voice (LRV), 93-4
Lynch, R., 216

M

MacIntyre, K., 213
Maile, S., 40, 213
Making Democracy Work (Putnam), 31, 32
Manchester

accountability and community organisation representation, 162-4

asylum seeker/refugee settlement and dispersal, 125, 193-7

networks of refugee organisations, 164-6, 167-8, 190-93

refugee organisation–officialdom relations, 169-70, 180-82, 184

structure and aims of refugee organisations, 152-60, *154*, 184-8

Manchester Refugee Support Network (MARSN), 167-8

Marcuse, P., 42

MARIM (Multi-Agency for Refugee Integration in Manchester), 155, 166

MARSN (Manchester Refugee Support Network), 167-8

Marx, K., 15

Masssey, D.S., 28

media

impact on image of dispersal policies, 117-18

Medical Foundation for the Victims of Torture, 73

membership (refugee community organisations

Birmingham, 132

Liverpool, 156

London, 77

Manchester, 156

Merseyside Refugee Support Network (MRSN), 155, 167

Merseyside Tamil School, 164

Midland Refugee Council, 183

Midlands, West *see* West Midlands

Midlands Refugee Council, *145-6*

migrant organisations

definition and characteristics, 12-14

see also networks, migrant; refugee community organisations

Modernising Government (Cabinet Office), 40

Molyneux, M., 207, 210-11, 216

Moran, R., 114

MRSN (Merseyside Refugee Support Network), 155, 167

Multi-Agency for Refugee Integration in Manchester (MARIM), 155, 166

multiculturalism, as tenet of UK policy, 22-3

N

NASS *see* National Asylum Support Service (NASS)

National Assistance Act, 1948, 39

National Asylum Support Service (NASS), 4, 41, 44, 46, 47, 48, 49, 109-10, 194

role and characteristics, 4, 41, 46, 47, 48

role in North West dispersals, 114-19, *115*

role in West Midlands dispersals, 111-13, *113,* 170-73, 179-81

National Lottery Community Fund, 82-3

National Refugee Integration Forum (NRIF), *54,* 55, 56, 99, 182

National Refugee Integration Strategy (Home Office), 26

Nationality, Immigration and Asylum Act, 2002, 37, 48-50, 55, 172, 196, 214, 219

NECARS (North East Consortium for Asylum Support Services), 59, 194

networks, migrant

and concept of social capital, 28-9, 206-11

refugee network relationships, 91-4, 141-7, 164-8, 190-93

theories of, 27-8

see also under title eg Bosnia Herzegovina UK Network

New and the Old, The (Home Office), 49

new institutionalism, approach to migrant integration, 25-6

New Labour governments

asylum and immigration legislation, 40-41

NGOs *see* Non-Governmental Organisations

NMSO (North Manchester Somali Organisation), 156

Non-Governmental Organisations (NGOs)

definition, 51

relations with refugee community organisations, 147-51

role in integration policy, 53

North East Consortium for Asylum Support Services (NECARS), 59, 194

North Manchester Somali Organisation (NMSO), 156

North West Consortium for Asylum Seekers and Refugees, 109-11, 181-2, 194

North West England
asylum seeker numbers, 119-20, *119*
socio-economic characteristics, 106-7
see also Liverpool; Manchester
NRIF (National Refugee Integration
Forum), *54,* 55, 56, 99, 182

O

Ockenden Venture, 51
One-Stop Service (OSS) (asylum
support), 79, 148
opportunity structure approach to
migrant integration, 25-6, 204-6
organisations *see* migrant organisations;
refugee community organisations;
voluntary organisations

P

Parsons, T., 12, 211
partnership
integration models, *54*
refugee community organisations, 91-4
see also networks, migrant
Pearl, M., 11, 60-62
Portes, A., 141
Praxis (umbrella refugee organisation),
96-7, 101
programme and quota refugees, reception
and dispersal, 37-8
Putnam, R., 31-3, 141-2, 207, 209, 216

Q

quota and programme refugees, reception
and dispersal, 37-8

R

race relations
policy framework, 22-3
see also assimilation; dispersal;
immigration
RAPAR (Refugee and Asylum Seekers
Participatory Action Research
project), Salford, 116
RCODP (Refugee Community
Organisations Development Project),
95-9
RCOs *see* refugee community
organisations (RCOs)
reception (asylum seeker and refugees) *see*
dispersal (asylum seeker and refugees)

Refugee Action, 51, *52,* 61, 95, 165
Refugee and Asylum Seekers
Participatory Action Research project
(RAPAR), Salford, 116
Refugee Arrivals Project, 51
refugee community organisations
(RCOs)
accountability 80-81
definition and characteristics, 11, 14-20,
136-7, 160-62, 188-90
relations with state, 23-5
see also migrant organisations
see also under Birmingham; Liverpool;
London; Manchester
Refugee Community Organisations
Development Project (RCODP),
95-9
Refugee Council, 51, *52,* 61, 73, 74, 91,
95, 144, 148
Refugee Legal Centre, 73
Refugee Training and Advisory Service,
73
Refugee Women's Domestic Violence
Network (London), 88
Refugee Women's Network, 88
Refugee Working Party (RWP), 93-4, 95
refugees
fear of, 2-3
see also asylum seekers; programme and
quota refugees
see also assimilation; dispersal;
integration
Refugees and Ethnic Minorities Support
Services (REMISUS), 161, 165
Renewal West London, 74-5, 192
representation, community
by refugee community organisations,
80-81, 85-8, 137-41, 162-4
Reproduction (Bourdieu), 29
research (refugee community
organisations)
methodology, 66-71, 75-9, *76*
resource mobilisation theory, as applied
to migrant populations, 26-7
Rex, J., 12-13
Ritchey, P.N., 27
Robinson, V., 2, 42, 47-8, 218
RWP (Refugee Working Party), 93-4, 95

S

Salinas, M., 18-19
Secure Borders, Safe Haven (Home Office),
37, 48, 51, 211, 214

Serra, R., 141
services, provision of (refugee community
    organisations)
    Birmingham, 133, 187-8
    Liverpool, 158, 187-8
    London, 78-9, 187-8
    Manchester, 158, 187-8
settlement (asylum seekers and refugees)
    see integration (asylum seekers and
    refugees)
Siisiänen, M., 30
SOCAT (Social Capital Assessment Tool),
    142
social capital
    definition and characteristics, 8, 28-33,
    141-2
    opportunities offered by refugee
    organisations, 89-91
    relationship with migration networks,
    28-9, 206-11
    relevance with refugee and state bodies,
    33-5
Social Capital Assessment Tool (SOCAT),
    142
social cohesion
    definition and characteristics, 211-13
    methods of achieving, 215-16, 218-20
    opportunities offered by refugee
    organisations, 216-18
    relevance to refugee policy, 213-15
*Somali Community in the United Kingdom,
    The* (Harris), 50
Somali Umbrella Group (SUG), 163-4
Sorenson, J., 15
Soysal, Y.N., 25-6
staffing (refugee community
    organisations)
    Birmingham, 133, 187
    Liverpool, 158, 187
    London, 78, 187
    Manchester, 158, 187
Stratham, P., 25
SUG (Somali Umbrella Group), 163-4
*Sunrise (Strategic Uplift of National Refugee
    Integration Services) programme*, 55

T

Tomlinson, F., 203, 216-17
Tonnies, F., 211
Treaty of Amsterdam, 43

U

Ujima, 92-3

V

Vertovec, S., 28, 211-12, 218
voluntary organisations
    role supporting refugee integration,
    51-2, 148
    see also migrant organisations; refugee
    community organisations
    see also under name eg Refugee Action;
    Refugee Council
Voluntary Service Unit (VSU) (Home
    Office), 19

W

Wahlbeck, Ö, 23-4, 205
Wardlow Road Resource Centre, 147-8
WDRS (Westminster Diocese Refugee
    Service), 94
Werbner, P., 22, 205-6
welfare benefits, policy regarding asylum
    seekers, 1-2
West Midlands
    asylum seeker numbers, 123-4, *124*
    socio-economic characteristics, 105-6
    see also Birmingham
West Midlands Consortium for Asylum
    Seeker and Refugee Support
    (WMCARS), 106, 107-9, 180-82, 194
Westminster Diocese Refugee Service
    (WDRS), 94
women, and construction of 'community',
    87-8
Woolley, F., 212, 216

Y

Yuval-Davis, N., 87-8

Z

Zetter, R., 11, 60-62, 67-8, 121